D1526125

Under the Radar Michigan
The Next 50

Here we go again!

Written by
Tom Daldin

Photographs and stories
about episode names by
Jim Edelman

Contributing prose by
Eric Tremonti

Scribe Publishing Company
Royal Oak, Michigan
First Edition

Under the Radar Michigan: The Next 50

Published by Scribe Publishing Company
29488 Woodward, Suite 426
Royal Oak, MI 48073
www.scribe-publishing.com

Cover photo by Debbie Sipes
Cover and interior design by Miguel Camacho
Edited by Inanna Arthen, Mel Corrigan and William Lacy
Printed in Korea

ISBN 978-0-9916021-4-8

Publisher's Cataloging-in-Publication

Names: Daldin, Tom, author. | Edelman, Jim, author. | Tremonti, Eric, author.
Title: Under the radar Michigan : the next 50 / Tom Daldin, Jim Edelman and Eric Tremonti
Description: Includes index. | Royal Oak, MI: Scribe Publishing Company, 2018.
Identifiers: ISBN 978-0-9916021-4-8 | LCCN 2017957530
Subjects: LCSH Under the Radar (television program). | Michigan–Description and travel.
| Cities and towns–Michigan. | Natural history–Michigan. | Wilderness areas–Michigan.
| BISAC TRAVEL / United States / Midwest / East North Central (IL, IN, MI, OH, WI)
Classification: LCC F566 .D35 2017 | DDC 977.4–dc23

TABLE OF CONTENTS

Each chapter follows the Under The Radar adventure, from the 51st episode to the 101st.
Missing episodes 1-50? Find them in our first book, Under The Radar Michigan: The First 50.
Use the index in the back for quick navigation.

Season 4

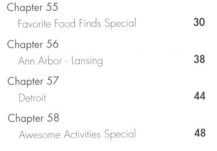

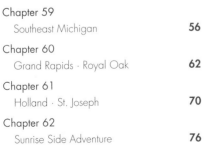

Season 5

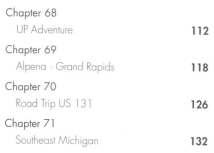

Season 6

Season 7

Foreword

a.k.a. Just in case your first book is lonely, we made another one.

Wow, one hundred shows! Who'da thunk it? When we started this crazy adventure seven years ago, we were just looking for a way to feed our families, pay the bills and hopefully help those around us until we figured something out. I mean, this could never last. We're not that lucky, right?

Well, here we are going into our eighth season on PBS Television, and the only thing growing faster than the number of our episodes is the number of incredible people, places and things we have yet to get to.

I remember when we first started Under the Radar. A friend of mine said, "You're doing a show just about Michigan? What are you going to do after one season?" Boy, did we show him a thing or two, or three, or eleventy billion. There is simply so much in this great state to discover and explore, it's overwhelming. You can turn to almost any page in this book and you'll find things that will delight, enlighten and enrich you. Heck, the food finds alone make it worth it.

Like so many people, in 2009 we lost our jobs and had to reinvent ourselves to survive as the economy slowly recouped. Now we and our growing family of newfound friends we feature are thriving because of our commitment to make Michigan the best place to live. And guess what? We succeeded.

I've said it before and I'll say it again: Michigan is an incredible place to live, work, play, set up shop and put down roots.

Photo by Debbie Sipes

Author's Note...
Important Reading.

If you have our first book, Under the Radar Michigan: The First 50, the next prose you peruse may sound a bit familiar, but the following wise words stand true for this book too.

Please remember that books are timeless, but people, places and things are not. Some of the many places we feature in this book may have, over time, changed, moved or simply ceased to be. So we can't stress enough that you always need to check ahead and contact any of these places before setting out to visit them. It could save you a long drive there and a very frustrating and disappointing drive home.

Another very important thing to keep in mind is that many resort community businesses and attractions are seasonal, and their open and close dates may fluctuate due to any number of reasons, including the weather. For this reason, we did not list dates, and you should always call ahead before setting out on your adventure.

> Be sure to use the index in the back if you're trying to quickly locate something we've featured in the book. You can search by city, category or name.

Contact information for each location has also been provided in this book, but given how easy it is to change phone numbers, email addresses and even locations, please be aware that this may have occurred as well.

You may notice that a few of the people, places or things we featured on the TV show are missing from this book. This is simply because, at the time of publishing, we became aware that a person, place or thing may have moved, changed or ventured into a different business. Also, a few of the people, places and things featured on the show wish to remain private or are not open to the public. For reasons of respect and privacy, they have been excluded from the book as well.

Thanks for your understanding. Have fun. Explore Michigan.

Not sure what Tom's doing with his hand on this cover? This time, he's showing off Michigan's Upper Peninsula! If you hold this book just right against the first book, you'll see the entire map of Michigan! If you don't have the first book, don't worry, you don't need to have read it to jump right in to this one. However, you're still missing out, so what are you waiting for?

Dedication

You never really accomplish anything alone in life. Sometimes we think we do, but that's just not true. We are influenced, encouraged, helped and even pushed by others to excel, succeed, create, concur, finish and endure. Without each other our lives would be unfulfilled and directionless. There are so many people who help make us who we are and help us get to where we are.

There are probably over a thousand reasons why Under the Radar Michigan happened and has become so successful. When I was just a little boy, my mother would tell me, "Tommy, some day you're going to have your own TV show." Of course I thought she was just being silly, but it stuck with me. Heck, when I was about twelve, I joined the "World Adventure Series Club" and she would drive me all the way down to the Detroit Institute of Arts so I could see my hero, Stan Midgley. He made fun and funny travelogue films about cool places all around the United States.

Jim, Eric and I have had countless experiences and crossed paths with hordes of humans who made this television series possible. It's almost impossible to properly thank everyone who played a part, but here's a sincere attempt.

One person in particular we again do need to recognize and thank is Gary Heidel from the Michigan State Housing Development Authority (MSHDA). Back when Under the Radar Michigan was just a concept, Gary sat down with us, understood what we were trying to do, saw the power and value in our program and has ever since been our biggest supporter by helping us spread the good word about Michigan.

Actually, we can't say enough good things about all the people at MSHDA. They have helped us and believed in us and the mission of turning Michigan around.

Pure Michigan and the Michigan Economic Development Corporation have also become wonderful partners to UTR. Emily Gerkin-Guerrant, Dave Lorenz, Kelly Wolgamott, Nick Nerbonne, Ryan Gajewski and Drew Mason are all a dream to work with. They challenge us to tell unique stories about great Michigan places and companies, and we're thrilled when we run across a story they haven't heard about.

Almost every call with them starts out the same way: "Have you heard about this place in _____ that does these really cool _____?" And then we're off, sharing cool people, places and things in Michigan.

Bob Fish, owner of Michigan's own Biggby Coffee chain, has also believed in us and supported us for some time now, and for that he deserves a sincere mention here.

We'd also like to thank the Detroit Public Television team for helping to bring UTR to the air. We are proud they think of us as more than a TV show on their station and that they include us in station events and allow us to report from the Mackinac Policy Conference every year. Rich Homberg, Dan Alpert, Fred Nahat, Jeff Forster, Jamie Westrick, Lauren Smith, Don Thompson, Laura Hinojosa, Nora Kadoo, Chris Jordan and Christy McDonald are the people who regularly touch the show and keep us moving forward.

We'd also again like to thank our incredibly talented team of "UTR Super Associates" who work so hard to make our show shine. Alexa DeCarlo (marketer on a mission), Chris Randolph (editor in chief), Cristin Trosien (super girl), Howard Hertz (lawman), Mike Sorrentino (who we account on), Marty Peters and Chris Hugan at Ozone (a sound decision), Jeremy Anderson (spins our web), David Wesch (groovy graphics), Matt Brunn (kept us focused "literally"), Greg Facca (a steady cam), with additional awesome edits from the likes of Elaine Danielian, Eric Carlsen and Dyan Bailey. Also a special thanks to Lynn Woodison for her dulcet tones and Susan Venen-Bock for helping to keep the wind in our "sales."

A special thanks goes out to the many people we have featured on the program. Without their inspiring stories of perseverance and success, these pages would be blank.

Thanks to all the great people who never gave up on Michigan and who are helping make it better, brighter and more braggable every day.

Last but not least is a sincere and heartfelt thanks to our families. They have stood by us, believed in us and supported us since day one. Without them, none of this would have happened or been so meaningful. We love you!

How to use this book:

Step 1: Purchase book.

Step 2: Read book and make notes.

Step 3: Throw book into one of the following: car glove box (with or without gloves), backpack, purse, briefcase, satchel, knapsack or huge pocket.

Step 4: Explore Michigan and have your own UTR-style adventures.

Step 5: Tell your friends.

Photo by Debbie Sipes

Chapter 51

Season 4, Episode 2

Family Fun Special

We get emails all the time asking, "Tom," (that's me) "where's someplace fun I can take the whole family?" Well, believe it or not, I actually have a family, a pretty nice one. So, I went through our first three seasons of UTR and picked some of the cool stuff we've featured that I thought my family would enjoy. So gather everyone around, because it's time for the first ever UTR Family Fun Special. First up, we hit season one and take you all the way back to Michigan's Jurassic Period.

Dinosaur Gardens
(989) 471-5477
11160 US 23, Ossineke, MI 49766
www.dinosaurgardensllc.com

It's called **Dinosaur Gardens**, it's just south of Alpena and it's an absolute trip… a trip back in time. The park is a walking tour that lets you see what dinosaurs must have looked like as they roamed the earth millions of years ago. It's set in a forest, so as you walk through, you get the feeling of what it would be like to see these giants doing their thing in a natural environment.

It's so awesome to walk right up to life-sized, realistic replicas of all kinds of dinosaurs. They even have some really cool caveman exhibits that show what their lives must have been like. My two favorites are the T-rex and the triceratops. They have them squared off across the path because apparently they used to fight, and believe it or not, the triceratops would win a good percentage of the time. Dinosaur Gardens is a wonderful family excursion, and it's something the kids will never forget. It's like going to Jurassic Park, only you'll have no trouble getting away from these dinosaurs: they don't move.

This next segment features another great place to take kids of all ages… even big kids like me.

Tollgate Farm
(248) 347-0269
28115 Meadowbrook Rd., Novi, MI 48377
www.experiencetollgate.com

Finally, a chance for me to feature something that's even sappier than I am! You read right, I said sap, and if you've always wanted to know what it's like to make real maple syrup, **Tollgate Farm** and Educational Center in Novi is the place to go. They know everything there is to know about tapping and sapping the mighty Michigan sugar maple.

First of all, when you visit Tollgate Farm, I highly recommend doing it with a bunch of kids, because you really start to feed off their energy and excitement. Watching them learn and discover is a real treat. Plus, it gives you the chance to pretend like you already knew it all.

The process of making syrup is a little bit of science, a little bit of magic and a whole lot of fun. We went with a wagon full of kids into the farm's maple forest, learned how and why the sap flows, actually tapped some trees and then made our way over to a real sugar shack to boil down the sap into delicious syrup. A guide was with us the entire way making sure the kids learned all about the process, because remember, I already knew it all… ha!

This was honestly the most fun I'd had in a long time. The kids were excited and wonderful, I actually did learn a lot, and when all was said and done, I had some freshly made syrup for my pancakes the next day.

Please note that the maple tapping season is in the spring and is very short and unpredictable, so by all means, call ahead to see when they'll be tapping and sapping.

Even though we went there for the experience of making maple syrup, Tollgate Farm is owned and operated by Michigan State University and is a real working farm with all kinds of activities and animals for the kids to see. They also offer an entire range of educational opportunities including youth education programs and camps, so I invite you to explore more about what this outstanding facility has to offer.

The Detroit Zoo
(248) 541-5717
8450 W. 10 Mile Rd., Royal Oak, MI 48067
www.detroitzoo.org

Next we went to the **Detroit Zoo** to see an exhibit I had heard about and always wanted to see. I'm telling you right now, this exhibit is so incredible that whether you're six or one hundred and six, you'll BEARLY be able to contain yourself.

It's called the Arctic Ring of Life, and it's North America's largest polar bear exhibit. What's also cool about this exhibit is that it's a complete four-acre arctic habitat that also houses arctic foxes and seals.

My favorite part about the experience is the spectacular seventy-foot-long Polar Passage, a clear tunnel that winds through a vast underwater marine environment. It's a twelve-foot-wide, eight-foot-tall tunnel that takes you underneath diving and swimming polar bears and seals!

For safety's sake and to keep everyone in one piece, the bears and seals are separated from each other by a transparent barrier, but it totally looks like they're sharing one aquatic environment. It looks so real, it's almost magic.

The Arctic Ring of Life was actually named the Second Best Zoo Exhibit in the US by the Intrepid Traveler's guide to "America's Best Zoos" and is open year round. So whether it's winter, spring, summer or fall, if you get the call of the wild, spend some quality time with your furry and feathered friends at the Detroit Zoo. Don't worry; they'll be waitin' for ya.

Next up is an event that brings together both families and our favorite furry friends all across the UP.

UP 200
(906) 228-3072
PO Box 15, Marquette, MI 49855
www.UP200.org

This time we came to Marquette to see something I'd never seen before, a two-hundred mile dogsled race called the **UP 200**. It's an Iditarod qualifier that brings mushers and their teams in from all over the Midwest. The race actually starts off right in downtown Marquette. The morning of the race, they bring in heavy equipment, dump tons of snow and actually build a dogsled trail right through the middle of the city. This takes a lot of time and energy, but when you see the start of the race, it's extremely cool.

The morning of the race we got to experience what's called the vet check. This is where every single dog is thoroughly examined by a veterinarian to make sure they're healthy and ready to run. I have to be honest; I had my reservations about how dogs were treated in this sport until I saw how happy and healthy all these dogs were. The relationship the dogs have with their owners is amazing. These dogs love two things: their owners and to run.

Putting on a race this size takes a ton of people who are dedicated to the sport. Students from Northern Michigan University even volunteer their time to help make the race happen. It's a total town effort that brings everyone together for fun and a ton of community spirit.

We had some time to kill before the race started, so we ran over to the NMU campus to see the Superior Dome. It's their stadium and field house, and it's one of the largest wooden dome structures in the world. Just walking into the dome is a real experience, but we got to do something really cool: take the catwalk all the way to the top. It's amazing that something this mammoth can be built entirely out of wood.

When it gets close to the start of the race, downtown Marquette really comes alive. More than seven thousand people line the streets to cheer on the mushers and their canine companions. They say the older you get, the more often you should do something for the very first time. If you've never experienced the UP 200, it's time you did.

The great thing about this trip north wasn't just the cool people I met, the things I learned or the places I saw. It was also about the inspiration it gave me to come back and discover more.

Now, if your idea of family fun is sand, sun and even more sand, get ready to travel to your new favorite place.

Mac Wood's Sand Dunes
(231) 873-2817
629 N. 18th Ave., Mears, MI 49436
www.macwoodsdunerides.com

When we went to Silver Lake, the first thing we wanted to do was get a lay of the sand, as it were, so we headed over to **Mac Wood's Dune Rides**. This is a great way to see some of the coolest dunes this side of the moon. The Wood family's been doing these rides for four generations now, and there's no other experience in the sand quite like it. You take off into the dunes with a tour guide and about twelve of your new best friends and go for an action-packed educational thrill ride in the sand.

I tell ya, our Mac Woods adventure was like a roller coaster ride combined with some of the best views in Michigan. Add in all the fascinating facts and good humor you get from your tour guide and you've got the makings of a pretty awesome Michigan experience.

When the ride was over, not only did I learn a ton about the dunes, my shoes were full of sand and my stomach hurt from laughing so much. It's good, old-fashioned family fun, and it's fun like this that makes the best vacation memories. Just don't forget who told you about it.

If you've got the kind of family that really likes to rock the boat, here's a way you can make all the kids happy.

Tall Ship Manitou
(231) 941-2000
13390 SW Bay Shore Dr., Traverse City, MI 49684
www.tallshipsailing.com

All my life I've wondered what it would be like to sail on one of those giant sailing schooners from the 1800s. Little did I know that in Traverse City, they have the **Tall Ship Manitou**. It's a 114-foot, double-masted ship that offers sailing adventures from two hours up to four days. They even conduct educational school programs onboard. Finally, a chance for me to get my sea legs and actually learn something.

Our captain, Dave McGinnis, knew these waters, knew his ship and probably knew right away that I knew absolutely nothing about sailing. In one word, Dave was great. He taught us a ton and even let me help out a bit. Imagine yours truly hoisting the main and trimming the jib. At least that's what I think I did.

I'd never been on a ship this size before, so I was also surprised to see that the galley was bigger than my kitchen at home. Nicer, too. I couldn't help but think how cool a four-day bed and breakfast sail on this ship would be. They also do shorter sunset cruises with gourmet edibles on board. Nice!

We had a great afternoon sailing Grand Traverse Bay aboard the Tall Ship Manitou, and it was another one of those experiences that reminded me how lucky we Michigan folk are. If you're looking for another outstanding adventure, whether it's just you, you and the wife or the whole family, set sail on the Manitou. And now that I'm an old salt, you can even tell 'em Tom sent ya. I promise they won't make you walk the plank!

If you want the kind of family adventure that involves sailing to a remote island with giant ancient trees and shipwrecks… guess what? You can do it right here in Michigan.

Story behind the name:
Family Fun Special
(Eff-Eff-Ess)

There are code names that make perfect sense (like "The 'Eagle' has landed"). Then there are government code names that make less than perfect sense. Turning letter sounds into words, like F to Eff, always made us laugh, so we combined our love of code names with made-up word sounds.

Chapter 52

Season 4, Episode 3

• Detroit

Every time I come back to Detroit, I discover more reasons to come back to Detroit. And, then I come back to Detroit, and discover even MORE reasons… and then I come back and wow, I think I just blew my own mind!

Detroit is a city that's headed only one way, and that's up. Tons of new businesses and young people are moving into the city to reclaim, redo and reinvigorate the economy. In every corner of the city you'll find inspired and motivated people who love this city and love what they do. When you combine smart and creative people with a powerful Midwestern work ethic, you can move mountains and make a city great. And this is definitely a great time to be in Detroit!

Dîner En Blanc
Phone: It's a Secret.
Address: It's a Secret.
Website: Still a Secret.
Tom's Bank Account: Not a Secret.

Our first stop in the Motor City was for a secret flash-mob event called Dîner en Blanc, which is a fancy French way of saying "Dinner in White." Now, here's how it works. A secret invitation goes out from a mysterious, anonymous person and at a predetermined time, a sea of diners wearing white converge at a secret location, and voila, Dîner en Blanc. They show up, set up, enjoy a self-brought gourmet dinner with all the accouterments, and when they're done, they disappear, leaving no trace that the event ever even happened. It happens once a year here in Detroit, and this time, it was at the field where the original Tiger's Stadium once sat.

I also found out that this culinary carting crowd has a lot more in common than just the color of their clothing. The concept is fascinating, the food people bring is incredible and the people are, well, pretty groovy. These are truly the innovative, creative and engaged people who care about this city and are returning its pride. As for me, all I kept thinking about was whether I could return my new white pants.

Dally in the Alley & Lightshow Bob
(313) 832-1949
N. Cass Corridor, Detroit, MI 48201
www.dallyinthealley.com

Next, we made our way over to something called **Dally in the Alley**. It's an earthy, urban community festival that's been going on in Detroit's Cass Corridor for forty years now. This home-grown event is raw, real and takes place in the neighborhoods just south of the Wayne State University campus. You won't find any corporate sponsors here, just Detroit-made people, products, music, food and all the Motor City atmosphere you can soak up. All kinds of people from all kinds of places come here to share their love for Detroit. This is an event you truly need to attend to fully understand. But, once you do, you'll totally dig it.

We also came to see someone who literally lights up this entire event. Now, if you're a Detroit musician, you probably already know the legend of Lightshow Bob. And who's Lightshow Bob, you ask? Well, simply put, he's the hardest working man in the lightshow business. For years now, Bob's been packing up, showing up, setting up, and with his massive amount of cords, lights, switchers and sequencers, he's been making Detroit bands shine brighter than they ever have before. If anyone puts heart and soul into what they do, it's this guy.

Bob is real, genuine and earthy, and when it comes to putting a spotlight on the bands that perform at the festival, he makes sure even people on the moon get a good view. So, as the sun set, Lightshow Bob took to the stage, whipped out his patented "lightar" (a guitar-like instrument covered with light switches) and took the band, music and entire crowd to a whole new level. Talk about light speed; Bob put on a show that totally lived up to his reputation. Lightshow Bob doesn't just light the show; he becomes part of it!

If you're looking for a festival that will totally enlighten you, Dally in the Alley is your kind of happening. And if you're looking for a guy who will just plain light you up, Lightshow Bob and his lightar will pretty much rock your world.

If you want to put a shining light on what's happening in Detroit right now, check out all the cool stuff **Shinola** is doing. They took a classic name, set up in the Argonaut Building and are helping build a better Detroit, one Michigan-manufactured product at a time. If you're looking for quality, you don't have to look far, because Shinola is right here in the Motor City.

Shinola creates everything from high-quality designer watches to classic bicycles, clothing, jewelry, leather goods and a whole lot more. And even though Shinola products are available at a variety of retail locations, they have their own stores in Detroit, Ann Arbor and Auburn Hills. These stores are worth checking out because they truly represent the company's image and mission.

I was most excited about Shinola's bikes. Designer Sky Yaeger came all the way from California to make bikes right here in the Motor City. On the show she even took me for a ride around Detroit. The bike was top notch and we had a blast.

If you're looking to improve your image and at the same time help improve this great city, check out the quality stuff at Shinola for world class products made right here in Detroit, Michigan.

Don "Doop" Duprie
(734) 301-6320
2909 Biddle Ave., Wyandotte MI 48192
www.donduprie.com

You're about to meet a local musician who made a ton of dough, so to speak. That's because he's **Don "Doop" Duprie**, a.k.a. The Rock & Roll Pie Guy, and for a few years, when he wasn't putting out fires as a fireman or gigging, he was knocking out some dangerously delicious gourmet pies in Detroit. He made some for us on the show and we were hooked.

Now Doop is back at work as a River Rouge fireman and has continued to establish himself as one of the premiere songwriters and performers in Michigan. His gift for story telling (and telling it like it is) is why we love him so much at UTR. The fact that he's one of the nicest guys you'll ever meet doesn't hurt, either.

If you're ever tooling around town and you see Don "Doop" Duprie on a marquee, head on in, sit a spell and let him sing your cares away. Oh, and he also performs as "Doop and the Inside Outlaws," so check them out as well.

Doop's newfound calling is his love and desire to see the town of River Rouge expand as a gem on the Detroit River by attracting more talented musicians and artists every day. As an unofficial ambassador to both Detroit and River Rouge, Don will tell you all about why you need to come to both of these great cities.

Story behind the name:
Ooh, La La

Dîner en Blanc. It's French. When speaking faux-French, always add "Ooh-La-La" to the end to let people know you're speaking French. It's a lot like adding "¡Olé!" to the end of a fake Spanish sentence, so people know you've been to Spain. We're not linguists, but we make ourselves laugh.

Chapter 53

Season 4, Episode 4

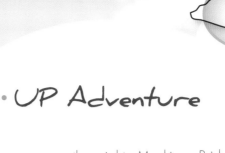

• UP Adventure

Every time we cross the mighty Mackinac Bridge into Michigan's beautiful Upper Peninsula, Jim and I always say the same thing: "Look, rocky outcroppings! It feels completely different!" And poor Eric always has the same response: "Oh, boy!" We may drive poor Eric crazy, but it really is different in the UP. There are miles and miles of unspoiled nature, tons of great towns and natural wonders to explore and a great mix of creative, hardy and happy people who love to share this paradise.

Kitch-iti-kipi Springs
(906) 341-2355
Hiawatha National Forest, Sawmill Rd., Manistique, MI 49854
www.cityofmanistique.org/big-springs-kitch-iti-kipi

Well, you know what I always say: "Nothing is too far, if you're having fun in the car." So before we knew it, we were there. Now, Florida has a natural spring called Weeki-Wachee and it's pretty cool, but Michigan has a cooler one called **Kitch-iti-kipi**.

The Kitch-iti-kipi Spring is located just a few miles west of Manistique in the Palms Book State Park. And when it comes to Michigan's natural wonders, I wonder why it took me so long to visit this place. It's extremely cool.

The spring is a surreal experience that will totally amaze you. And the best part is you just hop onto the self-propelled, open-bottom ferry, crank yourself out to the middle and watch the wonders of the spring. Over ten thousand gallons of fresh water bubble up through this spring every minute, and the water is so clear, it looks as if you're just over the bottom, but it's forty-five feet below. The water never freezes, and the coolest part is the spring is inhabited by huge, almost prehistoric lake trout that occasionally come up to say hello.

Kitch-iti-kipi Spring is the kind of place that's so cool, the second you get home, you tell everybody you know about it. So, don't worry if you can't say it right. Just make sure you get up there to see it. It's a real UP treasure.

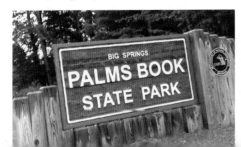

Shawn Malone - Lake Superior Photo
(906) 228-3686
211 S. Front St., Marquette, MI 49855
galleries.lakesuperiorphoto.com

I'm sure you've heard the old expression, "Nothing good happens after midnight." Well, you're about to meet a person who doesn't believe that at all. And that's because here in Marquette, Shawn Malone does some of her best and most incredible photography in the wee hours of the night. She owns and operates **Lake Superior Photo**, and when Shawn's not at the shop, she's out capturing some of the most breathtaking images you'll ever see of Michigan's awesome UP.

Now while Shawn is known for her stunning still photography, what originally put her on our radar was the incredible time lapse videos she takes while the rest of us are curled up in bed. I have to say: these videos are absolutely breathtaking. Very few of us ever really get to experience the true majesty of the night sky, and even fewer of us have seen the northern lights. But, until now, because of her incredible tenacity and technique, no one has seen the sky quite the way she captures it. Shawn is an incredible talent, and her photography is finding its way around the world. It really is hard to put her images and videos into words, so check them out for yourself. And next time you're in the UP and you hear something go bump in the night, fear not, it's just Shawn Malone and her trusty camera out there building incredible UP dreamscapes, one frame at a time.

Black Rocks at Presque Isle Park
Peter White Dr., Marquette, MI 49855
www.mqtcty.org/parks-presque-isle

Remember when your mom used to say, "If your friends all went and jumped off a cliff, would you jump, too?" Well, I finally figured out the right response: "HECK YEAH!"

And that's exactly what people of all ages do in Marquette at the tip of Presque Isle Park. The cliffs are called **Black Rocks** and they're an incredible formation of black cliffs that rise twenty feet above the crystal clear and frighteningly freezing waters of Lake Superior. Taking the plunge off these cliffs is a rite of passage for tons of Northern Michigan University students. It's also a yearly tradition for a lot of the locals and something my crew challenged me to do... hoo boy!

Presque Isle Park is absolutely beautiful and the view out over Lake Superior from Black Rocks is, in a word, incredible. These are one of the oldest rock formations in the world and a ton of fun to explore. This experience is a classic for your Michigan bucket list and a great way to feel one with nature.

Well, being the silly sod that I am, I thought, "Hey, wouldn't it be fun to make the jump off Black Rocks in a Superman costume?" So I slipped into a proverbial phone booth (if you're young, I'll explain what that is later), made the transformation into a pseudo superhero and took the plunge. Ahhhhhhhhhhh! Well, I thought dressing up like Superman would ease the impact and shield me from the frigid water, but all it did was make it more difficult for me to swim to shore. It's really tough to dog paddle with your Superman cape wrapped around your arm. But the truth is the jump was so much fun, Jim did it and Eric even did it twice. So, if you're up in the UP and you're up for the challenge, jumping off the cliffs at Black Rocks is an awesome experience you'll never forget. Take it from me: you'll feel like a superhero even without the crazy costume. Oh, and you'll also save $24.95!

The Copper Harbor Trail Club
PO Box 37, Copper Harbor, MI 49918
www.copperharbortrails.org

With a newfound sense of pride, courage and three soggy car seats we drove west to the Keweenaw Peninsula, turned right and drove north until we pretty much ran out of land. The town of Copper Harbor is as far north as you can go in Michigan and not get wet. It's a quiet little town nestled in one of the most beautiful places in the state. Copper Harbor sits at the northern edge of the Keweenaw Peninsula and looks straight north into mighty Lake Superior.

Now, if you're wondering what's bringing young people up here from around the world, it's not just the water. If you're into mountain biking, Michigan's UP is a great place to be. But if you're really into mountain biking, Copper Harbor just might be your new favorite pace. That's because the bike trail system up there is one of the best in the world. The **Copper Harbor Trail Club** is determined to put their trails on the world stage, and they've done just that by developing a system of trails that will satisfy beginners and blow the minds of professionals.

Sam Raymond, owner of the Keweenaw Adventure Company, got us biked up and hooked up with Aaron Rogers. Aaron is a true mountain bike enthusiast whose vision and sweat equity has put these trails on the world map. When Aaron's not traveling the planet spreading the good news about this area, he's right here in Copper Harbor hitting the trails (and hitting them hard!).

After a brief introduction we headed up to the trails. And speaking of "up," you won't believe how far up you get to go in Copper Harbor. Real mountains in Michigan, awesome!

Well, everything was going along great with the shoot, and we were all having a blast flying down the mountain when suddenly it happened. Gravity and momentum had their way with Jim. Yep, in the blink of an eye, Jim, his bike and UTR camera number one flew right off the switchback trail and fell more than ten feet straight down to the forest floor below. And even without a superhero costume, Jim walked away practically unscathed. So, ladies, if you're looking for a true man of steel, Jim can be reached at 734-beeeeeeep. Ha!

Once we picked up the pieces, coming down the backside of the mountain was a half hour thrill ride like I've never had before. Wow, mountain biking with real mountains. Not what I'm used to, but I could get used to doing this real quick. If mountain biking is your thing, you really need to think about coming up to Copper Harbor.

The Mariner North
(906) 289-4637
245 Gratiot St., Copper Harbor, MI 49918
www.manorth.com

When we finally hit bottom, we made our way back to **The Mariner North** to thank Peg Kauppi for putting us up for the night. She made sure we had everything we needed to recoup from a hard day on the mountain.

The Mariner North is right in town and a great place to stay. It's got plenty of rooms, cozy cabins and a restaurant that serves up hearty helpings. They'll make you feel right at home, even if you are practically in the middle of Lake Superior

The Jampot
6500 State Highway M26, Eagle Harbor, MI 49950
store.societystjohn.com

We packed up our stuff, left The Mariner North, and headed south on M26 along the coast, which, by the way, is one of the most beautiful drives in Michigan. On our way back down the peninsula, we stopped for a snack at a place I'd heard about and always wanted to check out, because when it comes to Michigan jams and jellies, this place is allegedly heaven on earth.

It's called **The Jampot** and it's a little bakery and jam shop on M26 just north of Eagle River. What makes this place so unique? Well, these sweet treats are made by genuine Catholic Byzantine monks. If you're eating corporate-made, mass-produced jams and jellies, consider this chapter to be your divine intervention. These heavenly, handmade spreadables and baked goods are made by authentic holy men, with nothing but your taste buds in mind.

When Father Basil isn't tending to holy matters up the road at the monastery, he's at this roadside bakery helping the other monks make mouthwatering spreadables and baked goods.

The smells in the kitchen and the treats we sampled were absolutely divine, and these gentle men of peace were probably some of the nicest, sincerest people we've ever encountered. If you're looking for the stairway to heavenly jams and baked goods, I strongly suggest a pilgrimage to The Jampot.

Oh, and if you're looking for a peninsula where you can float on a spring, fly like Superman, see the northern lights and mountain bike in real mountains, look up at the UP. After all, UP does spell up.

Story behind the name:
Holy Moly!
There Goes Jim!

Executive Producer-Boy Jim is our poster child for getting into situations where he should have been a lot more damaged than he was. In Muskegon, his luge slammed into the wall. He claims he was nearing eighty m.p.h. The luge staff say it was closer to fourteen m.p.h. They're going to agree to disagree on that point. In Copper Harbor, Jim's mountain bike dropped ten feet off the side of a bike trail. He was carrying a camera and audio equipment. Jim, the camera, the audio equipment and the bike were unscathed. We want to test Jim's level of luck and jump out of an airplane next summer.

Chapter 54

Season 4, Episode 5

• Harsens Island
• Grand Rapids

Harsens Island
At the mouth of the St. Clair River, MI 48028
www.harsensisland.com

Harsens Island: I've heard about it, seen pictures of it and know people who've been there, but now it was my turn. The people there call it paradise, and if you're a fan of boating, fishing or just a laid-back island lifestyle, that's exactly what Harsens Island is, with its nineteen square miles of beautiful waterways, historic homes and comfy cottages. Only about two thousand people live there year round, but in the summer, thousands more come to open their cottages, open cold beverages and escape the proverbial rat race. It really is the island life, Michigan style.

Champion's Auto Ferry
(810) 748-3757
1700 N. Channel Dr., Harsens Island, MI 48028
www.hiferry.com

Harsens Island is located at the top of Lake St. Clair, just a one hour drive northeast of Detroit, and unless your car can swim, there's only one way to get it onto the island. **Champion's Auto Ferry** owns a fleet of workhorse ferry-boats that run year round, around the clock, and the ride is just a short five minutes across the north channel from neighboring Algonac.

Dave Bryson's family has been getting people on and off this island for generations now, and he and his crews work long, hard hours to make sure this island thrives. Champion's Auto Ferry is an incredibly fast and efficient operation and a great way to meet some islanders. Dave even let me collect the ferry fares on our trip across. As you might imagine, I didn't fare so well.

Sans Souci
(810) 748-9798
3057 S. Channel Dr., Harsens Island, MI 48028

After leaving poor Dave with a mess of wrong change and crumpled up candy wrappers, we drove off the ferry and made our way across the island to the South Channel. This is where giant sea-going ships pass by so close you can almost reach out and touch them. It's also where we discovered the tiny town of **Sans Souci**. Now, if you're looking for a walkable town, you can't do much better than this. It's a wee town all right, but it's got everything you need for a fun day on the island.

You can grab a bite at the historic Sans Souci Restaurant, pack a picnic at the Sans Souci Market and find everything from cool island trinkets to incredible artistic treasures at The Waterfront Shoppe. It's a great place to explore and learn more about the island from the locals.

Harsens Island Historical Museum
(810) 748-1825
3058 S. Channel Dr., Harsens Island, MI 48028
www.stewartfarm.org/hiscfhs

Speaking of learning more, if you really want to learn about a place, a great place to start is back at the beginning. So we stopped by the **Harsens Island Historical Museum**, where Bernard Licata gave me a quick look back at the island. Turns out that back in the early 1900s, this island was the Mackinac Island of Southern Michigan. Every weekend thousands of Detroiters would board the legendary Tashmoo Steamer and travel up the Detroit River for a day of food and fun in the sun on the island. The Harsens Island Historical Museum really is a great place to get lost in this island's illustrious past. If you get a chance, stop by.

I was also curious about what life is like on the island today, so I spent some quality time with Artie Bryson. He's the township supervisor and was born here, so he's an islander through and through. Artie explained that the island is very laid back now, mostly residential and as "up north" as you can get in this part of Michigan. It only took a few minutes of conversation with Artie to realize how proud these islanders are and why this place is so special. Too bad Gilligan didn't get marooned here. I think he would'a dug it the most.

Well, now that I was becoming an expert on the island, I thought I should probably spend some time off the island and on the water. So, my good friend Captain Dave Baron and first mate Marty Peklo took us on a boat tour of the South Channel. Now this is where you really get a feel for how special this island is, with its beautiful homes right on the channel and an international waterway as your playground. The trip up and down the channel was thrilling and relaxing, all at the same time. It was at that moment I realized I could totally live there. Who knows? Maybe someday.

Harsens Island Schoolhouse Grille
(810) 748-9551
2669 Columbine Rd., Harsens Island, MI 48028
www.harsensislandschoolhousegrille.com

Well, all that boating made us hungry. Ever notice how just about everything we do on UTR makes us hungry? So we decided it was time to get educated on where to eat on the island. Now usually the thought of going back to school sends chills up my spine, but not this time. That's because they turned the island's original little schoolhouse into an actual restaurant. It's called the **Schoolhouse Grille**, and until 2005, it was a real island elementary school.

Kristin Bane reopened the school in 2009 as a place where she can show the whole world just how much she knows about the fine art of great food. This is a very cool place, because she left it looking so much like an actual school. The atmosphere is scholastic, the food is fantastic and it's a great, relaxing way to rub elbows and break bread with islanders. Heck, the school's old principal was actually there having dinner, and I didn't even have to stay after. There's a first time for everything.

Kristen is keeping the history of this great little schoolhouse alive for all the islanders to enjoy. She's also serving up the kind of fresh, local food we totally love on UTR… bonus! So, if you're looking for a uniquely Michigan island adventure, that's both close to and far from civilization, spend a day on Harsens Island. And, who knows, someday you just might pass by my cozy little cottage. Just don't forget to wave.

I say this a lot, but I'm gonna say it again: have you been to **Grand Rapids** lately? In fact, have you been to Grand Rapids at all? If you haven't, spend a day here, and if you don't love it, I'll come to your house and make you pancakes. But if you don't like Grand Rapids… no syrup.

Grand Rapids continues to be one of our favorite places to visit on UTR. If you like a city that's alive with great food, culture, sports, education and innovation, Grand Rapids is a place you just might want to live. It's a big city that's kept that small town sense of place, and it's attracting young people from across the country to help move it forward. It's a city on the move all right, and in all the right directions.

Dwelling Place
(616) 454-0928
101 Sheldon Blvd. SE #2, Grand Rapids, MI 49503
www.dwellingplacegr.org

If you had a company that created great affordable spaces for all kinds of people to live and work right downtown, what would you call it? How about **Dwelling Place**? Denny Sturtevant is the CEO at Dwelling Place, and he's the man with the urban plan to revitalize downtown Grand Rapids and its surrounding neighborhoods.

Now, Dwelling Place isn't an actual place; it's an organization that creates living spaces for people from all walks of life. From the elderly, less fortunate and special needs community to cool and creative live/work spaces, retail and high-quality rental places, Denny and his caring crew are continuing to make Grand Rapids a place anyone and everyone can call home. They even do entire neighborhood revitalizations. It's people like these who give entire communities a sense of place and make them a great place to be. Next time you're in GR, look around. You'll probably see some of their incredible work. Let's face it, everyone in our society deserves a sense of place in the community where they live, and Dwelling Place is just the place to make that happen.

Victor Axe & Tools
(616) 805-9133
www.victoraxe.com

There are a lot of old sayings out there I really love. "Don't count your chicken before it's cooked," "fight fire with water" and "a bird in the hand is worth its weight in gold" are a few. But, I didn't really understand the phrase "what's old is new again" until I met this guy.

Meet Victor Sultana, a young guy who took an old craft and turned it into **Victor Axe & Tools**, a relatively new company that takes the age-old art of working with your hands and handcrafts quality tools. Victor's specialty is bringing old axes back to life by retooling classic and reclaimed axe heads and fitting them with brand new wooden handles. These axes are as beautiful as they are functional and are the kind of things that become very individual and personal. While we were there, Eric bought one for his father, who cherishes it to this day. These axes are literally working works of art. Victor also offers handmade leather accessories that accompany his awesome axes. Youth and innovation always seem to go hand in hand, and Victor Sultana is the personification of that. Whether you fancy yourself a lumberjack or not, you can't help but admire what's happening at Victor Axe & Tools.

Grand Rapids Downtown Market
(616) 805-5308
435 Ionia Ave. SW, Grand Rapids, MI 49503
www.downtownmarketgr.com

Have you unfortunately acquired a taste for freezer burn? Yea, me too. That's why we both really need to change our lifestyle, and I've got a revolutionary old idea for you that'll help you eat fresh and expand your horizons.

It's called shopping local and buying fresh often, and the best new place to do that in these parts is the **Grand Rapids Downtown Market**. It's a state-of-the-art facility that takes the old concept of the farmer's market way into the new millennium. This modern market is bringing fresh and artisan foods to urbanites across the city. It has a huge open-air atmosphere that offers a number of restaurants with creative cuisine. You'll also find tons of artisan offerings, everything from cheeses and fresh baked goods to handmade candles, candies and coffees. And like every good farmer's market worth its weight in rutabagas, you'll find plenty of fresh and local meat and produce. Heck, you can even get cooking classes there.

The market was built on the site of the city's original farmer's market, and much of the new market was built with reused lumber and iron girders from the original structures. It totally gives the place a sense of history and creative connection to the past. The Grand Rapids Downtown Market is so much more than a market; it's a place for the community to meet, learn, shop and share. Every city should have a market like this. And everyone should come to Grand Rapids, because it's a city that's taking the solid traditions of the past and turning them into a bright future for all of us, and I like that!

Story behind the name:
What's the Opposite of an Axe Murderer?

When you're interviewing a guy who makes new handles for old axe heads, you hope beyond all hope that he's the opposite of an axe murderer.

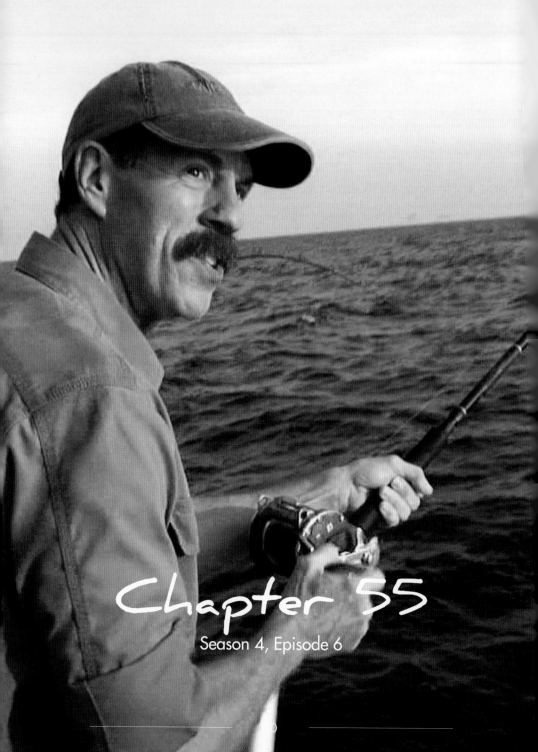

Chapter 55
Season 4, Episode 6

Favorite Food Finds Special

Do you like food? I mean, do you really like food? Good, then you're reading the right book, because we've put together some of our favorite food finds from our first three seasons. I guarantee you'll gain weight just reading this chapter. So hold onto your appetite, because first up is Muskegon and a delicious fish named Steve.

Margie J. Sport Fishing Charter
Great Lakes Marina
(231) 799-2229
1920 Lake Shore Dr., Slip B-2, Muskegon, MI 49441
www.fishmuskegon.com

There are two things I had never done before. One was to get up at four o'clock in the morning. I didn't know that time even existed. The other was to go charter fishing. And if you saw our Houghton Lake episode, you know that the only fish I ever caught came out of a bait tank.

When we showed up at the dock in the dark, all I kept thinking was, "Is this something you have to be a real fisherman to enjoy? I don't know the first, second or even the third thing about fishing." Well, as soon as I met Captain Drew Morris and his son Chris, I knew we were in good hands. They run the **Margie J. Sport Fishing Charter** in Muskegon, and they know everything you need to know, so you don't need to know anything. Which was good, because that early in the morning, I barely know how to tie my own shoes!

Right after Captain Drew confiscated our bananas (I guess they're bad luck on fishing boats), we set out for his favorite hot spot. Here's where I have to reiterate that you really don't need to know anything at all about fishing to have a great time on a charter like this. Drew and his son Chris were a boatload of fun. They had everything we needed for fishing, and they taught us everything we needed to know (not to mention they did ninety percent of the work for us). I did, however, burn my biceps a bit by proudly reeling in a fourteen-pound king salmon. During the thrilling man vs. fish fight, we affectionately named the fish Steve. Just seemed like a good name at the time.

Docker's Fish House
(231) 755-0400
3505 Marina View Pt., Muskegon, MI 49441
www.dockersfishhouse.com

The day was a blast, and the entire crew got to reel in a fish, including my son Anthony. We caught three huge king salmon and two magnificent steelhead. The coolest surprise of the day was that Captain Drew has a special arrangement with a great restaurant right on the water called **Docker's Fish House**. So we docked and gave the chef two of our catch, and he prepared a gourmet meal that totally blew us away. Actually, when we were done, a hurricane couldn't have blown us away; we were so full. But having your own catch prepared and served like that really brought the whole trip full circle and made this trip an exceptional Michigan experience.

Klenow's Market
(989) 362-2341
201 Newman St. E., Tawas, MI 48730
www.klenowsmarket.com

In the harbor town of East Tawas, a lot of folks told us we just had to stop by **Klenow's Market** right downtown. I guess they smoke more than the fish and beef there; apparently they also smoke the competition. They're a great little all-purpose market that has won some major awards for their smoked meats. They make incredible smoked salmon and even make their own smoked jerky and salami sticks. I had a salami stick with the jalapeno cheese inside… wow. Great folks carrying on a great, smoky tradition.

You hear us talk a lot about farm to fork on UTR. Well, when we were up in Petoskey, it was all about a great American Success story called "American Spoon." It's the story of two guys who took advantage of Michigan's tremendous resources and are now literally enjoying the fruits of their labor.

Monahan's Seafood Market
(734) 662-5118
407 N. 5th Ave., Ann Arbor, MI 48104
www.monahansseafood.com

Lunchtime at Kerrytown offers a number of really good options, but the one that hooked me and the crew was **Monahan's Seafood Market**. For more than thirty years now, Mike and Lisa Monahan have been selling and preparing fresh seafood for all of Ann Arbor to enjoy. You can buy fresh fish to go, get a quick carryout meal or sit, relax and enjoy any one of their aquatic entries.

Their philosophy at Monahan's is pretty simple: fresh, fresh, fresh. They don't bring in pre-cut filets; they buy whole fish, cut them up fresh and prepare their seafood dishes the old-fashioned way. I had a Vietnamese bluefish sandwich for lunch and the flavors were incredible.

Ann Arbor is the perfect place for Mike and Lisa to be doing their thing. The food scene there is way ahead of the curve. It's truly a foodie's paradise. I was trying to think of a clever way to say it, but I'll just say it: if you love fresh seafood that's expertly and creatively prepared, Monahan's Seafood Market is worth the drive to Ann Arbor and a trip to Kerrytown Market. If you already live in Ann Arbor… bonus!

A lot of people go to Saugatuck for sun, sand and shopping. But, you know us; we went for another fabulous food find.

American Spoon
(231) 347-7004
413 E. Lake St., Petoskey, MI 49770
www.spoon.com

Justin Rashid and his business partner Larry Forgione started **American Spoon** back in 1981, and it's been a sweet ride ever since. Larry and Justin shared a dream to produce the finest fruit preserves in the world from Michigan fruit. Larry developed the original recipes, and Justin selected varieties of Michigan fruit, and as the French say, voila. American Spoon was born.

It all started when Justin (a wild food forager) had a friend in New York (Larry) who was looking to become the great American chef. He wanted to use all American ingredients, so Justin started sending him morel mushrooms. When Larry asked, "What else do you have back there in Michigan?" Justin brought him to Michigan. Larry saw the tremendous agricultural resources, put down roots in Petoskey and the partnership was born. After deciding to concentrate on making jam, American Spoon came to be, and now they ship their incredible spreadables around the world.

The company credo is, "Make the best preserves in America using Michigan fruit," and that's exactly what they're doing. From humble beginnings to a fruitful enterprise, you'll taste a mouthful of Michigan with American Spoon.

Well, obviously we love our Omega 3s on this show, because in this segment, we're back in Ann Arbor and back to talking about fish. Hope Steve's watching. Wait, did we eat Steve?

Hungry Village Tours
(269) 857-1700
400 Culver St., Saugatuck, MI 49453
www.hungryvillagetours.com

Next, we were in for a real treat. We went on a relatively new tour you can take that shows you all the behind-the-scenes stuff that makes this area such a great food destination. It's called **Hungry Village Tours**, and if you're a foodie, David Geen will totally make you wish you lived there.

This is a small-group, personal-guided tour that takes you from place to place where you get to meet the people at the forefront of the food movement there. We had fascinating and in-depth conversations with everyone from coffee roasters and artisan cheese makers to chefs and organic farmers. If you're into knowing the who, what, when, where, why and how of what I like to call "real" food, this is something you need to experience. After hopping in their official van, our tour included the following fascinating food stops:

- Uncommon Grounds Coffee Roasters
  www.uncommongroundscafe.com

- A goat cheese farm called "Evergreen Lane Creamery"
  www.evergreenlanefarm.com

- Fenn Valley Vineyards
  www.fennvalley.com

- An organic blueberry farm called "Pleasant Hill Farm"
  www.pleasanthillblueberryfarm.com

- Lunch at "Salt of the Earth" Rustic American Eatery and Bakery
  www.saltoftheearthfennville.com

- Khnemu Studio and Fernwood Farm
  www.fernwoodfarmestate.com
  www.khnemustudio.com

- Summertime Market
  www.summertimemarket.com

It was a great day and our expert guide David Geen kept us tasting, laughing and learning the entire time. If you're looking for a totally unique and enlightening Michigan foodie experience, I highly recommend Hungry Village Tours.

Would you drive all the way up to Ishpeming in the UP for a great sausage? Maybe you should. We found one up there that was so good, I asked for the recipe.

Congress Pizza
(906) 486-4233
106 N. Main St., V, MI 49849
www.facebook.com/pg/congresspizzas

Another way to stay warm during the long, cold UP winters is to put on a few extra pounds, and you know me, I discovered a great way to do that, too. I stopped by **Congress Pizza** for a quick conversation with Paul Bonetti about a food that apparently everybody in the UP knows about but me. It's a spicy, mostly pork sausage originally from northern Italy called cudighi, and it came to Michigan's UP along with tons of Italian immigrants looking for work in the mines over one hundred years ago. The sausage was originally served with mustard and raw onions on a roll, which is exactly how we had it that day, and it was good-ighi. I may be half Italian, but I ate the whole thing.

Next up I'm in Leeland at one of Michigan's most romantic inns and restaurants... and I'm with the crew. Darn it!

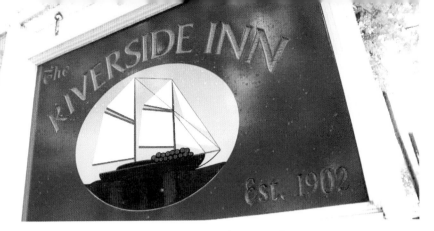

Riverside Inn and Restaurant
(231) 256-9971
302 E. River St., Leland, MI 49654
www.theriverside-inn.com

This was my crew's first trip to Leland, so we needed a nice place to stay and a great place to eat, and we also wanted to learn a little history about the area. So on a tip, we discovered the historic **Riverside Inn**. It's a 110-year-old inn and gourmet restaurant located right on the Leland River, just a block west of town. People say it's one of the most romantic places you can visit in Michigan. After seeing it, I agree.

Owner and innkeeper Kate Vilter made us feel right at home. The Riverside Inn is a perfect fit for Leland, and Kate has done an outstanding job of retaining its original beauty. The setting is absolutely beautiful and the dining experience is most certainly worth a stop there. The food truly is gourmet, with an emphasis on sourcing fresh and local. The menu is varied and very, very good. Their bar is also something you should check out. It's classic and extremely cool.

If you're planning a special weekend, a romantic getaway or if you just want to go someplace really nice, the Riverside Inn in Leland sure is a swell place.

Well, that wraps up our UTR favorite food finds chapter. Hope you enjoyed it. And if you feel full from just reading this, I sincerely apologize. Maybe next time we'll do a UTR exercise/workout special… I don't think so.

Story behind the name:
Food Baby

Have you ever eaten so much that it feels as if you've got a baby in your belly? At times like this (read: every time we shoot in a restaurant) Team UTR calls that feeling a "food baby." We just can't say no to bacon-wrapped anything.

Chapter 56

Season 4, Episode 7

• Ann Arbor
• Lansing

Ann Arbor continues to be one of Michigan's premiere hot spots for higher learning, creative living and loads of local eateries that'll expand your culinary consciousness. If you're looking for a place to live, work or play that has an intelligent energy and a casual vibe, this town has your future written all over it. Many people come here to learn, but it's the quality of life that makes them stay.

Frita Batidos
(734) 761-2882
117 W. Washington, Ann Arbor, MI 48104
www.fritabatidos.com

If you're into flavors that explode in your mouth, this island-inspired eatery is your new favorite place. It's cool, creative, casual and totally Cuban. Eve Aronoff took the heart and soul of Cuban food, gave it a modern twist and brought it right here to the streets of Ann Arbor. While visiting her grandma in Miami a few years back, she fell in love with the Cuban culture, studied their cuisine and is now serving up bold flavors from fresh, local ingredients. As strange as it may sound, this is gourmet Cuban street food, and you won't find these creative interpretations anywhere else.

If your entire Cuban food experience consists of a hybrid Cuban sandwich at some chain restaurant, come to **Frita Batidos** and taste all the authentic flavors you've been missing. And I guarantee: you'll be missing this food the very next day.

University of Michigan Museum of Natural History
(734) 764-0478
1109 Geddes Ave., Ann Arbor, MI 48109
www.lsa.umich.edu/ummnh/

Unfortunately, a lot of people avoid museums because they think they're boring. You know… they're all about learning. Well, if you've got the right attitude, learning can be a lot of fun. And if you pick the right museum it can be even more funnerer. I guess even I need some learning… darn.

Not only is the **University of Michigan Museum of Natural History** the right museum, it's an absolute treasure for people who live in Michigan. And until you come here, you forget just how much fun learning can be. I reached out to Amanda Paige, which is perfect because she's the outreach program manager at the museum and she had all the knowledge I was looking for. In only twenty short steps Amanda took me about eleventy billion years back to the time when dinosaurs were stomping the earth. She introduced me to a real Michigan mastodon and also gave me a close encounter with a T-rex. She even showed me a dinosaur that had a brain about my size. Wait a minute!

This museum is a real treasure and a great bargain. They only ask for donations and they have tons of fossils and dinosaurs on display. They also have all kinds of other cool natural history.

Amanda really made our trip to the museum so much fun, I completely forgot that I was learning. So, pick a day, exercise your brain, have some fun and spend a few hours at U of M's Museum of Natural History. After being here for a while you'll realize it's such a natural thing to do.

Ringstar Physical Arts Studio
(585) 307-0402
3907 Varsity Dr., Ann Arbor, MI 48108
www.a2ringstar.com

Have you ever been to a movie and watched a really great fight scene or swordfight? Or even better, Cirque Du Soleil? Acting is one thing, but where'd they learn to do that? Well, they learned it at a place just like Ringstar Physical Arts Studio, the place in Michigan to learn sword play, fighting, falling, silks and all the theatrical disciplines that make movies and theater come to life. Whether you're an actor or just an action enthusiast, this is a great place to learn.

Diane Miller is an expert aerialist and she saw a need, started Ringstar and is helping build action heroes, one student at a time. Oh, and she was nice enough to show me the ropes, so to speak. Next I had the chance to spend some quality fight time with Maestro Christopher Barbeau. He's one of America's premier master swordsmen, and he taught me some of the secrets to both real and movie sword play. It was a blast! Within minutes I was falling, fighting and lunging with my lightsaber (with safety and expert guidance). It was tons of fun, and as the night went on, I was so impressed with the level of commitment and concentration their students put into it. I was also lucky enough to learn some pretty stunning stuntery from the best. If you want to be the next action hero in the movies (or even just in your neighborhood), check out Ringstar Physical Arts Studio. And if you're looking for an enlightened city where you can expand your intellectual and culinary horizons, Ann Arbor just might be over your next horizon.

Lansing and East Lansing are cities of education and determination, with a deep commitment to move Michigan forward. Older businesses help carry on a great tradition here, while new businesses are popping up everywhere. Tons of young people are learning in Lansing and sticking around to make their mark. And that's a good thing for all of us.

Michigan Wine Competition and Gold Medal Reception
(517) 284-5733
55 S. Harrison Rd., East Lansing, MI 48824
www.michiganwines.com

The only thing that bothers me about people who "wine" a lot is when they don't call me when they're doing it!

Well, I got the call this time and it was to attend the **Michigan Wine Competition and Gold Medal Reception** at the Kellogg Hotel and Conference Center on the campus of Michigan State University. These are the movers, shakers and grape crushers of our great state, and these "winers" were there to pick, taste and celebrate the wines of Michigan.

Before I got to some serious tasting, I thought it would be a good idea to spend some time with Linda Jones. She's the executive director at the Michigan Grape and Wine Industry Council. She took me to college with her wine knowledge.

As one of the premier wine-producing states in the country, Michigan has become a wine lover's destination. Our wineries are winning awards everywhere, and more vineyards are being planted every year. Being a serious journalist who's dedicated to his craft, I thought it wise to fill a few carafes and try a great many of the Michigan wines offered at the reception. Once again, I'm sure glad Jim does all the driving!

Whenever I talk about wine, I always say there are only two kinds: the kind you like and the kind you don't like. Well, there's also a third kind: the kind you haven't tried yet. And if you haven't tried Michigan wines lately, you're in for a tasty surprise!

The Peanut Shop
(517) 374-0008
117 Washington Square S., Lansing, MI 48933
www.facebook.com/pg/the-peanut-shop-of-lansing-mi

Say you're a squirrel, you live in Lansing, you buried your nuts and now you can't find them. What do you do? Simple, you make a stop at **The Peanut Shop**.

Actually, this is where most Lansing land mammals come for salty, savory, nutty snacks. The Peanut Shop has been part of this community for almost as many years as they have nuts. They've got all kinds, and they roast them, shell them, box them, bag them and send hoards of happy people on their way every day. It's a tiny place that's absolutely nuts. Actually, their sign out front is almost bigger than the whole store!

If you want to step back in time and then step out with a tasty treat, Tammy Melser, Glenda Osterhouse, Michelle McClain and the rest of the nutty gang are ready to snag 'em and bag 'em for you. Honestly, the staff there is a blast and the savory, nutty aromas inside the shop are almost intoxicating. The Peanut Shop is part Planters museum, part party and a nutty place to visit. From almonds and pistachios to cashews and classic candy, they've got what you crave. So if you feel like a nut, do what we do on the UTR crew. Whenever we're in Lansing, we always stop at The Peanut Shop. It's even fun to say.

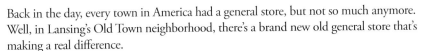

The Old Town General Store
(517) 487-6847
408 E. Grand River, Lansing, MI 48906
www.oldtown-generalstore.com

Back in the day, every town in America had a general store, but not so much anymore. Well, in Lansing's Old Town neighborhood, there's a brand new old general store that's making a real difference.

Lansing's Old Town is a place where young people are opening businesses and redefining the way we live, eat and shop. At **The Old Town General Store**, Rhea Van Atta took the old concept of a general store, modernized it, gave it her own creative twist and is helping an entire community connect. Yeah, it's a general store, but it's a whole lot more. It's the kind of place you walk into and you instantly belong.

In the short time we were there, not only did we get to talk to some of Rhea's loyal customers, we even got to meet many of her go-to folks for locally sourced foods. Whether you're looking for Michigan-made products, artisanal breads and cheeses or a place to connect with local artists and entertainers, this is your cool and convenient conduit. The Old Town General Store is what every town needs, a place where people in a community can support each other and get the everyday essentials they need. So whether you're looking for some great Michigan wines, a place to go nuts or a sense of place in your neighborhood, Lansing is a great place to be.

Story behind the name:
Hit Me! I'm Open!

When you get the chance to film an opening to the show on the University of Michigan football field, you take it. And you also bring a football with you, so you can play around on the field until security asks you why you're still on the field playing and not filming.

Chapter 57

Season 4, Episode 8

·Detroit

In this chapter we're back in Detroit, the city where I was born, got married, watched the Red Wings win the Cup and the Tigers win the World Series. It's no wonder this place is pretty special to me. It's also the place where I get to do my thing. What's my thing, you ask? Simple, you're reading about it right now. Detroit is a city that's creating better days right now. Not only is it one of the greatest sports towns in the world, it's also a place where you can find your niche, stake your claim and feel the effects of your influence. It's a big city getting big again. And now is a great time to rediscover it and be a part of the continued renaissance. The hip have already found the Motor City. They're just waiting for us regular folks to find it, too.

Center for Creative Studies
(800) 952-ARTS
201 E. Kirby St., Detroit, MI 48202
www.collegeforcreativestudies.edu

Detroit's **Center for Creative Studies** is a college where young people learn fine art and design. It's also a place that's so progressive and forward thinking that they actually looked back at an iconic building to move Detroit's design students into the future. I'm talking about the historic Argonaut Building in Midtown, where a lot of Detroit's illustrious design history began and where CCS students are exploring design today.

While we were there, President Rick Rogers explained that the Argonaut Building was designed by Detroit's own (and one of America's foremost industrial architects) Albert Kahn and built in 1928 as General Motors' primary research and design facility. It was also home to the legendary Harley Earl, who pioneered automotive design. Kids can start here as early as sixth grade and follow their design path all the way through college graduation. It's a groundbreaking new program that's turning academic heads and turning out tons of promising young talent.

OLLEGE for Creative Studies

With so much innovative design history between these walls, it's no wonder the faculty here is inspired to help move young Detroit designers forward. Professor of Product Design Steve Shock explained how students here actually work on real world campaigns and projects with actual corporations. Learning in this classic historic environment is something the students really enjoy.

Aside from design, the College of Creative Studies is also known for its Fine Arts program, and you'll never find a more inspirational purveyor of passion for the arts than Professor and Section Chair of Painting Gilda Snowden. I'm so sorry to say that Professor Snowden passed away not long after we filmed this episode, but we all feel sincerely fortunate and honored to have met and spent time with her. She made us laugh, think and reflect on the creative and artful part of the human condition. Her genuine and intense passion for art, free expression and her students was profound, and she will be deeply missed.

What CCS is doing for the future of talented young people and the rebirth of this great city is extraordinary. When it comes to fine art and design, you couldn't design a better school if you tried.

Ponyride
info@ponyride.com
1401 Vermont St., Detroit, MI 48216
www.ponyride.org

I get to meet a lot of really cool people doing Under the Radar. Most are cooler than me. Way more cooler. But I'd classify the guy you're about to meet as über cool. Heck, the word "cool" is even in his name. After traveling the world for years as a male model, Phil Cooley came to Detroit, became an entrepreneur, a restaurateur, an urban developer, and now with his nonprofit venture **Ponyride**, he's helping turn Detroit's Corktown into a place where young people and new businesses can spread their wings.

Phil explained how experiencing different cultures around the world made him eager to return to Detroit and help cultivate the creative culture coming back downtown. So after opening Slows Bar BQ (one of the Motor City's premier barbeque hot spots) he continued the motion by motivating young entrepreneurs through Ponyride. Ponyride is more than a concept; it's an actual 30,000-square-foot business incubator chock full of startup companies, makers and artists whose dream is to make their mark on Detroit's comeback. Phil Cooley walks the walk when it comes to revitalizing Detroit. He works here, eats here, sleeps here and dreams big here every day. He really is a shining example of the tons of young people who are helping to reinvent this great city and take our entire state into an even brighter future. If you've got an idea you want to take downtown, check out Ponyride.

Cadieux Café
(313) 882-8560
4300 Cadieux Rd., Detroit, MI 48224
www.cadieuxcafe.com

Have you ever heard of feather bowling? No? Well, read on, my UTR friend, because at the **Cadieux Café** on Detroit's east side, they're known for three things: steamed mussels, real Belgian beer and the ancient sport of feather bowling. And you know me; I tried to conquer all three.

But first things first: before I immersed myself in Flemish culture (whatever that is), I got my Belgian on with owner Ron Devos. He literally grew up in the place. His family has owned the Cadieux Café since 1962, and according to Ron, absolutely nothing has changed since then. Just walking into this unique and iconic place is like taking a step back in time. At one time there was a large Belgian population in East Detroit, and they brought the old-world ways with them, including this fun and unique sport. It's kinda like bowling, only you play on a hard packed clay lane with sloped sides, and you're rolling what looks like a wheel of cheese at a little unsuspecting feather. I guess Belgian farmers invented the game to pass the time. I was also passionately informed by a number of players that beer is a big part of the game (at least I had that going for me). Since the leagues didn't start until seven o'clock, the boys and I had some time to kill, so Ron made sure we killed it "Belgian style" with tons of tender steamed mussels and potent Belgian beers. We were politely informed that if you want to be part of the Fraternity of Flemish, this is pretty much mandatory… bonus! After arming myself with some knowledge, mussels and yet another Belgian beer, they let the games begin. This was an absolute blast. The bowling was fun, the league characters colorful and the atmosphere festive and traditional. They even have cool caricatures of past league champs lining the courts, and believe me, there's a story behind every one of them.

Well, after feather bowling, bowls of mussels and bottles of Belgian beer, the feathers weren't the only things feeling a little fuzzy. But, as always, we had an awesome UTR time, made some great new friends, and you guessed it: Jim was driving, so I could be Belgian responsibly!

Story behind the name:
Even My Mussels Have Muscles

The Cadieux Café, home to feather bowling and mussels. Lots and lots of mussels. So you see, the title of this show is a play on words, since muscles (the kind that we on UTR don't really possess) is pronounced the same as mussels (the kind that we enjoy eating).

Chapter 58

Season 4, Episode 9

Awesome
Activities Special

You know what I really love about Michigan? All the great activities we have here. Our first ever UTR Activities Special showed you some of our favorite activities from our first three seasons. First up is a great way to warm up winter.

Einstein Cycles
(231) 421-8148
1990 US 31 N., Traverse City, MI 49686
www.einsteincycles.com

Now for those of you who embrace winter and aren't afraid to get out and have fun in the snow, we've got a new sport for you. Fat tire biking is one of the fastest-growing sports in Michigan right now. What are fat-tire bikes? Simple, they're just what they say they are: bikes with big fat tires. But when it comes to riding in the winter, through sand or off the beaten path, these tires make all the difference in the world. Most normal bike tires are around two inches wide, but on a fat-tire bike, you're riding on tires four to five inches across.

We were dying to give these bikes a try, so we met up with Jason Lowetz at **Einstein Cycles**. Jason rents them, sells them and knows all the best places in and around Traverse City to ride them. Jason suggested a great system of trails not far from his shop, so off we went. Once we got out and on the trail and in the deep snow, I was simply amazed. The trails were completely snow covered and hilly, and we had a ton of fun on the fat tire bikes. It was unbelievable how smooth the ride was and how stable they were in the snow. I'm an avid cyclist during the summer months, so to be able to get out and ride like this in the winter was a real treat.

If you're looking for a new winter sport or just a bike you can ride through almost anything, fat-tire bikes are a blast. And believe me: you'll pick it up quick. After all, it's just like riding a bike!

Ishpeming Ski Club
PO Box 127, Ishpeming, MI 49849
www.ishskiclub.com

No one enjoys winter more than the hearty people who live in Michigan's beautiful Upper Peninsula, and if you don't believe me, read on.

Up in Ishpeming they've got the longest continually running ski club in the entire US. They call the **Ishpeming Ski Club** the birthplace of organized skiing in America, and there they have a monster ski jump affectionately called Suicide Hill. Since 1887, skiers and ski jumpers have been coming here to compete and learn to fly on skis.

When we were there, I was so very fortunate to spend some quality time with the late, great Coy Hill. Not only was Coy one of the club's most decorated jumpers, he personified this club's long and illustrious history. Coy was one of the precious old-timers who, back in the day (when it wasn't so easy), helped build this club and the giant ski jump. He was a true gentleman and a wonderful character whose enthusiasm and passion for this sport helped send some of our very finest to the Olympics. Coy passed away while the program featuring him was in the process of being edited. We feel lucky to have known him. He will be sorely missed.

If you can, you should come see this jump and witness what these incredibly brave and talented young men and women do. In my humble opinion, these ski jumpers are the rock stars of the ski world. They climb hundreds of stairs with giant skis on their backs, and then fly hundreds of feet through the air.

On the show, we suited me up and made it look as though I made one of these magnificent jumps. I acquired my genuine appreciation for these athletes when I carried those giant skis to the top of the jump and got a true perspective on the enormity of this feat. It looked like I did it, but I was really so scared up there. I respect those guys tremendously. Like I said, rock stars.

The competition we came to see that day celebrated the club's 125th anniversary, and ski jumpers from all over the world were there to compete. I've been watching ski jumping on TV all my life, but until I saw it in person, I didn't realize what an incredible sport it is. If you get the chance, get' to the UP and attend one of these awesome competitions. It's something I guarantee you'll never forget.

And remember, Michigan's Upper Peninsula isn't far if you're having fun in the car. So grab your imagination and your sense of humor. Get in the car and get up there. Before you know it, you'll be a Yooper too.

The Detroit Curling Club
(248) 544-0635
1615 E. Lewiston, Ferndale, MI 48220
www.detroitcurlingclub.com

As you know, Under the Radar is a TV show about Michigan, and we have a lot of fans in Michigan. But we have a lot of fans in Canada, too. So Canadians, this section's for you.

The Detroit Curling Club is in Ferndale, Michigan, and that's where we found tons of Americans playing this traditional Canadian sport. The club has been in existence for over 125 years, and believe it or not, the first record of people curling in the United States was on Orchard Lake in Southeast Michigan way back in 1832. Canadian or not, some Americans have been enjoying this sport for a long time.

Half the fun of belonging to any club is the people, and the folks at the Detroit Curling Club are fun, friendly and full of passion for this game. Curling is kind of like the Italian game bocce ball, only on ice and with a whole different set of funny words. It's pretty simple. You grab your broom, step on the slider, position your foot on the hack and deliver the stone. The object is to get the stone past both hog lines and closest to the button. See? Funny words, and it's a ton of fun.

They say once you try curling, you're hooked. So if you've got an addictive personality and you like to try new things, stop by the Detroit Curling Club. It really is a great sport that everyone should try at least once in their life, and I can't tell you how much fun the crew and I had that day. But I won't lie: the mostest bestest part of the entire experience was having a beer with all my new curling friends after the game. I got to hear some great stories about curling, and best of all, this all happened right here in Michigan. That, my friends, is what we're all about.

Third Coast Surf Shop
(269) 932-4575
22 S. Smith St., New Buffalo, MI 49117
www.thirdcoastsurfshop.com

If you're in Michigan and you hear someone yell, "Surf's up!" don't worry, you're not losing your mind. You're in Harbor Country.

Third Coast Surf Shop is a cool and funky sports store in New Buffalo where, believe it or not, they surf on Lake Michigan. That's right, I said surf, and if there's any other water sport that involves a paddle or a board, they'll teach you how to do that, too.

Ryan Gerard is one of the owners at Third Coast, and he's a true wizard of the water. When the conditions are right, he and his friends actually hang ten along Lake Michigan's southern shores. Even though surfing in Michigan is a bit under the radar, it's been going on here since the late 1950s. Winds coming across the lake can sometimes create swells as high as twenty-six feet and surfable waves up to ten feet high. Ryan's been riding Michigan's wide surf for over fifteen years.

Since the surf wasn't up that day, Ryan took me to a nearby river and showed me the fastest-growing water sport in the world: paddle boarding. You actually stand on what looks like an oversized surfboard with a two-ended paddle and propel yourself along the river. I honestly thought I was doomed to dunk, but it turns out paddle boarding was an absolute blast. It's almost like I was walking over the water. It was very different, and very cool!

If (or should I say when) you come to Harbor Country, stop by the Third Coast Surf shop. If it involves water, they'll make sure you have fun with it.

Port Austin Kayak and Bike Shop
(989) 550-6651
119 E. Spring St., Port Austin, MI 48467
www.portaustinkayak.com

Here's another awesome water sport that gets a big thumbs up from me (especially since the thumb is exactly where we did it).

Port Austin is quickly becoming one of the best places to kayak in the Midwest, so I met up with the man who could show me why. Chris Boyle owns the **Port Austin Kayak and Bike Shop**, and he rents everything from beginner kayaks to some pretty cool state-of-the art stuff. If you're into kayaking or want to learn, he's got everything you need.

Until we hit the water, I didn't realize just how much fun kayaking could be. The water was clear, calm and unbelievably warm. And the views were spectacular, but according to Chris, we hadn't seen anything yet. About a half hour into the trip we paddled around a rocky point, and what we saw was unbelievable. It was a huge rock formation called Turnip Rock, and I had no idea this kind of shoreline existed on Lake Huron. Turnip Rock is like a giant upside down triangle with trees growing on top. I'm not even sure how it stays upright.

We pulled into a little bay surrounded by cliffs and some pretty outrageous rock formations and took a few minutes for lunch. Chris lived in the Detroit area and vacationed in Port Austin as a kid. He started kayaking up there as an adult, fell in love with it and moved on up. I have to say that Chris is one of the nicest people you will ever encounter, in or out of a kayak. He made my first-time experience a blast. If you've got it in ya, get to Port Austin and get in a kayak. Just promise not to turn Turnip Rock right side up. :-)

The Great Lakes Pub Cruiser
(616) 319-1199
700 Ottawa Ave NW, Grand Rapids, MI 49504
www.greatlakespubcruiser.com

What do you get when you combine people, pubs and peddling? You get a portable party that's plenty of fun! The Great Lakes Pub Cruiser is like nothing we had ever seen before, and if you're looking for a powerful good time, this one's powered by people and pub juice.

You read right: The Great Lake Pub Cruiser is a people-powered, portable pub that the passengers pedal from place to place. It's basically a modernized wagon with seats on both sides, and each seat has a set of bicycle pedals that power the cruiser. As you and your friends pedal away, your tour guide steers the cruiser from pub to pub where you all enjoy some of Grand Rapids' finest microbrews.

The people keep the Pub Cruiser powered, and the social lubrication at the pubs keeps the night lively and full of fun. It's a great way to meet new people and discover Grand Rapids' exploding beer scene.

The best part of this crazy excursion is you're not driving, you're actually getting in a bit of a workout and you're getting a chance to work off your buzz before the evening is done. It's the healthiest way I can think of to go drinking with friends and family. So if you're going to partake, The Great Lakes Pub Cruiser is a great reservation to make.

Kiteman Jack's
(989) 362-4615
112 Newman St., East Tawas, MI 48730

If you're ever in East Tawas and someone tells you to go fly a kite, there's a place and a guy by the same name that's on the beach. **Kiteman Jack's** is right by the dock at the marina, and it and he have been an institution of fun for more than twenty years. The best thing about Kiteman Jack is if you buy it, he might even help you fly it. Flying a kite at the beach is oh-so easy. Just hook it up and let 'er go. I totally felt like a kid again. Buy it and try it for yourself.

With everything featured on the UTR Activities Special, now's the time to get up off that couch and get active. (That is, until Under The Radar is back on TV. Then feel free to return to the couch.)

Story behind the name:
Let's Get Physical

True Story: Tom loves Olivia Newton John. Loves her. So when we were looking for a show title for our Activities Special, we knew we had to let the world know about his crush.

Chapter 59

Season 4, Episode 10

Southeast Michigan

I've lived in Southeast Michigan all my life, and I'm still finding incredible things to eat, people to meet and places to visit all the time. It's no wonder why I stay. At least I'm not wondering!

Southeast Michigan continues to be the state's cornerstone for culture, history, innovation and inspired people doing amazing things. If you want an interesting and diverse place to discover your next favorite everything, this is a region that just keeps giving.

Peteet's Famous Cheese Cakes
(248) 545-2253
13835 W. 9 Mile Rd., Oak Park, MI 48237
www.peteetscheesecakes.com

When things get tough, some people take lemons and make lemonade. Well, here's a guy who took a tough real estate market and turned it into over ninety flavors of cheesecake. Bonus!

Meet Patrick Peteet, a man on a mission to save his family, revitalize the Michigan economy and feed us all his incredible cheesecakes. In an unassuming little shop in Oak Park he turned his life around and turns out awesome cheesecakes that are getting rave reviews.

Patrick and his family owned a successful real estate company that was doing really well until the market crashed. Then, like a lot of us (including yours truly), he had to reinvent himself to survive and provide for his family. Well, way back in high school, Patrick took home economics (because, as he explained, that's where the girls were) and luckily for him, what he learned stuck. So in order to make ends meet, he started making and selling scrumptious cheesecakes. Well, one tasty thing led to another. He opened up shop and now he's supporting his family and spreading creamy, cheesy goodness throughout the community with his cheesecakes. The family is doing so well, they've got two locations now. So, if family and a great slice of cheesecake are two priorities in your life, get yourself over, under, sideways and down to **Peteet's Famous Cheese Cakes**. Your first bite may be "petite," but I guarantee your next bite will be huge!

Miracle League of Michigan
(248) 506-4604
26000 Evergreen Rd., Southfield, MI 48076
www.michiganmiracle.org

We all know that some people don't believe in miracles, but if you know anything about this organization, they make miracles happen all the time.

The **Miracle League of Michigan** is an Easter Seals program in Southfield that gives kids with mental and physical challenges the chance to play baseball as a team member in a real organized league, a pretty simple thing that normally these kids would never get the chance to do.

Steve Peck is the founder and director of the program and one of the extraordinary and caring people who, every summer, helps bring a real sense of joy and accomplishment to these special young athletes. Just spend an afternoon with these exceptional kids and their families and you'll see what a miracle this league really is. I honestly don't know what's more of a miracle, the Miracle League of Michigan, or the fact that when they let me play, I actually threw a hittable pitch. Actually, I do know: it's the Miracle League hands down. As for me, I should probably stick to something I do well, as soon as I find it. If you'd like to witness a true miracle, get to Southfield and check out one of their games. I guarantee: cheering these kids on is one of the best feelings you'll ever have.

The Laundry
(810) 629-8852
125 Shiawassee, Fenton, MI 48430
www.lunchandbeyond.com

Being on the road as much as we are, you accumulate a lot of dirty clothes, so I thought we'd stop by **The Laundry** in Fenton and get a load of darks done. Was I in for a surprise!

Actually, The Laundry does clean up… when it comes to cool and eclectic dining, that is. It's funky, casual, sophisticated and a great place to see, be seen and select a meal that will knock your culinary socks off. It actually used to be a working laundromat back in the day. Now it's an eatery with an atmosphere so colorful and eclectic, you'll smile the moment you walk in.

Owner Mark Hamel spent time in Europe, noticed the food was better and came back to Fenton on a mission. Now he and co-owner Chad Brennan have created a place foodies across the Midwest are talking about. A lot of restaurants source local, but at The Laundry they're so good at it, they're sourcing from themselves with their own gardens, brewery and bakery. And Chef Jody Brunori prepares cuisine so creative, it'll be the star of your next selfie. She calls it "comfort food with a twist." Take some of their bread home, too. It's so good, it might be gone by the time you get there.

Now, if you go to The Laundry, you gotta do two things. First, say hi to Jon Foley behind the bar. He'll entertain, enlighten and prepare you some libations that may be from Michigan, but they're out of this world. And second, leave your laundry in the car, because at The Laundry, all you really need is your appetite.

Leader Dogs for the Blind
(248) 651-9011
1039 S. Rochester Rd., Rochester Hills, MI 48307
www.leaderdog.org

If you have any doubts that dogs are truly man's best friend, you need to read on, because when it comes to empowering blind or visually impaired people, **Leader Dogs for the Blind** in Rochester Hills is literally leading the way. Their canine companions are giving people around the world a better quality of life through independent travel.

After an absolutely fascinating tour of their entire facility and a little playtime with some future leader dogs (who doesn't love puppies?), I spent some quality time with Rod Haneline. Rod is the chief programs and services officer there and he totally personifies the passion that makes Leader Dogs such an incredible organization.

People from around the world come to Leader Dogs and live in their dormitories with their new companion for a full twenty-eight days. Then, after the two have bonded, they return home to live a fuller, more mobile life. Another amazing thing about Leader Dogs is that thanks to the generosity of their many supporters, all their programs are provided free to those who qualify. That includes meals, housing during training, travel, equipment and even your new best friend.

This really is a life-changing program. Just ask some of the unique people who go there and leave with a caring companion. Heck, they even tried to train me. The dog did fine; as for me, I don't think there are enough treats in the world.

The chance to experience what Leader Dogs is doing opened my eyes to the incredible services they provide and to the incredibly caring people who work and volunteer there.

So if you're looking for man's best friend, angels in the outfield, a cheesecake with a heart or a laundromat that'll wash your appetite away, spend some quality time in Southeast Michigan. It's got all that and a whole lot more!

Story behind the name: Field of Dreams

When you see the dreams (and tears of joy) that happen on the Miracle League of Michigan's Field of Dreams, there could be no other name for this episode.

Chapter 60

Season 4, Episode 11

Grand Rapids
Royal Oak

You know what the great thing is about Grand Rapids? It's a great place to do your thing. And if your thing is living in a cool and progressive city that has a lot of something for everyone, then look no further. When it comes to business, culture, food, entertainment and the arts, Grand Rapids is an urban adventure that young people continue to move forward. The city is full of cool places, awesome green spaces and every kind of shop and restaurant imaginable. You, my friend, would totally dig it there.

Meyer May House
(616) 246-4821
450 Madison Ave. SE, Grand Rapids, MI 49503
www.meyermayhouse.steelcase.com/house

If you think you have to travel across the country to see one of Frank Lloyd Wright's incredible works, think again, because the Meyer May House is right here in Grand Rapids. Frank Lloyd Wright is one of America's most well known architects. His lifelong philosophy was to design structures that kept humanity and the environment in complete harmony. It's a style he called organic architecture, and one awesome example is in a beautiful Grand Rapids neighborhood they call The Heritage Hill Historic District.

Don Dekker is the man in charge of keeping the Meyer May House true to Wright's original vision. Don knows all things Meyer May, and he explained that when you commissioned Frank Lloyd Wright to build you a house, everything in the home, from the structure to the window treatments, furniture and accessories, was designed by him. Wright wanted to shape your entire experience, because in one of his homes you were living in a functional piece of art.

Meyer May was a successful clothing merchant who liked to do things differently, so he had Wright design and build him this house in 1908. This is back when everyone else was building conventional box structures with gables and spires that stood out from the surrounding landscape. Wright's designs were low and linear and would blend in with the natural surroundings. The main entrances to Wright's homes were also not immediately detectable and were often hidden from people passing by. He believed that your home should be a place of privacy, serenity and tranquility. Every time I'm in a Frank Lloyd Wright Home it reminds me just how incredibly talented he was. It also reminds me just how much work my place needs. Darn it! The Meyer May house is pretty extraordinary, so take my advice. You may want to come see it. :-)

Grand Rapids Brewing Co.
(616) 458-7000
1 Ionia Ave. SW, Grand Rapids, MI 49503
www.grbrewingcompany.com

We all need to do our part to help save the planet and do things in a more organic and responsible way. So I plan to do my part by enjoying some organic beer. Responsibly, of course!

The **Grand Rapids Brewing Co.** is actually an old place that's become new again. It originally opened in 1893 when six local breweries combined their resources to produce great beer. Now it's returned as a hip new place right downtown where you can enjoy great food and beer brewed the way they used to do it: organically. The Grand Rapids Brewing Co. is Michigan's first organic brewery and one of less than two dozen in the entire US. While we were there, Head Brewer Jacob Brenner explained that organic beer is better because it's natural and not full of chemicals and pesticides. It's the way beer was made many years ago.

The approach they take with food there is also something that goes back to a time when things were simple, local and real. Executive Chef Adam Watts sources from local organic producers to make sure his ingredients are the freshest and of the highest quality. Good ingredients in, great food out!

Not only is this place being responsible by making organic beer and locally sourced foods, Autumn Sands explained how they even serve responsibly by reusing and recycling. Everything about this place is old school, but they're using new technology to lessen their carbon footprint. So if you want to make the world a better place, you can go to The Grand Rapids Brewing Co. and do it one beer at a time. Bonus!

Advanced Green Roof
(616) 298-4658
1197 Hoyt St. SE, Grand Rapids, MI 49507
www.agrgreen.com

Probably the most unusable part of any building is the roof. It's just a roof, right? Until you call these guys.

If you've got a relatively flat roof on your home or your business and you want to turn it into a living, breathing green space, Jeremiah Johnson and Erik Cronk are on top of it... literally. They started **Advanced Green Roof** in Grand Rapids, and the incredible green roof environments they're creating are showing up in some pretty cool and pretty high places.

Jeremiah and Erik got interested in Landscape architecture during their time at Michigan State University. Now they're adding beautiful and usable green spaces to rooftops across Michigan. These roofs are not only a great place to spend time, they also help protect and insulate the buildings they top. Green roofs have been around for a long time in Europe, but now thanks to these two energetic entrepreneurs, they're showing up everywhere.

So whether you're looking for a green roof, some awesome architecture or a responsible place to drink a responsible beer responsibly, Grand Rapids should be your next stop. And who knows? It's so cool there, you may forget to leave... on purpose. I've done it.

I've said it before, and I'll say it again, Royal Oak is so cool that when friends come in from out of town, it's where you take them. If you're young, young at heart or you just enjoy a hip and happening community, Royal Oak is the perfect place to set up shop or even your life. It's got awesome restaurants, cool shops, beautiful neighborhoods and a downtown that hums with a great, vibrant energy. And if you're looking for a city you can really connect with, there are tons of great places to live right in town, so you won't miss a thing.

Gayle's Chocolates
(248) 398-0001
417 S. Washington Ave., Royal Oak, MI 48167
www.gayleschocolates.com

Are you a chocolate lover? Are you an art lover? Are you a shoe lover? Well here at **Gayle's Chocolates** in Royal Oak, they'll blow your cocoa cranium. Since 1979 Gayle Harte has been turning high quality chocolate into incredible, edible art. She even makes high-fashion women's shoes out of chocolate. If you're looking for a fun and tasty treat that makes a statement about who you are, you are in the right place. This charming chocolatier turns almost everything and anything into chocolate. Gayle's love of chocolate started as a hobby, making small batches at home. But her ideas and ambitions grew into a place that now makes some of the best and most creative chocolate edibles you'll ever encounter. She's even got a hidden chocolate factory above her store Willy Wonka would be proud of. When you think about it, there's no flavor quite like chocolate. It's complex, satisfying and there's just something about it that soothes the soul. Next time you're rolling through Royal Oak, get into Gayle's and see just how much fun and how creative great chocolate can be. After all, it's eye and tummy candy.

Ray's Ice Cream
(888) 549-5256
4233 Coolidge Hwy., Royal Oak, MI 48073
www.raysicecream.com

You scream, I scream, we all scream for **Ray's Ice Cream**. That's right, next time you're in Royal Oak and you hear screaming, don't be alarmed. It's just me enjoying some Ray's Ice cream. When it comes to ice cream parlors, Ray's is authentic old school. Since 1958 they've been serving up homemade, handmade frozen fun that will melt all your cares away. This ice cream is the real deal.

The man with the perpetual scoop in his hand is Tom Stevens. He's the third of four generations who are keeping Ray's ice cream dream alive. He literally grew up in this place. And after going to school to become a dentist, Tom decided to come back to the family business and fill cones instead of cavities. Ray's is a fixture in the community because they give back so much. It's also pretty cool that they've maintained the original recipes created by his grandpa. Heck, they even serve a flavor called "Fat Elvis."

We were also lucky enough to spend time with the ice cream dreamer who's been there since the very beginning, Tom's dad Dale Stevens. This is a real family affair that's the kind of place we love on UTR. So next time you're in Royal Oak, go ahead and scream for some Ray's Ice Cream. Or you can just walk in and ask. That works too! :-)

Bastone Brewery & Jolly Pumpkin
(248) 544-6250
419 S. Main St., Royal Oak, MI 48067
www.bastonebrewery.com

If you're looking for a great restaurant, brewery or even nightspot where you can dance, I found all three on one cool corner in Royal Oak. That's right: all you have to do is walk into **Jolly Pumpkin** or **Bastone Brewery**. These two award-winning Michigan breweries have combined forces (and hops) to open my kind of comfortable, hip, casual and sophisticated place. Royal Oak is, after all, known for its great restaurants and entertainment venues, and these are two places rolled into one you should definitely know about.

Another reason the atmosphere there is so cool is that they took a classic, old building and renovated it into one of the coolest places to enjoy a frosty-cold adult malted beverage. It's not the beer making you look cooler, it's the building.

Now, believe it or not, my job also requires that I sit down and taste beers with brilliant brewers like Bastone's own Rockne Van Meter. And he knew exactly what I liked even before I did. He explained that when it comes to brewing Belgian beer there's a lot to think about. The flavors are intricate and complicated. And as I found out, really good!

If you're looking for a good reason to spend some time in Royal Oak, step into Jolly Pumpkin or Bastone Brewery and ask what they have to offer. When they're done telling you, I guarantee you'll be busy for the rest of the evening.

Ozone Music and Sound
(248) 298-2858
301 W. 4th St. #411, Royal Oak, MI 48067
www.ozonesound.com

It's not always easy to make me look good on TV, but right in the heart of Royal Oak, Marty Peters, Chris Hugan and all of our UTR super friends at **Ozone Music and Sound** at least make sure I always sound good. They own a sound design studio that offers an array of audio services you should check out. They also happen to be a couple of the nicest and most talented guys you'll ever meet. Next time you're actually understanding the silly stuff that comes outs my big mouth on the show, give a polite nod to these guys. They do great work, and for goodness' sake, they have to put up with me. Thanks, fellers!

Story behind the name:
My Roof's Green with Envy

Roof Envy.
We have it after learning about all the benefits of a Green Roof.

Chapter 61

Season 4, Episode 12

• Holland
• St. Joseph

If you've always wanted to go to Holland and meet real Dutch people, but the plane tickets were a little too pricy, don't worry. This is Michigan and we've got Holland right here.

Holland is an iconic Michigan town that was pretty much imported from the Netherlands. It's beautiful, clean, full of friendly people and is a favorite place for vacationers from around the world. The city was actually founded by some authentic Dutch immigrants way back in 1847, and the town's rich Dutch heritage continues to this day. It's a bit of the old country, with a lot of cool new places to shop, eat and stay for a while. And if you're so inclined, Holland is also a great place to take or even start a family. I liked it so much, I even changed my name to Tom Van Daldin. Couldn't help my van self.

Holland House Candles
(800) 238-8467
12350 James St., Holland, MI 49424
www.hollandhousecandles.com

If you had asked me before we visited Holland if decorative candles were my thing, I probably would have said, "Absolutely not." But after seeing these candles, I couldn't wait to light one up.

Now usually a candle is, well, just a candle, but if you want a luminary that's a wax work of art, **Holland House Candles** is the place to light it up. Valerie Nichols and her husband Bill have spent forty years developing a variety of incredible candles that are so unique they've even got a federal trademark. These handcrafted artisan candles are made one at a time and shipped all over the world. Valerie, along with black belt candle master Celeste Smith, gave me a quick lesson in the meticulous methods behind these marvelous candles.

Now usually you have to apprentice for two years before you can competently carve one of these creative candles correctly, but you know me, I'm pretty much good at everything. Not! But they let me try anyway.

These candles are so incredibly beautiful, artistic and intricate that you have to see them to believe them. And being able to watch as these talented artisans create them is a real treat. It's a true challenge because they have to be carved very quickly while the wax is still warm and workable. Well, when all was said and done and our candles were carved, I'll be honest: the one I did didn't look half bad. It looked completely bad. But just trying gave me a real appreciation for the amount of training and concentration that goes into every one of these masterpieces. If you want to light up a room, buy a regular candle. But if you want to watch people light up when they walk into a room, Holland House Candles have no match. Except, of course, the ones you use to light them with. :-)

de Boer's Bakery and Restaurant
(616) 396-2253
360 Douglas Ave., Holland, MI 49424
www.deboerbakery.com

I'm sure you've heard of the Wright Brothers, the Blues Brothers and even the Marx Brothers, but if you want great baked goods in Holland, Michigan, you gotta go see The Dutch Brothers.

In 1956, fourth-generation baker Jakob de Boer came to Holland, Michigan from the Netherlands, had three sons, Jacob, Sam and Mitch, and voila, the Dutch Brothers were born. If you've got a hankering for some old-world goodness done right, you're in the right place, because the mantra at **de Boer's Bakery and Restaurant** is, "Come hungry… we have lots." These young guys craft incredible artisan breads, pastries and cookies the original Dutch way, and you can totally taste it. Their passion for both pastry and people is the primary reason for their popularity. I love the fact that the kitchen is completely open, so you can look back and see the brothers baking and making magic.

They also have a full-service restaurant there that's full of happy, hungry people. These guys love each other, love what they do and are loved by the entire community. Another thing they like to say at de Boer's is, "We're all family here," and that's what makes the atmosphere so awesome. So whether you're looking for some outstanding artisan baked goods or an outstanding homemade meal, The Dutch Brothers will not disappoint. And if you go Dutch, you'll only be paying for yourself… bonus!

The DeZwaan Windmill at Windmill Island Gardens
(616) 355-1030
1 Lincoln Ave., Holland, MI 49424
www.windmillisland.org

There's one thing that ties Holland, Michigan back to the Netherlands more than any other thing, and it's a pretty big thing.

The DeZwaan Windmill (meaning "the swan") **at Windmill Island Gardens** is probably the most famous landmark in Holland, Michigan. It was originally built in 1761 and was brought to Holland from the Netherlands in 1964. It's the only authentic, working Dutch windmill in the entire United States. And even though it's amazing and was an incredible feat of engineering for its time, believe it or not, the windmill is the second reason we came to Windmill Island.

The first is Alisa Crawford, who totally cast her fate to the wind by (get this) becoming the only Dutch-certified journeyman miller in America, the only woman member of the Netherlands' professional corn millers guild and the sole miller of this 253-year-old Dutch windmill.

We traveled five floors up with Alisa, who explained how this huge, incredible structure still mills flour. You could feel the huge windmill vibrate from the turning of the colossal wooden blades in the wind. This was the last windmill to be allowed to leave the Netherlands, and you can still see bullet holes in its sides from World War II. Alisa actually went to Europe, learned Dutch, apprenticed for years and now teaches history and preserves the past in this monument to man's early ingenuity. What I found fascinating is that all the gearing is wooden and that the entire thing is still lubricated with beeswax.

This is definitely one for your Michigan bucket list. Oh, and while you've got your bucket, be a good sport and bring some grain into the mill. :-)

So whether you want to light up your life, dine with some Dutch Brothers or Mill about a beautiful island, you may as well do it in one of Michigan's prettiest towns. Sure, we got plenty of 'em, but I don't think they'll mind if you start in Holland.

Ever visit a town that's so nice, you wanna go there twice? Well, when it comes to **St. Joseph**, three times won't even do it. In fact, this place is so nice, you might even want to live here. The downtown is classic, quaint Americana, the beach and the parks are absolutely beautiful, the people are friendly and welcoming and there are enough great restaurants and shops to keep you full and happy for a long, long time. And it's the kind of town where you feel like you're on vacation every day of the year. The town is built on a beautiful bluff overlooking Lake Michigan, so by the time you get back to town, all the sand is off your feet... bonus!

Silver Beach Pizza
(269) 983-4743
410 Vine St., Saint Joseph, MI 49085
www.silverbeachpizza.com

A lot of different things inspire people to start their own business. Now here's a business that was inspired by a frosty-cold adult malted beverage. I'll drink to that!

Silver Beach Pizza is the place to go in St. Joe for great people, atmosphere, pizza and a famous frosty-cold adult malted beverage called a Schooner. It's also a great place to go if you want to catch a train, because this place happens to be a real, working Amtrak Station. All aboard!

Jay Costas came up with a beer-inspired plan to serve great drinks and food to all who seek it. Now his son David is helping to turn this mission into a bona fide St. Joseph tradition. This is the town's prominent beachside pizza party place. It's a great restaurant with a casual atmosphere, and the coolest part is that as you sit enjoying your beverage, trains are pulling in right next to you at the station. It's a very fun and unique experience. So whether you drive, take the train or even swim to shore, Silver Beach Pizza will faithfully fulfill all your carbohydrate needs. Even the liquid ones... now that's what I'm talking about!

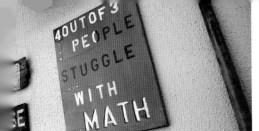

Dave Smykal & Chartreuse Gallery Art Co Op
(269) 983-0931
304 State St., Saint Joseph, MI 49085
chartreuseartgallery.com

Sometimes the best way to learn the personality and flavor of a community is through a local artist, and I found one who has a plethora of personality. Easy for me to say.

You'll find Dave Smykal and what he calls his "crazy wall of craziness" at the **Chartreuse Gallery Art Co Op** in downtown St. Joseph. All the artists here take turns running the gallery and must live no more than fifty miles away. The gallery is full of wonderfully expressive pieces that truly reflect the creative spirit of this town. If you want get a real feel for this area, the eye candy here is an absolute taste-tempting treat for that big thing that sits on top of your shoulders.

Dave is what he calls a "mixed medium outside artist," meaning that he has no formal art training. But what he does have is tons of talent. He's become known and admired for his creative signs and wonderfully wacky sense of humor. His art will make you think and laugh out loud. There is some of his art hanging on the wall right above me as I write this book.

Dave is also doing something else that's very special. He mentors a talented and aspiring artist named Brian Cooley, who is autistic. And as Dave will tell you, Brian "has it going on." His art is colorful, whimsical and has a childlike quality people absolutely love. Check him out.

Dave and Brian display a ton of both art and heart at the Chartreuse Gallery. They really personify the creative spirit of this part of Michigan. So if you're looking for a town where you feel like you're on vacation all year round, for goodness sake, get yourself to St. Joseph. And don't worry. We'll keep a Schooner cold for ya!

Story behind the name:
Thumbs Up
Now, Kate

Walking around Holland, Michigan at the Tulip Festival, you see lots of people in their Dutch clothing. Kate must have been five years old and was watching us shoot the opening to the show. When a cute little girl, dressed up in Dutch clothing, asks if she can be in your show, you never say no. Got it?

Chapter 62

Season 4, Episode 13

Sunrise Side Adventure

In our official UTR Sunrise Side Adventure, we explored the east side of Michigan's magnificent mitten. And I just figured out why they call it the Sunrise Side. The sun actually rises on this side of the state everyday... go figure!

Michigan's Sunrise Side continues to be our state's biggest under-discovered treasure. The people, places and things you'll find when you explore these shores are exceptional. No matter what you're into, the great towns and awesome natural resources make this part of Michigan a wonderful place to play or even stay for a lifetime. It's also less crowded over here, so there's lots of room to stretch out, kick back and relax. The Sunrise Side is definitely worth a UTR-type adventure, so let's get 'er done.

Mulefoot Gastropub
(810) 721-1019
244 E. Third St., Imlay City, MI 48444
www.themulefoot.com

You've heard the old expression, "Go west, young man." Well, you know us on UTR; we're rebels. So we went east, and our trip started with a feast the likes of which we'd never had before. Now if you say **Mulefoot Gastropub** to a regular person, they'll probably ask you if it's contagious. But if you say it to a foodie, they'll know exactly what you're talking about, and that's because the Mulefoot Gastropub is a sophisticated, funky, cool and casual eatery in Imlay City. And believe me, this place is attracting attention from genuine food lovers across the country. Identical twin brothers Mike and Matt Romine are living their dream and dreaming up incredible locally grown edibles that are filling stomachs and blowing minds. Youth is not being wasted on these guys; they have infinite energy and passion for what they do.

The restaurant is named after a very rare breed of a pig that's famous for the quality of its pork. The meat is actually more of a red color and there are only about six hundred in the entire United States. Mike and Matt have some of these pigs on a forty-acre plot north of town where they roam free (the pigs, not Mike and Matt).

Even though these guys are still in their twenties, they've already worked at some of the best restaurants around the world and gained great experience and an incredible perspective on the entire food experience. While we were there, Mike also explained that a gastropub is a unique concept: gastro for gastronomy (or the art of choosing, cooking and eating good food) and pub as in a public house. It's a blending of high-quality food and creative and high-quality adult beverages. The great thing about the Mulefoot is the laid back atmosphere without all the attitude. The place is earthy and casual, yet still sophisticated. And they source and serve "hyper local," so everything comes from only a few miles away. Mike and Matt are what I like to call extreme foodies. They make their own pickles, mustard, mayo and ketchup all from scratch. Even their homemade steak sauce is barrel aged for two months. From their fresh-caught smoked trout pâté that actually comes to the table in a jar of smoke to their toasted hay-flavored ice cream with smoked root beer, these guys will take you off the known taste spectrum and transport you to the fourth dimension of flavors (what I like to call the UTR happy place). So I totally take back what I said before… the Mulefoot Gastropub is contagious.

Quite honestly, these talented young guys could be doing this anywhere in the world. But they decided to keep it real and keep it right here in Imlay City. Well played, gentlemen.

Mai Tiki Resort
(989) 739-9971
3322 N. US Highway 23, Oscoda, MI 48750
www.maitikiresort.com

When I want to relax and kick back in a tropical setting, I head north to the **Mai Tiki Resort**. That's right, I said north, because hey, this is Michigan and anything is possible.

Just south of Oscoda on US 23 and right on the shores of Lake Huron is the Mai Tiki Resort. And if you've ever driven by this place, I'm sure you did exactly what we did: a double take! The Caribbean on Lake Huron?

When you walk onto the grounds, you're instantly transported to the tropics. From the grass hut umbrellas and big, beautiful white sand beach to the little pastel cottages all in a row, this place warms you up and slows you down. And suddenly, as Bob Marley would say, "Every little thing is gonna be all right."

Teresa Landino is Mai Tiki's proud proprietor. And she makes the tropical magic happen there every summer season. I don't think I've ever seen anyone put more energy and passion into making sure guests kick back, relax, have fun and lose themselves in this tropical paradise in a temperate zone. The accommodations are comfy, clean, colorful and whimsically tropical. You can sip a Mai Tai at the tiki bar in the evening, enjoy movies in the moonlight on the beach with your kids or even have a full tropical wedding there. It's Jamaica just where you want it: in your own backyard. So next time you've got a taste for the tropics, save the airfare, tune out and then check into the Mai Tiki Resort. It's a place where life's a beach… every single day.

Legends of Thunder Bay Shipwreck Tour
(888) 469-4696
500 W. Fletcher St., Alpena, MI 49707
www.alpenashipwrecktours.com

We were in Alpena on a Friday the thirteenth, so we decided to go out onto Lake Huron in a glass bottom boat to see some of Michigan's most famous shipwrecks… a little scary and kind of ironic!

On UTR, even though we like to live dangerously (not) this two-hour tour is fun, safe, fascinating and über educational. It's the **Legends of Thunder Bay Shipwreck Tour**, where you get to explore some of the Great Lakes' most famous sunken treasures without getting wet. This glass-bottom boat tour is part of the Great Lakes Maritime Heritage Center in Alpena and sets sail (so to speak) seasonally, so always check ahead.

Lady Michigan

The tour is narrated by knowledgeable volunteers who share tons of historic information during the entire trip. My first mate for the day was Stephanie Gandulla, and her passion for this unique experience is unparalleled. She explained that there were so many shipwrecks there because back in the 1800s this was one of the busiest waterways in the world. Combine that with shallow shoals and abundant bad winter weather (hence the name "Thunder Bay") and you have a ton of boats becoming un-buoyant. The cold fresh water is what keeps the wrecks preserved so well.

The great thing about this tour is that the staff really cares about the quality of your experience, and they make sure that you're learning and laughing the entire time. We saw some absolutely fascinating shipwrecks that were so close you could almost reach out and touch them. We even got to get up close and personal with a classic freighter that was in port loading its cargo. If you're looking for a way to meld your mind with Michigan magnificent maritime memories, you might want to head to Alpena for the Legends of Thunder Bay Shipwreck Tour. Oh, and make sure you spend some time at the Great Lakes Maritime Heritage Center. It really is an awesome place to get a sense of Michigan's great shipping history.

Tall Ships Celebration
(989) 895-5193
Downtown Bay City
www.tallshipcelebration.com

If you've always wanted to sail the seven seas, but you kinda like living in Michigan, have I got a festival for you! **The Tall Ships Celebration** is an absolutely incredible summer event that happens right on the river in Downtown Bay City. Now, it doesn't happen every year, so you need to check ahead, but if you can catch this great festival, you'll witness some of the most majestic masted ships still sailing the Great Lakes.

These are the giant wooden multi-masted ships from yesteryear, and some come from as far away as Norway to be part of the festival. Shirley Roberts is one of the dedicated people who work so hard to make this fantastic floating festival fun for all. She got us up close and personal as the ships started entering the harbor. You'll witness incredible sights and sounds as these mighty classic monsters come in to dock with their sails flapping and cannons firing. My goose bumps got so big I thought they were barnacles. Another awesome thing about this event is that you can actually board and tour some of the ships, so it's fun, exciting and educational for the whole family. The extra added bonus is that the ships dock right in town, so you have all of downtown Bay City's restaurants and shops to explore.

Not only are the tall ships in Bay City a fascinating celebration of our illustrious maritime history, they're also a heck of a lot of fun!

So if you're in the mood for some incredible food, a sandy tropical getaway or even classic ships on both sides of the water, the Sunrise Side is a part of Michigan you really need to explore. Remember: the more you see, the more you've seen. Think about it!

Story behind the name:
Tiki Sunrise

Ever since season one, whenever we were on the Sunrise Side of Michigan, we'd pass Mai Tiki and say, "We need to learn more about that place." Fast forward three seasons later and we finally arrived with cameras in hand. The sunrise did not disappoint, and it's also the location that Producer-Boy Jim Edelman met his bride. Owner Teresa and Jim became smitten, romance blossomed after our shoot and wedding bells rang out in 2017 for the happy tiki couple!

Chapter 63

Season 5, Episode 1

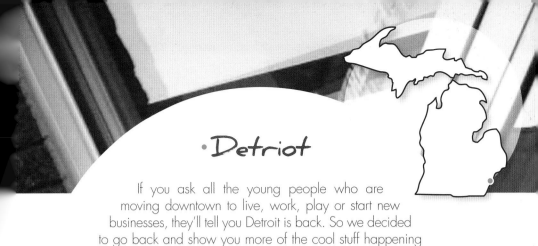

·Detriot

If you ask all the young people who are moving downtown to live, work, play or start new businesses, they'll tell you Detroit is back. So we decided to go back and show you more of the cool stuff happening there. I think that's called logic.

T
he Motor City is revamping, refueling and reenergizing itself with tons of urbanites who want to invest in a better future for themselves and this great city. You don't have to look hard to find hard evidence of this great renaissance. And the harder you look, the harder it is to leave once you get there.

Detroit City Football Club
(313) 265-3630
2750 Yemans St., Hamtramck, MI 48212
www.detcityfc.com

If you're in Detroit and you hear thousands of people yelling, cheering and having a great time, there's a good reason for it. Meet the **Detroit City Football Club**, a relatively new minor league soccer team whose passionate fan base is growing faster than you can say, "Let's have some fun." The team's nickname is La Rouge, and before every home game, their most ardent fans get together at a local restaurant and watering hole called Harry's. This is where team fans lubricate their lungs (so to speak) and get pumped for the battle on the field. This is also where we ran into The Northern Guard. The Guard is a group of hardcore super supporters that opposing teams fear because of the intensity of their cheer. This group has endless enthusiasm. They dress up, get fired up and fueled up for the big game.

About a half hour before game time the battle cry begins with smoke, drums and cheers from The Northern Guard, and a massive parade over to the soccer field at Cass Tech High School gets underway. This is an awesome sight to see and a unique thing to experience: hundreds of people marching, chanting and cheering the half mile to the stadium, all with great passion and good fun (oh, and some colorful language, so be warned). Sean Mann is one of the founders of the team and league, and one of the passionate people who bought this incredibly cool spectacle to the Motor City. He explained how it all started with Detroit neighborhood leagues and evolved into the exciting semipro league it is today.

So with families on one side and the entire Northern Guard on the other, the game got under way. And I have to tell you: not only was the quality and speed of the game impressive, the way The Northern Guard intimidates the other team is a show all by itself. If you're one of those people who thinks soccer is boring, you haven't been to see The Detroit City Football Club yet. Trust me, once the smoke clears, it's something you'll be talking about for a long, long time.

Mudgie's
(313) 961-2000
1300 Porter St., Detroit, MI 48226
www.mudgiesdeli.com

Hey gourmet food lovers, if you're ever in Detroit's historic Corktown neighborhood and you get the munchies, you gotta go to **Mudgie's**. It's marvelous!

Mudgie's is a funky, cool, casual place where all kinds of people come for real food that's so good, it'll make you want to move next door. My daughter Andrea brought me here a while back, and I had a sandwich so good, I wanted to adopt it. Just so we're clear, we're not just talking sandwiches here. From breakfast to dinner to dessert, Mudgie's is serving it up right. And if libations are your inclination, you'll also find a huge selection of Michigan brews and a wine list with prices that are sure make you smile. They serve a Bloody Mary there that will tickle your tongue and melt your mind.

Greg Mudge is the man behind this authentic artisan deli, and he has an interesting story. He actually worked there back when it was called Eph McNally's, and when the place suddenly closed, he pulled up his apron straps, bought and renovated the building and got busy turning it into a cool and creative Corktown eatery. The staff bends over backwards and the cooks are bending cuisine forward with their unconventional approach to deli food. I dare you to try and find a favorite. There are just far too many things to love.

Greg genuinely loves what he does and you can totally tell by the way he interacts with both his staff and his customers. If you're looking for a cool place to quell your munchies, get yourself to Mudgie's.

Slow Roll
info@slowroll.bike
www.slowroll.bike

Normally Detroit is the Motor City, but on Monday nights in the summer, if you lose two wheels, you can gain a whole lot of new friends.

It's called the **Slow Roll**, and thanks to Mike MacKool and Jason Hall at Detroit Bike City, over a thousand cyclists of all kinds meet, greet, mount and slowly roll through the city. And let me tell you, you can hear them coming: talking, laughing, ringing their little bike bells and making new friends mile after mile. Not only is the Slow Roll good for you, it's good for Detroit, good for Michigan and a good time too. Just ask the folks who roll with it. Each ride starts at a different location, and then miles of slow-rolling fun begins. This is not a race. It's a chance to tour the city, make new friends and help create a sense of place in the community that includes people from all walks of life. It's a great way to remind yourself that we're all the same, only different. And that sharing and understanding will bring us all together.

The night we went, the ride started at Detroit's Campus Martius Park right in the center of the city. And once all the rollers were rallied, Mike, Jason and a sea of volunteers took us on an hour and a half slow roll that was as much fun as all the people in it. I made new friends, ran into old ones (almost literally) and got a real sense of how Detroit's becoming a community again. I saw every kind of person imaginable on the roll, even a couple like me. And some of the tricked out bikes will amaze you.

Mike and Jason have done a very cool thing here. This is so much more than just a bike ride. It's a movement that will enlighten you. So if you want to connect with Detroit and be cool all at the same time, do what I do on Monday nights in the summer: the Slow Roll.

Signal Return
(313) 567-8970
1345 Division St., Detroit, MI 48207
www.signalreturnpress.org

The printed word is probably one of the most important inventions mankind has ever made. It helps us relate, create and communicate. And what they're doing at **Signal Return** just might have me returning for some classes.

Signal Return is a hip, new place that's keeping the age-old art of screen printing and letterpress alive. It's a for-hire exhibition and education space in Detroit's Eastern Market that's helping this city rediscover its creative roots.

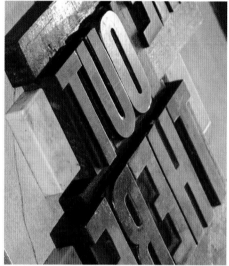

Lynne Avadenka is an accomplished artist whose passion and incredible talents energize everyone who comes through the front door. She explained that people from all walks go there to take classes, teach, create, buy art and share the experience. The moment you walk into Signal Return, you want to start doing something. Screen printing and typesetting are such a tactile and different experience than working with a computer, and more and more young artists are attracted to this physical, hands on, old-school approach.

We spent so much more time there than we thought we would and even left with a few things to proudly hang on our walls. I guarantee you've never been to a place quite like this, and I highly recommend taking a class there.

Signal Return is actually about two kinds of communication: the kind where you combine art with a meaningful message and the kind where you get together, communicate and share with other people in your community, and that kind of communication is worth a thousand words. Just please don't make me type set them.

Supino Pizzeria
(313) 567-7879
2457 Russell St., Detroit, MI 48207
www.supinopizzeria.com

Now, pay attention. This is important. If you walk from Signal Return to the south, you'll end up at the western part of Detroit's Eastern Market. What will you find there? A pretty darn good piece of pizza, that's what!

Supino Pizzeria has become a legend in these parts, partly because owner Dave Mancini is a real Italian and partly because he serves up really good pizza. But mostly because he really cares about this city, and it shows. Dave is the hardest working man in the gourmet pizza business. Heck, he spent years just developing and perfecting his dough. He also came by his knack for making the best honestly. It's simply in his Italian DNA.

After spending some serious time in Italy, Dave fell in love with food and decided to forget about grad school and open an eatery in Detroit. The restaurant is named after his father's hometown, which is just outside of Rome. Dave lives downtown, loves the city and, when you think about it, is in the perfect place. Everything he needs, from meats and cheeses to fresh flour and produce, is right there at Eastern Market. Bonus! From traditional to cool, brave and creative twists on the proverbial pie, Dave's pizzas are, in a word, magnifico. So if you're in the market for a great piece of pizza, get down to Eastern Market and just say the name Supino. I guarantee someone will point you in the right direction.

Story behind the name:
Rock n Slow Roll

We joined two thousand bicycle riders on a slow roll around Detroit. It rocked. This episode pretty much named itself!

Chapter 64

Season 5, Episode 2

·Plymouth
·Port Huron

I've got a proposition for you. Come to Plymouth, Michigan, spend a day here, and if you don't like it, I'll make you one of my famous liverwurst and chocolate syrup sandwiches. Don't worry; I think you'll like Plymouth.

Plymouth is one of those towns that's real easy to describe, because all you have to do is list off all the things you'd want in your home town: great location, cool shops, awesome restaurants, green space right downtown and beautiful surrounding neighborhoods with tons of friendly families. Plymouth is one of those special places you should, could and would probably want to live. Heck, even if you can't live here, come for a visit and take some Plymouth love back to your town.

The Peace Pedalers
(734) 589-7627
www.peacepedalers.net

There's a new way to get around downtown Plymouth, and it's green, friendly and a whole lotta fun. Andy and Diane Webster call themselves The **Peace Pedalers**, and if you're looking for a way to relax and enjoy the sights and sounds of downtown, this person-powered ride is cozy, comfortable and a completely convenient way to cruise around town.

It's a carriage in the back, a bicycle in the front and tons of fun facts in the middle. Andy and Diane live in and love Plymouth, so they're the perfect pedalers to prime you for all the great things to do there. Whether you want a complete tour of town or just a relaxing ride to get ice cream after dinner, this is a great and unique way to do it. You'll have a blast and at the same time lessen your carbon footprint. Bonus!

So if you're looking for a way to make your special evening even more special, the Peace Pedalers are the perfect way to make Plymouth just that much more fun.

FootGolf at Fox Hills Golf and Banquet Center
(734) 453-7272
8768 N. Territorial Rd., Plymouth, MI 48170
www.foxhills.com

Well, after all that riding and relaxing, I thought it'd be a good idea to work up an appetite for dinner. What I didn't know was I was about to work up an appetite I'd need three restaurants to satisfy.

A lot of people play golf, some well and some like me. So I decided to try a sport on the golf course I can really get a kick out of. It's called FootGolf and if you can kick a soccer ball, you're well on your way to playing one of the fastest-growing sports on the planet. **Fox Hills Golf and Banquet Center** had an awesome course that was calling my name, and Director of Golf Mark Runchey had all the knowledge I needed to get me kicked into gear.

Mark explained that this sport first took hold in Europe because of the popularity of soccer there. The rules are exactly the same as regular golf, except you play on a special course where the hole on each green is large enough to accommodate a soccer ball. It's a simple switch, and no matter your skill level, it's a blast to play.

Well, with a quick stretch for safety and consistency (and my sciatica), we hit the links. And I'll be honest: FootGolf is fun. You play par 3s, so the fairways and the learning curve are pretty short (so is my attention span).

Well, we were all having a friendly competition, getting some exercise in the sun and having more fun that you can kick a soccer ball at, when suddenly it was time for me to make the shot that would break the club record. Unfortunately, I kicked the ball right into the lumberyard (if you know what I mean).

So if you're looking to try something new, try FootGolf. Who knows, you just might become a club pro like me... NOT!

The Sardine Room
(734) 416-0261
340 S. Main St., Plymouth Township, MI 48170
www.thesardineroom.com

Imagine coming to a town and loving it so much you open three restaurants there. Well, that's exactly what the Yaquinto family did, and the people of Plymouth welcomed them with open hearts, minds and especially stomachs. They opened their restaurants right downtown on the same block and all in a row. There's Fiamma's for a fancy and flavorful night out, Compari's for classic and comfortable Italian and **The Sardine Room**, a contemporary raw bar and a whole lot more.

Before sampling the food ourselves (which we like to do on UTR) Ryan Yaquinto gave me some food for thought on why these restaurants are so loved. First of all, Ryan's aunt actually still makes all the pasta by hand in their basement kitchen (very Italian) and everything is made as if you were sitting in their kitchen at home. The family lives in town, is connected to the community and prides themselves on helping to create a true sense of place there.

The Sardine Room is the newest of the bunch and getting rave reviews, so I decided to sit down with Ryan's brother Frank to see (and hopefully taste) what all the fantastic fuss was about.

A raw bar is a place that specializes in oysters and seafood. But The Sardine Room is so much more. They've got a wide and wonderful menu of small plates that cater to big appetites. They also have a great selection of craft beers and cool cocktails. It's one of those comfortable and cosmopolitan places where it's cool to just be seen. Raw bars have always kinda fascinated me, so I jumped both feet first into the oyster pool with shuck-meister general Scott Rochon. This guy is a real pro who pridefully and properly prepares as many as fifteen hundred oysters in a single evening. After a quick lesson (or six) on how it's done, he even let me try a couple. You can probably imagine how well that went... hoo boy.

Well, after mastering the fine art of not cutting my finger off, we wove our way back and forth between the three restaurants to get a general consensus of overall diner delight. People who were full and fulfilled is what we found.

Regardless of the level of fanciness you prefer, there's no doubt you'll find it at one of these great restaurants. The only tough part will be deciding which one's your favorite.

As for us, we couldn't imagine a better way to cap off a great day exploring the friendly and beautiful town of Plymouth. We met some great people, toured the town, had some fun in the great wide open and ate like kings. And that, my friends, beats my favorite liverwurst and chocolate syrup sandwich any day of the week.

When I want a city that's on the water, has a great past, a vibrant present and a bright future, two words immediately come to mind: Port Huron. If you've never been to Port Huron, you're missing out on one of Michigan's most popular ports. The city stretches seven miles along the St. Clair River at the base of Lake Huron, and it's a boater- and water-lover's paradise. It's also an international border crossing marked by the spectacular Blue Water Bridge. The downtown is bustling with new restaurants, shops and great places to enjoy this awesome city. It's a great destination for the day and a place you might even want to stay. Even the aqua blue color of the water there will amaze you. I've always loved it there, and that's why we went back!

Boatnerds
(810) 479-4719
51 Water St., Port Huron, MI 48060
www.boatnerd.com

Port Huron really is filled with fascinating people, places and things, and this time we found all three.

If you're tired of being a generic nerd like me and you want to specialize, here's something that'll float your nerd boat. They're called **Boatnerds**, and they've got their own website called boatnerd.com. Heck, they've even got their own command post at the Great Lakes Maritime Center right on the water in Port Huron. If you're fascinated by the formidable freighters floating on the Great Lakes, this is a club you should contact.

Frank Frisk (a.k.a. Freighter Frank) is a celebrated photojournalist, lecturer, philanthropist and boatnerd numero uno there at the center. If it navigates the Great Lakes, it's on Frank's radar.

Frank is one of the principal people who make this a wonderful place to be, whether you're a boat nerd or not. The Maritime Center is very unique. It's the wishing well of everything maritime. You can research the freighters there, get Great Lakes history there and connect with other lake and boat lovers.

One of the coolest things about the center is that volunteers announce fascinating facts about each massive ship as they slowly pass by so close you can almost touch them. It really brings these classic cargo carriers to life. They tell you the name, cargo, place of origin and eventual destination of each of these floating fortresses. So if you get a chance, stop by the Great Lakes Maritime Center and be a bona fide boatnerd for a day. They've got lots of food, friendly people and even found-object art made from stuff retrieved from the bottom of the river. Very cool!

The Riverwalk
(810) 294-4965
51 Water St., Port Huron, MI 48060
www.scriver.org

Port Huron is one of those cities really taking the time to do its waterfront right, most recently with a brand new addition to their riverwalk. **The Riverwalk** is one of my favorite things about Port Huron. I mean, what's not to love about beautiful blue water, mighty ships passing by and majestic views of the Blue Water Bridge. If you want to take a walk that'll raise your spirits and lower your blood pressure, try a stroll up or even down the St. Clair River. It's a great way to reset your psyche.

The Exquisite Corpse Coffee House & Gold Rodent Gallery
(810) 989-5242
410 Water St., Port Huron, MI 48060
www.facebook.com/pg/exquisitecorpsecoffee

After some quality time reconnecting with Port Huron's waterfront, we made our way downtown for a cup of coffee at a funky, cool place that's actually two businesses in one. On one side it's an awesome art gallery called **Gold Rodent Gallery**, and on the other it's a gourmet coffee shop called **The Exquisite Corpse Coffee House**. I guess you'd say it's the "art" of good coffee. Get it?

The cafe sits in a great old building that's been meticulously brought back to life by Rick Mills from East Lake Builders. He's one of the main men behind many of Port Huron's historic preservation projects. Rick is helping take some of Port Huron's most iconic buildings into a very bright future.

I know I say it a lot on UTR, but it's true: they'll never, ever make buildings the way they used to, so we need to preserve and protect the classic and historic ones we have left. Rick explained that old buildings like the one we were in have so much more atmosphere and character, and that the history and stories that come along with these old beauties are priceless. Heck, the bricks that surrounded us there were put into place way back in 1817.

It had been a few years since we visited Port Huron, and from everyone we talked to, it's impossible not to pick up on a true sense of pride and commitment to restoring, reviving and re-energizing this great city. If you haven't been there lately, you owe it to yourself to go for a visit. Just be prepared though, because once you get there, you may never want to leave. I sure didn't.

Story behind the name:
I Get a Kick Outta You

We're punsters here at UTR. Soccer balls on the golf course take us to Sinatra songs. It only makes sense in Producer-Boy Jim's head.

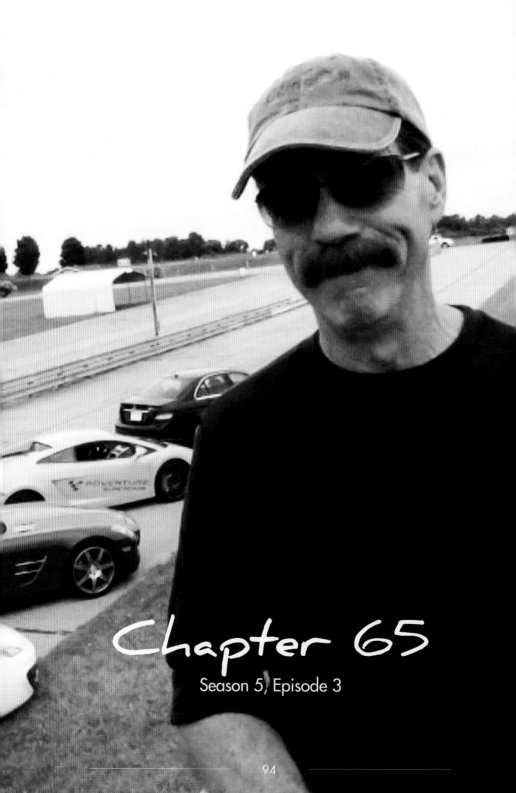

Chapter 65

Season 5, Episode 3

• Grand Rapids
• South Haven

Well, we went back to Grand Rapids, and for a very good reason (actually, for three). Picking only three things to feature is always a challenge in Grand Rapids because there's so much happening there. Every time we come back, more inspired and motivated people are doing incredible things. If you haven't experienced this great city, it's time you did. You won't find a better place to live, eat, work, play or stay in the entire US of A. Grand Rapids really does have something for everybody. And last time I checked, everybody includes you.

Malamiah Juice Bar
(616) 730-1532
435 Ionia Ave. SW, Grand Rapids, MI 49503
www.malamiahjuicebar.com

If you want to drink every day and still feel good about yourself, you gotta find the right bar, and we found a great one. In the heart of Grand Rapids' new Downtown Market you'll find Malamiah Juice Bar. This cool and colorful place is where the fruits and vegetables of labor are turned into healthy beverages that'll totally surprise you with their taste. Jermale and Anissa Eddie wanted to share a healthier lifestyle with their family and all of western Michigan, so they tossed the dice (and a few veggies) into a blender, and voilà, a business was born. Heck, this is such a family affair that they even named the place by combining the names of their two boys, Malachi and Nehemiah.

This cool, young couple always dreamed of owning their own business, and now with the healthy nutrition of their kids to think about, juicing seemed to be a natural way to go. The flavor profiles are profound, the colors amazing and the way you feel after you drink them is awesome. Anissa combined every kind of fruit, veggie and herb imaginable for us to try while we were there. As we enjoyed our juice, Jermale went on to explain that they also combine integrity, excellence and kindness into the way they do business and treat others. Not only were Malachi and Nehemiah two of the brightest and cutest kids I've ever met, they also happen to be two of the luckiest, because with motivated and caring parents like this, they'll go far. If you want something that's good for your mind, body and soul, seek out Malamiah Juice Bar. It's a bar you can belly up to any time of the day.

La Taqueria San Jose
(616) 284-2297
1338 S. Division Ave., Grand Rapids, MI 49507
www.facebook.com/Taqueria-Sanjose

If you like food from below the border that's the real deal, sometimes you gotta go under the radar to find out where the locals eat. And you know us. We totally found it.

Juan Barajas owns and operates **La Taqueria San Jose**, and if you're looking for a raw, real, authentic and genuine Mexican taco, you came to the right place. There are no frills here, just an honest and sincere family making some of the best food on this side of any border. The only thing American about this food is the people eating it. Juan does everything the way he learned back home in Mexico. And lucky for us, he now makes his home right in Grand Rapids.

Like all great places, this is a total family affair. They work hard, use honest authentic Mexican ingredients and as Juan's daughter Mayra will tell you, they cook from the heart. If you're feeling adventurous and you're in the mood for some straight-ahead tacos, head straight to La Taqueria San Jose. This is what real tacos taste like!

John Ball Zoo
(616) 336-4300
1300 Fulton St. W., Grand Rapids, MI 49504
www.johnballzoosociety.org

Looking for a place where you can learn about the natural world? Well, there's no better place than the zoo. And we found a great one!

Just west of downtown Grand Rapids you'll find one of the coolest zoos this side of the jungle. **The John Ball Zoo** combines a modern approach to caring for animals with a rich history of giving back to this great community. The zoo also sits high atop some beautiful hills that overlook the city.

To get up, up and into the park you get to ride in a real funicular cable car. This is a very cool experience. While we gained some altitude into the park, I had the pleasure of getting to know Brenda Stringer. She's the director of institutional advancement at the zoo and a big part of why this place is so special.

Once up top we discovered one of the coolest habitats for man or beast. The forest environment you walk through up there is very cool. And after a bit of goofing around (you know me) Brenda got me up close and personal with one of my favorite creatures. The tiger exhibit there is extraordinary. It's what's called a "soft habitat" so the tigers have plenty of space, differing terrains and elevations to enjoy. But that was just the beginning of our adventure. I also got to ride on a real camel, pet a slippery stingray and even talk to a couple of chimpanzees I believe may be relatives of mine. As we walked through the zoo, every habitat Brenda showed me was cooler than the one before. And the way the zoo is designed and laid out, every exhibit is tucked away in its own little forest habitat. Very natural and very cool.

Our morning at the zoo really was an awesome experience. So if you want to learn more about the animals that inhabit this planet, inhabit your car and plan a family expedition to the John Ball Zoo. And if you're looking for a healthy, all-natural juice to wash down those four incredible tacos you just so vigorously ingested, come to Grand Rapids. They've got the three things you just read about, and about eleventy billion more.

I f you're looking for one of the best lakefront communities south of heaven, I think you'll find it in **South Haven**!

When we pulled up to the Old Harbor Inn in South Haven and saw not only how nice it was, but that it was also right on a marina, I knew this was going to be a great trip. This is one of Michigan's best boating communities, and we were spending the night right in the middle of it. Perfect. And the beach there on Lake Michigan is beautiful.

As for the rest of town, it's your quintessential, classic resort beach town, and it's vibrant year round. You couldn't ask for a more beautiful or relaxing place to live, play or stay (and that's exactly what we did).

GingerMan Raceway & Adventure Supercars
(269) 253-4445
61414 County Rd. 388, South Haven, MI 49090
www.gingermanraceway.com

If driving a super expensive exotic sports car at a high rate of speed is on your bucket list, get your bucket, throw it in the trunk and drive (at a responsible speed, of course) to South Haven. Because for a few days every summer, a company called **Adventure Supercars** comes to **GingerMan Raceway** and lets regular Joes like you and me press the pedal to the metal in cars most of us can only dream of owning. And these guys don't mess around. They bring some major auto bling from Audi, Lamborghini, Mercedes, McLaren and Nissan. Just choose your chassis, and after a brief safety session, you get to attack the track just like the pros.

Before driving my dream, I hopped a high-speed ride with Director of Operations Nick Isakovic. He took me out in the Mercedes SLS AMG (whatever that is) and gave me some great insight into what drove these guys to do this. Fun!

Well, with a few passenger laps under my belt (and my equilibrium completely rearranged), I picked my pleasure: the Lamborghini Gallardo LP550-2 Balboni Edition (whatever that means). Then with Adventure Cars Co-Founder and CEO Aleks Djuric as my wing man, I tore up the track, Tom style. I think I must've hit about sixty. Actually, I was holding on so tight, I don't even know how fast I was going. I do know it was faster than I've ever gone before and an absolute thrill.

GingerMan Raceway really is the perfect track to have an experience like this. Heck, you can even race your own car on this incredible track. So if you want to drive your dream car, check in with the guys at Adventure Supercars. And if you want to eat food that tastes good in a town that's so cool it's just south of heaven, try South Haven.

Story behind the name:
Drive FASTER!

We got the chance to drive a gaggle of supercars. Tom's driving instructor kept yelling at him to drive faster (and his left turn signal was on the entire time on the track).

Chapter 66

Season 5, Episode 4

UTR
Holiday Special

In this chapter, we take you to some of Michigan's coolest Christmas celebrations. So, ho, ho-hold on, because here we go.

Christmas in Ida
www.christmasinida.com

Have you ever heard the old expression, "Big things come in small packages?" Well, here's a tiny town that celebrates Christmas in a huge way.

Ida is a small farming community in Southeast Michigan, and every year, it attracts holiday festival goers from all over the US for **Christmas in Ida**. How do they do it? Well, one way is with their incredible Parade of Lights celebration. For an hour and a half the entire community puts on a nighttime parade made up of over 150 Christmas floats that bathe the entire town in colorful lights. It's a sight to see you can probably see from space!

As many as fifty thousand people converge on this tiny town for an incredible weekend of Christmas cheer. The floats in the parade are awesome and so are the people that put them together. It takes the community an entire year to plan and prepare for this heartwarming event, and it shows.

Before the parade starts, they kick off the evening with a spectacular fireworks display right over town. That night, it was so close you could almost feel the light. If you'd like to light up your holidays this season, check out Christmas in Ida. We had so much fun, I'd a go again. Get it?

Charles W. Howard Santa School
(989) 631-0587
2408 Pinehurst Ct., Midland, MI 48640
www.santaclausschool.com

Even though our show is about Michigan, in Midland, I got to go to the North Pole and meet Santa. Actually, to be more accurate, I met about two hundred of them. The Charles W. Howard Santa Claus School is the world's oldest institution completely dedicated to the art of being Santa. Once a year, jolly gents from around the world go there to spend three days learning all things Santa.

The school is right in downtown Midland, and you'll know it by the sea of Santas strolling up the twinkling front walk every October. The inside of the Santa house is almost surreal. It's like something out of a fairytale. Dozens and dozens of Santas singing carols, eating Christmas cookies and learning to be the best Santa they can be. This has got to be the coolest Santa house this side of the North Pole.

The school was started over seventy-five years ago by Charles Howard. Howard was the original Macy's Thanksgiving Day Parade Santa. He saw a need for better Santas, and the rest is history.

If anyone has the spirit of Santa in them, it's Tom Valent and his wife Holly (a.k.a. Mr. and Mrs. Claus). Together they run the school and are keeping the legend of this jolly man alive and well.

Whether you're a first-timer at the school or a seasoned Santa, getting together once a year like this is a great way for these guys to share, grow and be the best Santa they can be. These guys are the real deal, with real beards, real bellies and a real desire to keep the spirit of the holidays happy and pure. Now these guys may look just like Santa, but inside they're really just big kids with really big hearts.

With a little coaxing, tugging, shoving, tying and gluing, they even made me up to look like Santa. When I was done and everything was in place, I almost felt like the jolly old gent. Every one of these Saint Nicks was the nicest guy you'll ever meet. I was overwhelmed with their kindness and good cheer.

I'm sure Santa at the North Pole would be very proud of all these guys. They're helping keep the spirit of Santa alive and bringing holiday cheer to kids all over the world, some small and some not so small, like me.

North Pole Express
(989) 725-9464
405 S. Washington St., Owosso, MI 48867
www.michigansteamtrain.com/npe

Do you believe that there's a train that goes from Owosso, Michigan all the way to the North Pole? I believe, and now you will too.

The Pere Marquette is one of only a handful of steam-powered locomotives still in operation, and it's right in Owosso. It's the 1225 **North Pole Express**, and every year around the holidays, it hauls thousands of cheerful kids and their families on a magical journey to the North Pole. It takes an army of proud and dedicated volunteers to keep this behemoth on the rails and running, and Engineer Rich Greter is one of the proudest to be keeping this part of railroad history alive. He explained that the 1225 was built in 1941 and once hauled freight and munitions between Detroit and Chicago.

After a fascinating conversation, it was time to head north. So with the fireman stoking the fire and steam shooting high into the sky, the train pulled forward into the station, and the passengers boarded the North Pole Express.

Now, if you've seen the classic Christmas kid's movie, The Polar Express, you've seen the animated version of this very train. The Pere Marquette was the actual inspiration for the train in the movie. In the film it takes little Billy all the way to the North Pole to help him believe in Santa Claus again. And just like in the movie, kids and even entire families make the trip sporting their favorite pajamas.

While on board I had the pleasure of chatting with Conductor Bob Marsh about this unique holiday adventure. He was the real deal and dressed in an authentic period uniform. This enchanted trip is all about recreating the experience little Billy has in the movie The Polar Express. And just like in the movie, on the way to the North Pole, the train actually stops to pick little Billy up. He boards the train in his PJs and walks the entire length of the train to greet all the kids on board. Very authentic and very cool.

The train travels about an hour west to the little town of Ashley, where the entire community shows up to greet the train. The locals turn the town into an awesome Christmas Village with all the holiday trimmings, from holiday shops and little North Pole eateries to a place where you can even rub antlers with some reindeer. The kids love it. I loved it, and Santa even showed up to give away the first gifts of Christmas.

After two fun-filled, holiday action-packed hours in Ashley, everyone boards the train and it chugs from the North Pole back to Owosso. And when the kids return to their seats, they each discover a little jingle bell, just like the bell Billy has in the movie to help him believe. I took a walk back through all the vintage passenger cars, and I have to tell you, I've never seen so many happy families in one place before. Everything about this trip is all about the kids. Heck, they even have magic elves on board to make sure everyone's in good holiday cheer.

This really is a nostalgic and wonderful way to celebrate the holidays with your family. If you believe in the magic of Christmas, I believe this is one of the best ways you can share it with your kids.

Holiday Nights at Greenfield Village
(313) 982.6001
20900 Oakwood Blvd., Dearborn, MI 48124
www.thehenryford.org/current-events/calendar/holi-day-nights-in-greenfield-village

Are you one of those people still living in the past? Well, perfect. You should come to **Holiday Nights at Greenfield Village**, because Christmas past is what they specialize in there. Every holiday season, The Henry Ford decks out Greenfield Village to be a total holiday experience from the late Nineteenth and early Twentieth Century. You really get a feel for what early American life must have been like with cooking demonstrations, classic street vendors and vintage shops. And the streets are full of lovable characters dressed in period clothing who bring the entire experience to life.

When we were there I was lucky enough to catch up with the senior manager of creative programs at The Henry Ford, Jim Johnson, and he put this past into my present. He explained that this experience is almost like Dickens's A Christmas Carol crashing into the classic holiday film It's a Wonderful Life. You feel as though you're inside a vintage holiday card getting a fun and fascinating history lesson. It feels so real because everything is as it was over a hundred years ago. Another thing that's so great is that the atmosphere is very laid back. You can wander around and immerse yourself in all the merriment at your own pace. You also get to go inside some of the old log homes end see what life was really like back then. What an awesome historical holiday experience this entire evening was. From the horse-drawn wagons and Model T rides to the fascinating fireside stories, it was an amazing night. And to top it all off, we even got a surprise shout out from the jolly big man himself. That's right; Santa is there for all the kids.

The whole night was a one-of-a-kind experience I guarantee you'll be talking about for years to come. So take it from the host of Christmas past, go to Holiday Nights at Greenfield Village, because the past there would make a nice present for your future. Wow, I think I just went into the fourth dimension.

The Big Bright Light Show
(248) 656-0060
www.downtownrochestermi.com/the-big-bright-light-show

This next holiday happening will blow your merriment-filled mind. It's called **The Big Bright Light Show**, and it happens every year between Thanksgiving and New Year's. Back in 2006 the DDA's Executive Director Kristi Trevarrow had an idea, and that bright idea has helped put Rochester, Michigan on the map across the country. Now get this: they wrap almost the entire downtown with over 1.5 million brightly colored holiday lights. Each building has its own color and is covered with strands about every two inches. The entire town is wrapped in an explosion of color.

When you drive into Rochester, it's almost like you're driving right into a cartoon, and standing in the middle of town during the Big Bright Light Show is a surreal sensation that's nearly impossible to describe. The lights come on every night around sunset and stay on until the wee hours. It takes two months to put them up every year, but it's totally worth it. The show brings people into Rochester from across the country to eat, shop, take photos, get engaged—you name it. If you're looking for a unique holiday experience, you've got to experience the Big Bright Light Show in downtown Rochester.

Oh, and if you're looking for a great town to live, work or play in, Rochester has everything you need for a wonderful quality of life, Michigan style! Well I ho-ho-hope you enjoyed our first ever Under The Radar Michigan holiday special. If you got this book as a gift, make sure to take the person who got it for you someplace cool. You've got plenty to choose from now.

Story behind the name:
Is this Actual TeeVee?

Little kids provide the best moments on UTR. When the little boy in Ida for the Christmas Parade of Lights asked us if this was "Real TeeVee," we knew the kid was onto our scam.

Chapter 67

Season 5, Episode 5

Restaurant Special

Hey there food lovers, here comes another one of our official UTR best-of restaurant specials. This time we dug deep into season three for some totally awesome eateries. If you're on a diet, drop this book right now, because here we go.

Fralia's
(989) 799-0111
422 Hancock St., Saginaw, MI 48602
www.fralias.com

The locals told us that if you want a seat with your meal at **Fralia's**, you gotta get there early because it fills up quick. They also told us that if you like great food, this is the food to fill up on.

High school sweethearts Jennifer and Adam Bolt own, operate and orchestrate this finer diner. If you're looking for a hip place where they put heart and soul into some great sandwiches, this is it. Everything is fresh, from scratch and made with an artistic and creative twist. Adam was an art major who started cooking for his college roommates, dove into the culinary arts and hasn't looked back since.

Fralia's is the place where people meet, eat and exchange ideas in Saginaw. Jennifer and Adam's philosophy is simple, "Serve fresh, creative food from the heart, and creative and caring conversation will follow." And it's working. There really is a positive vibe about this place that makes you feel like you belong.

So if you want a whole community rolled up in a killer sandwich, frequent Fralia's. That's what the rest of Saginaw does.

Java Joe's
(906) 643-5282
959 N. State St., Saint Ignace, MI 49781
www.javajoescafe.com

If there's anything about St. Ignace you want to know, the place to go is **Java Joe's**. Java Joe's is a tuned-in, turned-on, psychedelic little café with great coffee and excellent food, and it's run by two of the most interesting and energized people you'll ever meet. Joe and Sandy Durm make this place go, go and then go some more. Just walking into this place is a trip. It's an explosion of color, content and creative stuff, and Sandy's wild collection of themed tea pots will amaze and delight you. They're all available for purchase… bonus!

As for Joe, he is such an interesting and intelligent character that I don't even know where to start. He's politically active, socially stimulating, philosophically fascinating and will tell you everything you need to know about the area. Whether you agree with him or not, you have to respect the man's integrity and mental stamina. He's great fun to talk to, and he and Sandy are two of the nicest people you will ever encounter.

If you want great food in a comfortable, casual, cozy and crazy environment, or you just need to know where in St. Ignace to go, it's all at Java Joe's. Don't 'cha know?

Ernie's Market
(248) 541-9703
8500 Capital St., Oak Park, MI 48237
www.facebook.com/erniesmarket

Next, we went to Oak Park to meet a guy I guarantee you will love, or my name ain't Baby. When you walk into **Ernie's Market**, you can't help but feel the love, because for decades Ernie's been at the heart of this neighborhood, and for good reason: he fills your tummy and feeds your soul. Also, be prepared to take on a new identity, because the second you walk in, your name will instantly be changed to "Baby," because that's Ernie's endearing term for all he meets.

At Ernie's, it's all about two things: feeling good about yourself and a good sandwich for a great price, and people come from far and wide for both. They say you should never eat anything bigger than your head, but at Ernie's, if you get a #6, get ready to smash that rule. And, if you've never been to Ernie's before, you can't get your sandwich cut in half. As Ernie says, "If it's your first time, you gotta fight it, Baby!"

Ernie truly is a bigger-than-life, one-in-a-million personality who makes even bigger deli sandwiches to order. His place is simple, real and takeout only. Everyone in the neighborhood knows Ernie and he knows them. His philosophy is that people in a community should help each other, watch over each other and care about where they live. The bonus with Ernie is that you get a great sandwich while he's caring about you.

If you do go to Ernie's, get ready to be called Baby. Get ready for a man with more positive energy than the sun with a smiley face painted on it. And get ready for a sandwich that will most likely hold you until tomorrow. Believe me, until you meet this extraordinary man, you won't know what you're missing. Now, what do you want on your sandwich, Baby?

West Texas Barbeque Company
(517) 784-0510
2190 Brooklyn Rd., Jackson, MI 49203
www.westexbbq.com

If you're familiar with West-Texas-style barbeque, you know that it means no frills, down home, real-deal barbeque, and that's exactly what **West Texas Barbeque Company** is. Dan Huntoon and his son Justin make magic at this place, and quite simply, these meat men are the men to meet. They took a chunk-a Texas, slow smoked it and brought it all the way to Michigan for all y'all to enjoy. And all I can say is them's some good eats!

You can carry out, or if you like, have a seat at their "BBQ Joint" right on the premises. This is authentic Texas style pit barbeque and the pits are fired using only seasoned oak and hickory. They don't use gas, electricity or charcoal, and they never rush what they're cooking. They always cook it low and slow. Getting hungry yet?

Even though this place is a bit under the radar, barbeque lovers from all over are finding it, and they're also finding it to be just the place they've been looking for. These guys can caramelize the fat on a beef brisket like there's no tomorrow, and their ribs, BBQ turkey and smoked sausages are (as my foodie friends would say) "to die for." Dan spent time with some of the best pit-men in Texas, perfected what he learned and brought it up north for us Yankees to munch on. So un-restaurant-chain your brain and come meet some real barbeque people. In the vernacular of the West Texas countryside… it don't git nun not no better.

Turkey Roost
(989) 684-5200
2273 S. Huron Rd., Kawkawlin, MI 48631
www.turkeyroostrestaurant.com

Imagine if you could eat Thanksgiving dinner any and every day you wanted to. No questions asked—except maybe what side you wanted with it. Well, stop imagining because at **The Turkey Roost Restaurant**, you can… and we did! This little pink building in Kawkawlin, Michigan is a landmark for people who know what they love, and what they love is a great turkey dinner with all the trimmings whenever they want it.

The owner Todd Ballor eats, thinks, sleeps and serves turkey. He worked there as a kid, came back to buy it and is carrying on the tradition of serving delicious homemade turkey dinners. Not only do the locals love this place, people from all over the Midwest make the pilgrimage there all times of the year. The Turkey Roost is an icon, a tradition for thousands and an anchor to this town. We came hungry and left full with a real appreciation for what Todd and the Turkey Roost are all about: friends, family and community. Oh, and a homemade turkey dinner any time you want it… bonus!

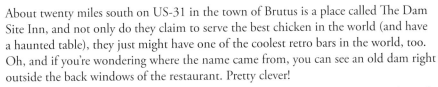

The Dam Site Inn
(231) 539-8851
6705 Woodland Rd., Brutus, MI 49716
www.damsiteinn.com

About twenty miles south on US-31 in the town of Brutus is a place called The Dam Site Inn, and not only do they claim to serve the best chicken in the world (and have a haunted table), they just might have one of the coolest retro bars in the world, too. Oh, and if you're wondering where the name came from, you can see an old dam right outside the back windows of the restaurant. Pretty clever!

Four generations of the East Family carry on a tradition at the Dam Site that's brought in the likes of astronaut Buzz Aldrin, our own Michigan rocker Bob Seger, and yes, even me, the fantabulous Tom Daldin from UTR.

The bar at the Dam Site Inn is like something right out of a Hollywood movie. It's circa 1960s, totally looks like a place George Jetson would stop for a martini after work and was made partly of Naugahyde car upholstery. The groovy chairs in the bar were designed by Eero Saarinen, who also designed the St. Louis Arch and the JFK airport. It's a must see.

The kitchen there is also completely open to all patrons for inspection. And I have to say, it was one of the biggest, cleanest kitchens I've ever encountered. As promised, they sat us at the haunted table, but to be honest, we were so hungry and the food was so good, I don't remember ever seeing a ghost. I barely saw the food it was so good.

If your dream restaurant has great fried chicken, a funky retro bar, a haunted table, an awesome family and a dam right outside the back window, take a trip to the Dam Site Inn. You'll be darn glad you did… ha!

Well, hope you enjoyed this UTR "best of" restaurant section. Now get out there and enjoy Michigan's awesome eateries yourself. I know it's hard to believe, but I promise we'll leave some food for ya.

Story behind the name:
Yum, Yum Eat 'em Up!

Food. 'Nuff said.

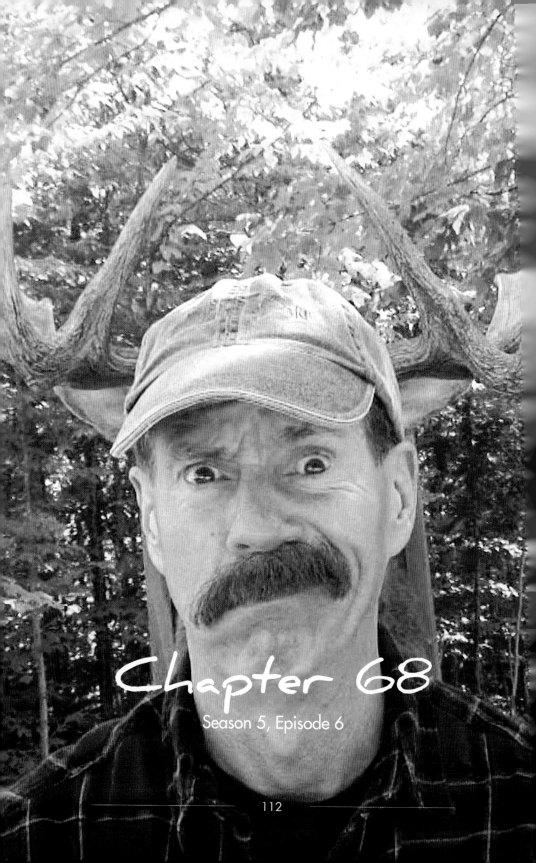

Chapter 68

Season 5, Episode 6

• UP Adventure

Are you a down-state flatlander who has yet to make it to Michigan's beautiful Upper Peninsula? Well, we're gonna make it easy in this chapter and feature stuff on the eastern half because it's not that far to get to. Be honest. Do you drive to the airport, hop on a plane and head west every time you want rugged fun and adventure? Well, if you do, cut it out! Michigan has an entire (and huge) upper peninsula that has enough fascinating stuff to discover for a lifetime. From great lakes and large land mammals to pristine forests and friendly folks with fantastic food, the UP has everything the modern explorer needs to feel alive again. I call it our own "out west," and that's why I'm taking you back UP right now.

Mackinac Bridge

The Tip Top of The Mitten. Right where I-75 hits the water.
www.mackinacbridge.org

Have you ever wondered what it would be like to go to the very top of the suspension towers on the Mackinac Bridge? Well, I hadn't either, but the guys on the crew made me go up there and find out. And I'll be honest… I was ascared!

That's right, Jim and Eric made arrangements and then told me what we were about to do… travel by ladder and tiny elevator to the top of the mighty bridge's south tower. Not a feat for the week of heart, mind or stomach. Well, that was three strikes for me, but there was no way I was getting out of this one. So before I took the steep steps into the stratosphere, I checked in with Bob Sweeney at the bridge authority for some basic bridge talk. He explained that at the top of the south tower, we'd be standing almost six hundred feet above the water. Gulp! Thank goodness they had us wear protective orange vests. D'oh!

Well, after stalling for as long as I could (and calling my wife to let her know where I left the TV remote) we took a way less than little elevator and a labyrinth of tunnels and ladders to the very top. It's there that you open a huge submarine-like hatch and step up and out onto the platform high above the Straits of Mackinac.

The word "wow" doesn't even begin to describe either the view or the feeling you get when you step out onto this small platform. And I can't even begin to tell you what an extraordinary experience this is. You're standing on a platform no bigger than an average patio with just a waist high railing between you and the hereafter. We had a beautiful sunny day, so you could see forever.

Climbing to the top of the mighty Mackinac Bridge was an incredibly scary and exhilarating experience all at the same time, and it really gave me a deep appreciation for the true majesty of this incredible monument to man's ingenuity. It also gave us great views of our next UP adventure. Next stop is the home of the Soo Locks, Sault Ste. Marie.

Antlers Restaurant
(906) 253-1728
804 E. Portage Ave., Sault Ste. Marie, MI 49783
www.saultantlers.com

It never ceases to amaze me how many amazing places amaze me on our TV show. And at this next place, you'll be amazed.

Antlers is a cool and rustic restaurant in Sault Ste. Marie where just about every land mammal imaginable watches you enjoy your meal. If you're looking to turn your next dinner out into an adventure, get ready because when you come through the door you'll be welcomed with more than just open arms. As folks enter the restaurant, bells, whistles and sirens sound from behind the bar. It's a wild way to welcome newcomers to this wacky place where wild animals adorn the walls. The bells and whistles were once used to warn illegal imbibers of an impending raid during prohibition. Now they're just used to make sure you have a good time.

This place has a great atmosphere, good food, ample amber ales and a history more fun and colorful than a barrel of bootleggers. Just ask owner Chris Szabo. He'll tell you that since 1948 the place has been a taxidermy orphanage of sorts, and that the original name of the place was the "Bucket of Blood Saloon." I guess back in the day, if your place didn't have a tough name, no one would go. Antlers is now a respectable place that serves what they call "Northern Cuisine," like locally caught white fish and venison. They also have lots of other great stuff on the menu for low-plains flatlanders like me. So next time you're feeling a little wild and crazy and hunger hits, head north to Antlers in Sault Ste. Marie. Just don't order the furry fish that's mounted on the wall. It's a little dry.

Tahquamenon Falls State Park
(906) 492-3415
41382 W. M-123, Paradise, MI 49768
www.michigan.org/property/tahquamenon-falls-state-park

Tahquamenon Falls. You know about it. You've seen pictures of it. But have you been to see it for yourself yet? Yeah, I hadn't either, and that's why we went.

Just west of the little town of Paradise in the eastern UP is one of the most beautiful places in Michigan, and yep, I had never been there before. So to finally get up close and personal with Tahquamenon Falls, I checked in with Park Ranger Theresa Neal, who started by showing me Tahquamenon's incredibly awesome lower falls.

The lower falls are an absolutely beautiful area of cascading falls that circle around both sides of a small, hikable island, and what you can do there is very cool. For only a few bucks you can rent a rowboat and row a couple hundred yards over to the island. There you can either hike the short quarter-mile trail around the island, or if the water level is low enough (and you are so inclined) you can hop right in the water and play in and on any one of the dozens of waterfalls. I actually went back up later that summer with my family, and the water was so warm and the levels so low we sat under some of the smaller falls with the warm summer water falling around our shoulders. The lower falls really are an awesome and interactive place. The natural beauty along the quarter-mile trail around the island is wonderful and the views of the cascading falls and the river are breathtaking. Unfortunately, the lower falls is something a lot of people miss entirely, and that's too bad. I don't think I've ever been in a more beautiful place in Michigan. It was totally worth the trip.

Well, now it was time to see the granddaddy himself, one of the largest waterfalls east of the Mississippi. So, after a beautiful and hardy hike upriver, there it was. And I was impressed. I had seen Tahquamenon Falls a hundred times in photographs, but when you see it in person, it's so much bigger and awe inspiring. The falls are fifty feet high and about two hundred feet across. You can climb a set of stairs down to the edge of the falls or view it from a plethora of places along the edge of the gorge. Now, if you're wondering when you get there why the water is an awesome root beer color, it's from the tannic acid given off from the hemlock trees in the area. The water is very clear. Besides, I like root beer.

Don't forget that this is also a 50,000-acre state park with camping, tons of trails and lots of other natural beauty to explore. So next time you're planning a trip, skip the airport and check out Tahquamenon Falls State Park in the UP. It's a tremendous sight to see. But to see it, you gotta get up there.

Oswald's Bear Ranch
(906) 293-3147
13814 County Rd. 407 (H-37), Newberry, MI 49868
www.oswaldsbearranch.com

When there's no one left to care for a bear, where do they go? **Oswald's Bear Ranch**, that's where.

Just north of Newberry in the Eastern UP is Oswald's Bear Ranch, and if it wasn't for this place, the bears you see would have probably ceased to be. They call Dean Oswald "Bear Man" and for good reason. His love for these gentle giants has helped create a sanctuary for orphaned and abused bears that otherwise would have probably met their end.

This is also a place where man and beast come together to gain a mutual respect for each other. Young and old come to Oswald's Bear Ranch to have an up close and personal experience with Michigan's beautiful black bear. The entire Oswald family is part of the process, working around the clock to keep these bears happy and healthy. As for Dean? Well, he's probably one of the most interesting people you'll ever meet.

Since 1984 Dean has been rescuing bears and giving them a safe and natural place to live out their days, but before that he was a marine, a policeman, a fireman and even a professional boxer for eleven years. Now he's a momma bear to dozens of grateful furry friends. If he gets them small enough, he even bottle feeds them.

Dean speaks in a low, gentle, earthy yet commanding voice that I believe could sooth even the most savage beast. But truth is, bears are by nature very gentle creatures, and if anyone was ever the "bear whisperer," it's this guy. The huge habitats he's built are so expansive that they even come with their own streams and waterfalls, and these bears eat well. All the restaurants in the area donate fresh food and produce to the ranch. I even got to get into a small area and feed a baby bear some treats. Oswald's Bear Ranch is a great place for the whole family to laugh and learn about these mighty and majestic animals. If you're wondering who man's best friend is, if you ask Dean, he'll tell ya. Cause, he's got about thirty of 'em.

Muldoons Pasties
(906) 387-5880
1246 M-28, Munising, MI 49862
www.muldoonspasties.com

If you're a Yooper, a pastie is a taste-tempting, savory meal you can hold your hand. And if you're not a Yooper, well, they're pretty much the same thing. It's just that you don't get to eat them as often.

So to get our flatlander hands on one, we headed west on 28 to marvelous Munising and found **Muldoons**. If you're looking for a classic, traditional pastie, Donna Grahovac, Peggy Cromell and their league of extraordinary pasties preparers will totally take care of you. They also just happen to be some of the nicest people you will meet on any peninsula.

When we got there I got straight into the kitchen and commenced to prepare pasties. If you've never had one before, they are simply a savory pastry that's made to eat with your hands. Traditionally they are filled with ground beef, potatoes, onions, carrots and rutabagas. These convenient luggable lunches were invented in England way back in the day so men could take them to work, into the mines or wherever. No muss, no fuss. It was like a pot pie in the palm of your hand. The reason pasties became a staple in Michigan's Upper Peninsula is because of all the mining that was done up there. Now they're simply a delicious UP treat.

Making pasties with Donna and Peggy was an absolute blast and I did so well, they even promoted me to prep boy and let me cut and clean about eleventy billion carrots. At least, I think it was a promotion. If you go there, try the gravy that comes with them… it's yummy! So if you want to experience the original UP fast food, there's nothing faster than a portable potpie you can pull out of your pocket. And trust me, at Muldoons, just one of these tasty mounds of crust-covered meaty goodness and you're set for a while.

You'll also be set for a while on adventure when you visit the UP. Where else can you get high on Michigan, eat with antlers, see big black bears and wander through waterfalls. You know where. So, do what we do on UTR, hop in your car, drive past the airport and head north to the UP. *Excelsior!*

Story behind the name:
I Ain't Ascared
of Nuthin'

We don't get many angry letters around the UTR ranch, but let me tell you, a few people really hated our use of the word "ascared." We got letters telling us it's not a real word. No Kidding. People must really hate that word. We love it.

Chapter 69

Season 5, Episode 7

·Alpena
·Grand Rapids

Alpena is another one of those Northern Michigan towns that kinda has everything: a vibrant downtown with cool shops, awesome eateries with fresh local cuisine, tons of the great activities and outdoors to explore and more beautiful Lake Huron shoreline than you can shake an anchor at. It's a boater's paradise and an internationally known dive destination with hundreds of historic shipwrecks right off shore. If you're looking for something cool to do, you won't have to look hard there.

Art in the Loft
(989) 356-4877
109 N. Second Ave., Suite 300, Alpena, MI 49707
www.artintheloft.org

To me the arts are like the icing on the great cake of life, and you know me, I like a lot of icing. If you're a lover of the arts, whatever kind you're into, **Art in the Loft** will teach it to you, display it for you, sell it to you and even let you just look at it for a while. To say this space is cool is a huge understatement. The gallery is located on the third floor of the historic Center Building in a spacious loft setting overlooking downtown Alpena and Lake Huron. The loft has a great atmosphere that blends small-town charm with a great cosmopolitan vibe.

There was a culinary arts class I really wanted to check out that day, but before I got aproned up, I spent a few artful minutes with Linda Suneson. Linda explained that whether you're into painting, sculpture, glass or jewelry, it's all there waiting for you. This place really is an ultra hip, one-stop art fulfillment shop. You can learn it, love it or take it home from there. From students to seniors, the whole community uses art to connect in this fantastic space.

I really do appreciate all the arts, but the one I enjoy the most is the one that when you're done, you get to eat a ton. Cheryl Bates is one of the culinary arts instructors at Art in the Loft, and her specialty is food that tastes good and is über good for you. Bonus! After letting me into her cooking class, she found out pretty quick that I actually play a fourth-degree foodie on TV. After some chopping, mixing, laughing and learning, we produced a healthy and artful meal fit for a TV show host, and there's no better way to enjoy your work than to sit down and enjoy it with great people. When all was said and we were done, Cheryl gave me a job truly fitting of my talents in the kitchen… she let me wash the dishes.

Just like laughter is the natural byproduct of a good joke, art is the natural byproduct of the human spirit. It's how we celebrate life. And at Art in the Loft, they celebrate life every day.

The Fresh Palate
(989) 358-1400
109 N. Second Ave., Alpena, MI 4970
www.thefreshpalategourmet.com

So often kids graduate from school and move away from their hometown to explore the world. Well, here's a young guy who moved away and then came back with some really good food. Bonus!

Eric Peterson lives, breathes, sleeps and cooks great and healthy food for this community. He's created a food destination called **The Fresh Palate**, and foodies from farther than far are finding it. The atmosphere is positive and energetic, the diners are delightfully diverse and the menu is so fun and creative it won't even dawn on you that you're doing your body right. And speaking of bodies, everybody we talked to loved everything about this place because Eric has combined great taste with fresh, healthy, organic and locally sourced ingredients. That's right: we're eating again, but at The Fresh Palate it's so easy to do because the food is so darn good. Eric studied the culinary arts in Oregon, San Francisco and even Hawaii and then brought his knowhow home to Alpena. So if your pallet needs some freshening, stop in and see Eric at The Fresh Palate. He's got plenty of healthy and creative plates that'll please ya!

Rockport State Park
(989) 734-2543
101750 Rockport Rd., Alpena, MI 49707
www.visitalpena.com/adventures/rockport-state-recreation-area

Just outside of Alpena is a pretty cool and interesting place to go explore, so I got a pretty cool and interesting person to take me there. Not only is Mary Beth Stutzman the head of the CVB in these parts, she also happens to be an avid lover of the great outdoors and even an amateur geologist. And she was my pick to show me a fascinating state park there called **Rockport**.

Rockport is a wonderfully bizarre and surreal combination of landscapes because it used to be a limestone quarry, hence the name Rockport. Back in the day, ships would dock there to collect the stone and then transport it around the world. There are even some of the old mining structures still partially intact. It's a very unique place, and in parts of the park, you'll swear you're walking on the moon. This is not your typical state park for a lot of reasons. Yes, there are hiking and biking trails, but you'll also find sinkholes to explore, a bat hibernarium (bedroom for bats) and, get this, there's even a trail that will take you about four hundred million years back in time to the Devonian Period. That's when this area was at the bottom of a giant coral sea. There you'll find incredible and fascinating fossils of all sizes. And I don't mean you'll just find them; there are so many that you'll be tripping over them. As a matter of fact, there are so many that the park service lets each visitor leave with as many as twenty-five pounds of fossils. Jim hit his limit with just one giant one. I know because I helped carry it out.

If you get a chance and you want to see what life was like back, back, back, back in the day, check out Rockport State Park. It's another world right here in Michigan.

Some people call **Grand Rapids** Michigan's city of tomorrow... today. Well, I call it the city of tomorrow, yesterday, today and even the day after tomorrow. What I'm actually trying to say is that when it comes to a good-sized city, Grand Rapids has a good amount of everything you need for an awesome quality of life. From its great restaurants and braggable breweries to its rich history and booming business climate, this is a world-class city that's right in your own backyard.

Another thing I love about Grand Rapids is that it's such a museum-rich city. Right downtown you've got an array of awesome institutions where you can expand your mind and get completely lost in human accomplishments and expression.

Grand Rapids Art Museum
(616) 831-1000
101 Monroe Center St. NW, Grand Rapids, MI 49503
www.artmuseumgr.org

The **Grand Rapids Art Museum** offers an incredible look into the art of man, and the building is almost a work of art itself. It's a LEED-certified, green-friendly structure that's specifically designed to connect you with the art. This place has a fascinating and diverse collection of works from around the art world, and all ages come to enjoy and learn from it. Just being in this building makes you feel creative. They even have some cool and progressive programs that will get the whole family up to their elbows in art.

Grand Rapids Children's Museum
(616) 235-4726
11 Sheldon Ave. NE, Grand Rapids, MI 49503
www.grcm.org

Don't worry, we haven't forgotten about you kids. The **Grand Rapids Children's Museum** is a place for the whole family where kids can explore the world around them. This place really celebrates childhood and the joy of learning. And the cool thing is it's an interactive, hands-on environment that totally inspires learning and discovery. It also helps kids with development and self-expression. This place has it all: art, science, engineering and math, and it's all in fun and colorful spaces that encourage young minds to grow. Sometimes mom and dad actually learn something too… bonus!

Gerald R. Ford Presidential Library and Museum
(616) 254-0400
303 Pearl St. NW, Grand Rapids, MI 49504
www.fordlibrarymuseum.gov

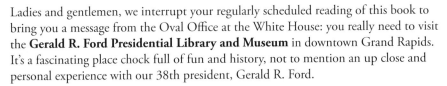

Ladies and gentlemen, we interrupt your regularly scheduled reading of this book to bring you a message from the Oval Office at the White House: you really need to visit the **Gerald R. Ford Presidential Library and Museum** in downtown Grand Rapids. It's a fascinating place chock full of fun and history, not to mention an up close and personal experience with our 38th president, Gerald R. Ford.

While we were there we met up with Kristin Mooney. She's a Public Affairs Specialist at the museum and her mission was to make sure I both learned and behaved. As you walk through the museum, you're surrounded by the historic sights and sounds of the '70s. And with some exhibits, you can walk right into the history. Even if you weren't alive during the '70s this is a great way for you to experience some of the most influential people, places and things that helped shape the world you now live in. They have an exact replica of the Oval Office and a cabinet room you can walk right into. They even have an entire section of the infamous Berlin Wall that came down in 1989.

Not only does this museum give you an up close and personal experience with a fascinating decade, it really gives you a sense of the importance and complexities of the presidency, as well as the accomplishments of Gerald Ford. If you're looking for a place to feel presidential, pop into the Gerald R. Ford Library and Museum. Oh, and the Oval Office really is oval… cool.

Pal's Diner
(616) 942-7257
6503 28th St. SE, Grand Rapids, MI 49546
www.palsdiner.com

There are some really cool classic diners out east in New Jersey that I'd love to show you, but I can't because UTR is all about Michigan. Well, guess what? Someone bought one and brought it all the way to Grand Rapids!

It's called **Pal's Diner** and it's a cool, classic diner that was built way back in 1954. That's when they made the finer diners. It's a one-of-a-kind find, and Barry Brown and his wife Sam were kind enough to buy it and bring it all the way back for us to enjoy.

Barry will tell you that the move was monumental because they moved it all in one piece. The place is an explosion of pastel colors and the finer diners there are just as colorful. We met so many wonderful and genuine people there. Pal's truly is a piece of Americana that serves up all the classic diner favorites. From shakes and burgers to liver and onions, the menu will totally take you back.

So if you get a chance, check out Pal's Diner. You'll leave full, happy and with a whole lotta new friends. It's classic diner done right, right in Grand Rapids.

Sinuous Guitars
info@sinuousguitars
www.sinuousguitars.com

If you're like me, you like things that are made locally. Well, here's a guy who's making guitars right here in Michigan that are being played around the world.

Greg Opatik at **Sinuous Guitars** is a designer by day and musician by night who's combined his talents to make one of the most unique guitars you'll ever strum. Greg and Jeff Armstrong are working hard to make this Michigan-made guitar a star in the music world.

These guys are making unique instruments because they're concentrating on what the other guitar companies aren't doing. They build beautiful custom guitars that actually fit your body. That way, it almost becomes a part of you. These guitar designs will really make you stop and take notice. They look and feel different because Greg and Jeff are looking at the entire process differently. It really is exciting on UTR when we catch a new business like Sinuous making such a big splash so quickly. The energy and enthusiasm these guys have for what they do is why we keep making UTR and why we love Michigan. Once you pick up one of these guitars, it's pretty hard to put down… unless you're me. People actually asked me to put it down.

And once you come to Grand Rapids, you'll see why it's such a great place to expand your horizons, your waistline and your love for innovation. So, do what we do on UTR: get in the car and explore our great state. I guarantee you'll be amazed.

Story behind the name:
Hey! I Found a Fossil!

Rockport State Park, home of eleventy billion fossils. Seriously, you cannot pick up a rock that is not a fossil. That's why it's funny that Tom would be excited about finding a fossil in a place where it's harder to find a non-fossilized rock. But that's Tom.

Chapter 70

Season 5, Episode 8

Road Trip
US 131

Welcome to a special chapter we're calling Road Trip.
It's a pretty simple concept. We pick a Michigan road, drive
along it for a couple days and see what cool stuff we discover
along the way. Even I should be able to handle that.

O n this road trip we picked Michigan US 131. It runs north and south
through the Lower Peninsula's western interior and takes you through some
beautiful parts of the state that are chock full of awesome Michigan treasures.
So we headed up and started our trip just north of Kalkaska, a town known for its
friendly people and great places to catch the mighty Michigan trout. We hit the road
and before we even got up to speed, we found something we just had to check out.

Robinson's Scenic Gardens
(231) 258-2459
7350 US-131, Mancelona, MI 49659
www.facebook.com/pages/Robinsons-Scenic-Gardens

It was a wonderfully weird place called **Robinson's Scenic Gardens**, and if I hadn't
"scenic" for myself, I wouldn't have believed it. This crazy concrete statuary is full of
everything and anything you've ever seen (or might wanna see) made out of cement,
and they're all for purchase. For over forty-two years Sally and Larry Robinson
have been mixing, pouring, molding and painting every kind of concrete creature
imaginable. They've come up with over two thousand different kinds of lawn and
garden ornaments, and according to Sally, they ain't done yet.

Sally and Larry were supposed to retire, but they just couldn't sit still. They make all their own
molds and have everything from big pink elephants to nice little gnomes for your garden.
Sally said it gives her a chance to finally be creative. It also gives the grandkids a great place to
learn about the work world. If you're looking for some crazy, cool and colorful concrete eye
candy to adorn your castle, or even if you're just looking, look for Robinson's Scenic Gardens
just north of Kalkaska. Believe me; you won't have to look hard to find it.

After 26 Depot
(231) 468-3526
127 W. Cass St., Cadillac, MI 49601
www.after26project.org

Once again, we hit the road heading south, and on the way down US 131 we got hungry, and you know us, any place we eat has to be kinda special. So we pulled into the beautiful town of Cadillac to see what was cookin', and after a quick refresher course on just how cool this town is, we found a place that truly was special.

If you want a great meal that'll fill your stomach and warm your heart all at the same time, have I got just the restaurant for you. In the heart of downtown Cadillac sits **After 26 Depot**, a renovated classic train station that may not take trains anymore but does train special needs adults by giving them a meaningful and rewarding place in the community. Yep, it's a restaurant all right, but it's a restaurant that's doing the right thing.

Andrew MacDonald and David Gaunt are two of the passionate people who helped turn this wonderful idea into an eatery that's changing some very special lives. They explained that in the State of Michigan, developmentally disabled and cognitively impaired individuals can stay in school until they're 26 years of age. After that, the question is what happens to these people (hence the name). Well, After 26 Depot answers that question in a big way by giving these special individuals a place to contribute, connect and belong. They earn a living and it gives them a genuine purpose that helps serve the community where they live. The food and atmosphere are both great and just being there gives you a feeling I just can't put into words. I'll be honest, I got a little teary eyed watching the heartfelt give and take that takes place there. They say that food brings people together. Add a noble cause to that and you bring an entire community together. We had a great lunch, made some special new friends and left feeling like family. If you're ever in Cadillac, stop by After 26 Depot. It's a heartwarming experience that comes with a great meal. Bonus!

Blue Cow Café
(231) 796-0100
119 N. Michigan Ave., Big Rapids, MI 49307
www.bluecowcafe.com

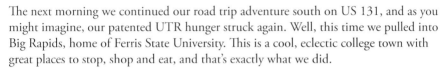

The next morning we continued our road trip adventure south on US 131, and as you might imagine, our patented UTR hunger struck again. Well, this time we pulled into Big Rapids, home of Ferris State University. This is a cool, eclectic college town with great places to stop, shop and eat, and that's exactly what we did.

Now, you know how much we love to find farm-to-fork food on UTR. Well this time, we decided to do something different. This time we're getting it from a blue cow. The **Blue Cow Café** is a place where fresh, local and seasonal is an everyday thing. You'll know it by the blue cow out front.

Connie Freiberg personifies the passion for food at this elegant eatery and she's found a welcome home in Big Rapids. She named the restaurant Blue Cow because she feels so many wonderful things come from cows, from butter to ice cream. She is also a member in good standing of the SLOW food movement, meaning they source ingredients that are sustainable, local and organic. Connie is also a devout locavore and believes in sourcing as close to the restaurant as possible.

Next, I headed back to the kitchen to confront the wizard of true blue cow cuisine. This is where Chef Joel King does his culinary thing. He's from a family of chefs and his Champagne Chicken has people coming from far and wide. This dish is (as they say) to die for, and Chef Joel is a great guy doing great things in the kitchen.

There may not really be such a thing as a blue cow, but there really is a restaurant in Big Rapids that's got great food, an awesome atmosphere, a friendly staff and a big blue cow out front. Now mooooove over, cause we got more driving to do.

Herman's Boy
(616) 866-2900
220 Northland Dr. NE, Rockford, MI 49341
www.hermansboy.com

It really is an awesome drive heading south along US 131 with its rolling hills and classic Michigan farms. We were all just relaxing and enjoying the fall colors when suddenly it happened: SNACK ATTACK. We needed something to munch on and wake us up, so we pulled into a place called Rockford. This is a beautiful little town that's got everything you need to enjoy classic Americana. So we drove through town and put our landing gear down at a place that would satisfy all of our munching needs and then some.

The place is called Herman's Boy. My dad's name was Herman, and I was his boy. So I guess this segment was just meant to be.

When you first walk into **Herman's Boy**, it can be overwhelming. Everywhere you look are incredible spreadables and edibles. It's five unique businesses all rolled into one, with one family making it all happen. I'm telling you, this place had a little bit of everything we needed, and everything looked good.

Jeff Havemeier, or Herman's boy's boy (more on that later), explained just what the heck was going on in this cool and colorful place. They took a bunch of businesses that may not have survived on their own and put them all together into one cool and classically eclectic place. Now they're all thriving. You can get everything there from state-of-the-art outdoors cooking equipment and every kind of kitchen gadget to dozens of fresh roasted coffees, authentic Mackinac-Island-type fudge and even a huge array of gourmet deli-style hot and cold sandwiches, cheeses and soups. Gosh, I'm winded just typing that sentence. They even do a series of gourmet outdoor cooking classes in the summer. Three generations are working hard every day to make sure we all have fun with food. If you go, you have to try their patented "bagel dog."

After a couple times giving the entire place a once-over and a few unauthorized snacks, I had the privilege of sitting down with Herman's boy himself, Floyd Havemeier. His father started the business, so he grew up in it being called "Herman's boy." Floyd eventually paid tribute to his dad by giving it this awesome name. With one family, five unique businesses and a whole community that loves having them there, Herman would be mighty proud.

Nick Fink's Tavern
(616) 784-9886
3965 W. River Dr. NE, Comstock Park, MI 49321
www.facebook.com/nick.finks

Well, with new-found friends, fond memories and a Herman's Boy bagel dog in my pocket, we headed down US 131 for the last stop of our official UTR road trip. And just north of Grand Rapids in a cool community called Comstock Park, we found a classic place to kick back and end the episode (and this chapter).

This place has been a hotel, a barbershop, a post office and even a house of ill repute. It's **Nick Fink's Tavern** and it's got more history and character than you can shake a swizzle stick at. That's right, Nick Fink's is one of the oldest neighborhood bars in Michigan, and if the walls there could talk, I can only imagine what they'd say. Lucky for us Nick's manager Matt Rule talked real good. He loves this place so much, he bought the house right next door. This awesome and earthy watering hole has been an anchor in this community since 1888. It's the kind of place where you come in, order your favorite libation, sit at a table or sink into a booth and instantly become a local. It's the real deal all right, and you can almost feel the crazy past that's gone on between these walls. As luck would have it, a couple members of the famous Fink family were actually there that night, and to them this place is a lot more than just a bar. As we enjoyed a few beverages, they shared stories and tall tales about many of the photos behind the bar. It was truly a special evening. If you want a heaping helping of history, character and characters with your next adult beverage, you'll find it all at Nick Fink's Bar in Comstock Park.

And if you haven't taken a road trip since college, throw your family or some friends in the car and head up (or down) US 131. Where else can you see silly cement, special people, a blue cow, Herman's Boy and even have a drink with a Fink, all in one trip? So go make your own UTR-style road trip adventure. Who knows, we just might see you out there on the open road.

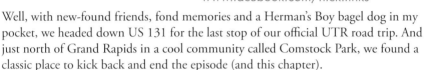

Story behind the name:
Roadie

Someone has to carry the equipment. Eric and I voted that someone to be Tom. Don't forget our shaving kits, buddy.

Chapter 71

Season 5, Episode 9

Southeast Michigan

If you're looking for a place to live, work and play that will satisfy your mind, body and spirit, Southeast Michigan is the place to be. Everything you need for both quality and quantity of life is all around you. Now, on this program we've shown you tons of great reasons to check out this part of Michigan, and guess what? We've got four more.

Thunder Over Michigan Air Show
(734) 483-4030
Event Locations Vary
www.yankeeairmuseum.org/airshow

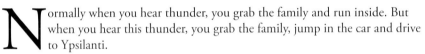

Normally when you hear thunder, you grab the family and run inside. But when you hear this thunder, you grab the family, jump in the car and drive to Ypsilanti.

The **Thunder Over Michigan Air Show** is one of the premier air shows in the entire world that features some of the rarest and most fascinating flying machines made by man. If you've got a wow counter, you might want to bring it, because this show is incredible. Thunder Over Michigan takes place every August at Willow Run Airport in Ypsilanti. It's also home of the historic Yankee Air Museum where you can totally lose yourself in the history of the war birds built on this very site.

As the props were firing up the day we were there, I had a chance to chat with Event Director Kevin Walsh. To say he flies high with enthusiasm for this event is a huge understatement. This is one of the most historic airfields in the nation, and over five hundred volunteers help make this event fly. He reminded me that during World War II, 8,600 bombers were built on this very site and that the Yankee Air Museum is a great place to learn and honor the efforts and sacrifices made by our brave veterans.

It was a real thrill to be this close and see these massive WWII bombers and fighters firing up their engines. You could almost feel what it must have been like to be here back in the day. During WWII, thousands of women stepped up, rolled up their sleeves and became a powerful part of the American wartime workforce. Collectively, they became known as Rosie The Riveter and worked in factories right alongside the men to help keep the US war machine running. These brave and determined women welded, riveted and carried a heavy load to help build and maintain America's arsenal. They were and still are true American heroes. At the air show I was lucky enough to run into a real, genuine Rosie the Riveter, Mary Louise Blanco. She was amazing.

When we left our Rosie, things were relatively quiet. Then suddenly you could hear the thunder as the sky became filled with vintage warplanes: classic fighters, bombers, cargo and troop planes, all flying by so close you could almost see the faces of the pilots. First they came by in formation, and then it was a fantastic free-for-all of flight. The sounds and sights were astounding, and just when I thought it couldn't get any cooler, it happened with a boom: the US Air Force Thunderbirds came screaming overhead in their F-16 Fighting Falcon jets. For the next hour these incredible pilots did acrobatic and precision flying like I've never seen before. It was an absolutely awesome and incredible way to wrap up a thrilling day at the air show.

At least I thought it was, until I was invited to take the ride of a lifetime in a real B-25 Bomber. It's called the Yankee Warrior, and it's the last remaining B-25 still flying that actually flew combat missions in World War II. This was very cool.

In seat number one was Delane Butafucko. She's a commercial pilot whose love for classic aviation put her in the captain's seat of this vintage bomber. And just watching her and co-pilot Bill Clark go through the pre-flight check was absolutely fascinating.

The flight was incredible, loud and full of emotion and amazement. I don't remember the last time I did something this cool. Actually I don't think I ever have. Flying along at only 1,800 feet, you get the real feel of flying. You can almost feel the spirit of the brave men who flew these planes into combat. If you're ready for a once-in-a-lifetime experience, make time in your life for this!

If you get a chance to experience this air show, I guarantee you'll be a totally different person after you leave.

The Creature Conservancy
(734) 929-9324
4940 Ann Arbor-Saline Rd., Ann Arbor, MI 48103
www.thecreatureconservancy.org

When it comes to the animal kingdom, if you want to have a close encounter of a meaningful kind, I've got a place near Ann Arbor where the animals will be wild about you. **The Creature Conservancy** is not a zoo, it's not a nature center and it's not an animal park. It's a wildlife education center that focuses on creating personal connections between people and some of the rarest and coolest animals you'll ever see. If you're tired of just looking at animals and want to truly understand them, this is a fascinating place to visit.

The day we were there, the prestigious Columbus Zoo was on hand to help celebrate the grand opening of this unique facility, and in between all the hoopla we managed to track down the man who made it all happen, Steve Marsh. Steve is an animal enthusiast and wildlife expert who, years ago, woke up to an alligator being left on his doorstep. And the rest, as they say, is history. The Creature Conservancy will get you up close and personal with everything from kangaroos and emus to armadillos and even that same alligator that got left on Steve's doorstep. He's quite a bit bigger now. Steve and a passionate army of volunteers are rescuing animals and educating humans, all in a safe, fun and fascinating environment. Whether you're a school group, a family or just a curious person, and you want a more meaningful meeting with some of the world's most exotic animals, The Creature Conservancy in Ann Arbor should be your next expedition. Who knows, you might even see the rare, elusive and endangered TV show host. Don't worry; they're not smart enough to bite.

Scribe Publishing Company
www.scribe-publishing.com

If you're looking for a Michigan publisher, we found a great one for you. Actually, she found us. Jennifer Baum heads up **Scribe Publishing Company**. She's young, bright, professional, full of energy and enthusiasm and, like a lot of us, reinvented herself to become a great Michigan success story. And when it came time to write the first (and even this) UTR book, if it weren't for Jennifer, it may never have happened.

Jennifer grew up as a healthy, happy bookworm and became a writer and freelance editor. A few years ago she noticed that there wasn't much publishing going on in Michigan. That's when her husband (and really cool guy) Tom said, "Why don't you start your own publishing company?" Well, the light bulb went on, she did some research and set up shop. It wasn't long after that Tom came home from work one day with another idea. He said, "Hey, I checked the Under the Radar Michigan website and those knuckleheads don't have a book out yet." (I added the "knucklehead" part). Soon thereafter, Jennifer called us and walked us through the entire process with amazing coordination and precision. Quite honestly, if she had never called, you'd have nothing in your hands right now. Jennifer sure must know what she's doing, because nearly half of the books she's published have won national awards, and it's easy to see why. She puts all of herself into every project she takes on. She also displayed incredible patience and understanding with me, because me write real slow and sumtimes not 2 good.

Chef Brian Polcyn & Schoolcraft College
(734) 462-4400
18600 Haggerty Rd., Livonia, MI 48152
www.schoolcraft.edu/campus-life/dining-at-schoolcraft/
american-harvest/meet-our-chefs

There are a ton of chefs all across Michigan creating great food. But here's one who creates great food and other great chefs. **Brian Polcyn** is what you might call a super chef. He's published, highly decorated, has opened a half dozen successful gourmet restaurants, perfected the ancient art of charcuterie and still finds time to teach and inspire young chefs at **Schoolcraft College's** state-of-the-art facility in Livonia. When it comes to the

enlightened food movement sweeping the country, this guy is in perpetual motion. Almost two hundred future chefs go through the Schoolcraft program every year, and they learn so much more than just how to cook. Students also learn how to become critical thinkers and fully understand all their ingredients. If you want to feel great about the future of food, just spend some time with the motivated young people who are passionately pursuing this proud profession. Their energy is contagious.

Chef Polcyn's expertise is in charcuterie. This is the ancient art and science of drying, salting and curing meats. If you think about it, refrigerators have only been around for a hundred years or so, but food has been around forever. So, way, way, way back in the day, people needed to invent methods to keep food fresh for long periods of time. As Chef Polcyn so poetically puts it, there's a magic to charcuterie that gives its complex flavors soul. The cured meats and sausages we sampled that day were, in a word, heavenly.

It became increasingly obvious why Chef Polcyn is so revered in the culinary community and why his passion and personality inspires so many young people. This guy knows food and is driven to help others discover its essence.

I learned more about charcuterie and food preparation from Chef Polcyn and those young people than I ever had before. And when all was said and class was done, we enjoyed the meats, breads, vegetables and fruits of the students' labor at the American Harvest Restaurant. It's a full-service teaching restaurant that's right there at Schoolcraft College, and it's open to the public. They serve up student-made gourmet meals that help inspire these young chefs, help fund the program and are absolutely delicious. It's a great experience I highly recommend you try.

Like I said before, if you want to create a great quality of life or even a great vacation for your family, check out the creative people, places and things of Southeast Michigan. I mean, where else can you fly like an eagle, play like an animal, write your own destiny and even find future food fit for a king?

Story behind the name:
Why'd the Toad Cross the Road?

Tom gets to play with giant toads. Look at that picture... it's a giant toad. If that crosses the road, you don't ask questions.

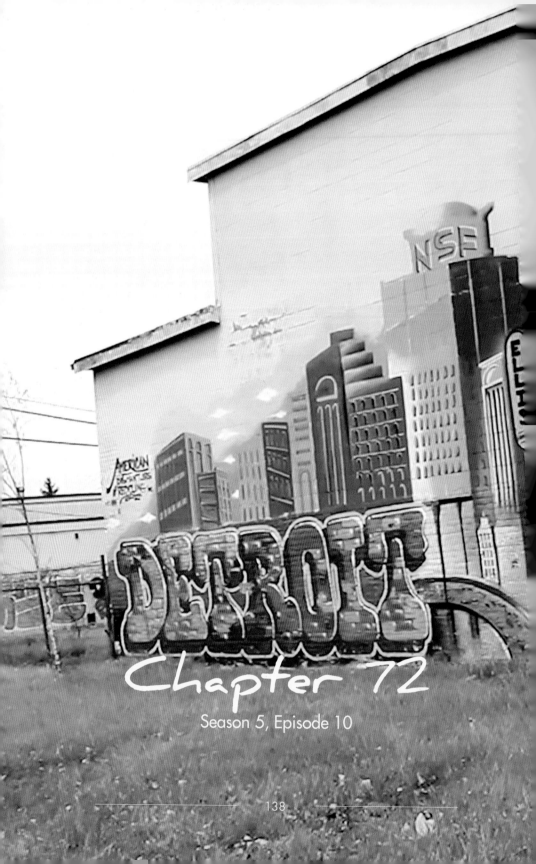

Chapter 72

Season 5, Episode 10

· Detroit

Well, it's time for another patented UTR urban adventure, so we're back in Detroit to show you more reasons why we continue to be excited about this great city.

The rebirth is happening so fast there you'd think we just had triplets. There are so many exceptional, interesting and unusual things to experience. From the iconic people and places that have been there through thick and thin to the new eateries and urbanites embracing and investing in the city, Detroit is an incredible place to explore and get to know better. And I feel more connected to this city every time I go back.

Oneita Jackson

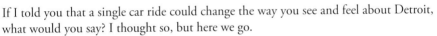

If I told you that a single car ride could change the way you see and feel about Detroit, what would you say? I thought so, but here we go.

Oneita Jackson is an award-winning writer who gave up her first dream for her second: to give inspirational tours of Detroit. For eleven years she was an editor and columnist at The Detroit Free Press. Now she's a driver, a fixer, a concierge and bigger-than-life ambassador for the city she loves. If you want to know the real Detroit, you need to know Oneita.

While explaining her transformation from writer to Detroit's ultimate driver and urban expert, we even transitioned through a car wash to make sure we were cruising clean. Because when you're exploring with Oneita, style and substance go hand in hand. And speaking of style, just for the nostalgic fun of it, Oneita decided to take me over to see her good friend La France Harper for an old-fashioned shoe shine and some great conversation. Now, if you take one of Oneita's tours, you'll see that she's high energy, high on Detroit and a woman of many words, which is great when you've got a thirst for information like me. So if you take one of her exciting and informative Detroit tours, don't bring your word counter, because it'll probably overheat. I honestly thought I knew a lot about Detroit, but after Oneita's short, sweet, fast and furious tour of the new and classic businesses downtown, I realized I've got a lot more exploring to do. There's not one place she did not know.

The Heidelberg Project
(313) 974-6894
3600 Heidelberg St., Detroit, MI 48207
www.heidelberg.org

So with our wheels turning and my head still spinning with tons of great new places for me to come back to, we made our way over to what has become an icon known around the world, **The Heidelberg Project**. This two block, ever-changing art environment all started back in 1986 when renowned local artist Tyree Guyton decided to help express this tattered community's hopes and dreams by turning found objects and abandoned homes into an explosion of artistic colors and concepts. Today the Heidelberg Project features community programs and educational workshops that all promote positive energy, art and a sense of community. Oneita gave me her own personal and passionate tour and even showed me two of the dots she painted on one of the houses in support of the project. The ultimate goal is for this neighborhood to eventually become an actual self-sustaining art village where Detroit kids can grow, learn and love their fellow man. If you're looking for a cool and colorful Detroit adventure or even an artistic way to express your love for this great city, contact The Heidelberg Project. They'll tap into all the positive energy you can give.

Le Petit Zinc
(313) 963-2805
1055 Trumbull St., Detroit, MI 48216
www.lepetitzincdetroit.com

Well, after feeding our brains for a while, it was time on Oneita's Detroit tour to feed our stomachs. So she took me to a place that was both halfway around the world and right over in Corktown.

If you're searching for a quaint little place to enjoy some authentic artisan French countryside cuisine, **Le Petit Zinc** is what the French would call magnifique. After a warm cup of foamy French roast, I sat down with owner Karima Sorel for a quick and enlightening conversation. Lucky for me it was in English.

Originally from Detroit, Karima spread her wings and traveled the world. From New York and Europe to Brazil and beyond, she made her mark. Then in 2009, Karima came home, strengthened her family roots and brought this little piece of Paris to Detroit. She loves this community and her approach to food is fresh, simple and honest, all with a fantastic French twist. Karima has even now partnered with Black Bottom Brewing Company, a local Corktown microbrewer. Now you can enjoy a tasty brew with your baguette. Bonus!

From the flower-filled garden dining outside to the cozy indoor decor, this place is an awesome oasis. The food and atmosphere at Le Petit Zinc was just what the doctor and Oneita ordered. We left feeling full, a little more French and fresh for the rest of our adventure.

Belle Isle State Park
(844) 235-5375
2 Inselruhe Ave., Detroit MI, 48207
www.belleisleconservancy.org

As we got back up to speed, Oneita proclaimed that she was now taking me to one of her favorite places in the entire city, the park island of **Belle Isle**.

On the island, we were lucky enough to hook up with Park Manager Karis Floyd at the botanical gardens inside the Anna Scripps Whitcomb Conservatory. He's heading up the DNR's new efforts there and making a real difference on the island.

Karis is the perfect person to help with the rebirth of this great gathering place because he practically grew up on the island. A lot of people say that Belle Isle is a hidden gem, but actually it's right in the middle of the Detroit River and hard to miss. It's bigger than Central Park in New York City and is one of the largest urban parks in America. From the beautiful botanical gardens and the awesome views of both Detroit and Windsor to America's very first aquarium, this awesome island has tons of fun for any family. You can hike, bike, swim, kayak or canoe, and the iconic fountain at the west end of the island is definitely something to see. Belle Isle adds so much to the quality of life all of us share here in Southeast Michigan and we are so lucky to have it. And now with all the new renovations underway, it's going to get even better.

Craft Work Restaurant
(313) 469-0976
8047 Agnes St., Detroit, MI 48214
www.craftworkdetroit.com

Next we made our way off Belle Isle and straight to where Oneita makes her home, West Village. This is a great little community in Detroit that's alive with new businesses and restaurants. It also happens to be home to our last stop on the tour. How convenient! **Craft Work** is a relatively new eatery in Detroit's West Village, and from what Oneita told me, it's a neighborhood favorite for neighbors far and wide. If you're looking for a classic gathering place where you can settle into some great food and conversation, you'll feel right at home at Craft Work.

The awesome establishment is basically split into two rooms with one simple purpose: to make you feel cool and comfortable. On one side, you've got a classic (and classy) public house, complete with a vintage wooden bar and some long wooden tables that are perfect for casual communal mixing. The woodwork there is original from the 1920s, so you can literally feel the history. Another nice touch is the iconic personality photos on the walls. Happy hour alone makes this place a more-than-worthwhile watering hole to wander into. I guarantee you'll make some new best friends.

The restaurant room has a warm and earthy elegance that really helps you melt into the eclectic atmosphere of this hip and historic neighborhood. No TVs there, just good cuisine and conversation. The food is simple, classic and creative American. It's a limited menu, so each dish is given a ton of TLC, and the flavor profiles are profound. They continually feature whatever is fresh and in season, so check out their menu and strap on your bib. Craft Work is just one of eleventy billion reasons to have an urban adventure in Detroit. So get in the car and get down to Motown. You'll be glad you did.

Story behind the name:
Lady Cab Driver

We are doing a story on writer/cab driver Oneita Jackson. We won't get a second chance to use the Prince song "Lady Cab Driver" as a show title.

Chapter 73
Season 5, Episode 11

• Holly
• Traverse City

This town may be small, but it's really big in a lot of the things that make Michigan such a great place to be. Holly totally takes you back to a time when your town was where you went to belong. It's got a fascinating and colorful history that's been brought into the future with interesting shops and great places to unwind and reboot. From historic and infamous Battle Alley, a place for pugilism and frequent fisticuffs in the 1800s, to its illustrious past with the Grand Trunk Railroad, Holly is a great place to explore. And if you're looking for quaint, you can sure get a cup full there.

Detroit Model Railroad Club
(248) 634-5811
104 N. Saginaw St., Holly, MI 48442
www.dmrrc.org

The following is an official UTR Public Service Announcement: this is Tom Daldin from Under The Radar Michigan, and this message is for you kids (as well as you adults). You should never, ever play on railroad tracks. It can be very dangerous. That is, unless you play on these railroad tracks!

Right in downtown Holly is the **Detroit Model Railroad Club**, and you won't believe this place until you see it with your own eyes. Dozens of club members and volunteers operate, build and maintain tons of trains, tracks and tiny towns for all to enjoy. If you're looking for a fantastic place to take the kids or a place to feel like a kid yourself, this place is a Michigan must.

When we got there, the festivities and official announcements were just about to get started, so I took a quick moment for some train talk with Weldon Greiger. The club started way back in 1935 and has been in Holly since 1976. That's when they started construction on the track there. This tiny railroad is what they call "O" scale, which means that a forty-foot boxcar is ten inches long in their world. Wow, that would make me one and a half inches tall. Do the math. They've laid down miles and O scale miles of tiny terrain, towns and trains to fascinate your family. It truly is a magical place for the little ones.

Just as we were getting ready to pack up and head off to our next Holly adventure, the candy train pulled into the station and the kids' waiting faces said it all. If you wanna have a terrific time with tiny trains in a cool town, contact the Detroit Model Railroad Club.

Note: the club is only open to the public on select days from November through March, so be sure to check their website or contact them directly before you go. All aboard!

Historic Holly Hotel
(248) 634-5208
110 Battle Alley, Holly, MI 48442
www.hollyhotel.com

Say you're in the mood for a wonderful dinner out, but you're also in the mood for some fascinating history, a great atmosphere and a few scary ghosts. Well, there's a place in Holly that will not disappoint.

The **Holly Hotel** isn't a hotel anymore but continues to be a destination for people who are looking for a genuine, authentic dining experience. Everything about this place is old-school cool, and George and Chrissy Kutlenios personify the passion that keeps this Michigan landmark alive and well.

In 1978 George was transferred to Michigan and house hunting in Clarkston when he saw on the front page of the Detroit Free Press that an historic building in Holly burned nearly to the ground. Being a self-proclaimed junkie for old architecture and always up for a good challenge, he went to see it. It was love at first blight. So with all the money he had, George bought the hotel and began resurrecting its brilliance and charm.

George and Chrissy are two of the most genuine and passionate people you will ever meet. They live by the motto, "Do the right thing," and boy are they ever with this incredible place. When you enter the Holly Hotel you step back to a time when a night out was truly a special occasion. The ambiance is über romantic, the service sensational and the food is always up to George's impeccable palate. The breads are baked fresh and everything is done in house. If you want to impress your significant other, other than a quick stop at a jewelry store, this is a pretty safe bet. You should also know that the Holly Hotel is nationally registered as one of the single most haunted places in America. So when you dine there, be sure to ask your waiter about some of the friendly spirits who still go bump in the night. Don't worry, I asked. They're all very nice.

After a great conversation, we ate, laughed and became yet another part of George and Krissy's extended family. Next time you're looking for more than just a meal, head for the Holly Hotel.

A lot of people will tell you that **Traverse City** is one of the greatest places you can live or vacation in Michigan. The food scene is awesome, the beer and wines are incredible and the natural surroundings are beautiful. Well, I'm not gonna tell you that… read on and see for yourself!

Every time we're in Traverse City, I start making plans to move there. The city is big enough to make you feel alive, but still small enough not to get in the way of all the natural beauty. It really is the best of both worlds, a cosmopolitan community with a vast cultural and culinary landscape that still maintains a small-town vibe. It's quintessential Michigan living, if loving life is what you're looking for.

The Little Fleet
(231) 943-1116
448 E. Front St., Traverse City, MI 49684
www.thelittlefleet.com

Food trucks used to be something you'd grab a sandwich and a coffee off of and head back into the plant, but now they've become a foodie phenomenon, and they found their way to Traverse City. Meet Gary Jonas, an energetic and enterprising young guy who has helped change the food landscape in Traverse City. He opened a hip and eclectic bar called **Little Fleet**, created a culinary corral for Traverse City's finest food trucks and gave the community a place to meet, eat and connect. In one place you've got the hub of Traverse City's new food truck scene and a year-round indoor/outdoor bar that serves up everything from local craft brews to classic and designer cocktails. Gary is definitely onto something.

If you're wondering what came first, the bar or the food trucks, according to Gary, they both just happened. He explained that the food truck culture has taken off because it's a great way for budding and aspiring chefs to create and cultivate their craft before investing in a brick and mortar. Plus these new food trucks are anything but boring. They're colorful, creative and make for a fun and festive atmosphere. Plus at Little Fleet, you can choose from a wide variety of cuisines, from Asian to Tex Mex to classic burgers. Imagine: food from around the world, your friends all around you and a round of your favorite beverages. Sounds like a double helping of heaven to me.

Whether you're a foodie, fun or libation lover, move your feet to Little Fleet. There's something there for everyone and everyone there will be just as happy as you they found it.

Tree Sturman
(231) 883-1413
161 E. Grandview Pkwy., Traverse City, MI 49684
www.experience231.org

I'm always talking about how Traverse City sits smack dab in the middle of some of Michigan's most beautiful natural surroundings. So I thought a walk in the woods was in order to remind me and show you just how true that is.

Once I got into the woods, I couldn't see "Tree" for the forest, so I used my excellent survival skills to track down **Tree Sturman**. Tree (yes, that's his real name) is an admitted nature expert, an extreme outdoor enthusiast and a bona fide conservationist who's helping to keep green stuff around for future generations. When Tree's not teaching kids, he's showing folks Michigan's best flora and fauna with a series of eco-tours at a place called Experience 231.

The farther into the woods we got, the more I realized how much Tree truly "walks the walk" when it comes to preserving and appreciating nature, and this guy knew everything. Around every bend, Tree shared either an interesting insight or a great story about the natural beauty surrounding Traverse City. They say a walk in the woods is good for your body and soul, but when you're with an enlightened nature lover like Tree, it's just as good for your mind.

In the pristine forests just outside Traverse City you can see mink, otter and even the elusive bobcat. You just need to know (or know someone who knows) where to look. From tall timber to wild flowers and lowbush blueberries, a walk in the woods up there offers discoveries around every trail bend. When you decide it's time to reconnect with the great outdoors, give the trails and parks around Traverse City a try. And if you want to actually know what you're looking at, give Tree a try at Experience 321. He leaves no leaf unturned, and he just might turn you into a nature lover.

148

Grand Traverse Pie Company
(231) 922-7437
525 W. Front St., Traverse City, MI 49684
www.gtpie.com

A lot of things in life are easy as pie, but when you've got a pie company this successful, something tells me it wasn't that easy.

Grand Traverse Pie Company makes some of the best pies this side of Orion's Belt, which you'll probably have to loosen after a couple pieces. They also helped put this part of Michigan on the pie chart around the world. Mike Busley is a Michigander who took the long way to Traverse City to find his slice of heaven.

Like a lot of young people, Mike graduated from college and headed west to California to find fame and fortune as an engineer. What he didn't find was the passion, so after an illustrious career, he and his wife Denise headed back home to Michigan in search of their collective calling. After deciding to reside in Traverse City, they set out to open a small business that was connected to the community, where they could see the daily fruits of their labor. Since they were smack dab in the middle of the world's cherry capital, they started with cherry pies, and as they say, the rest is a delicious history.

The Grand Traverse Pie Company is something all of us in Michigan can be proud of. And knowing that you're supporting a company that supports its community just tastes, well, as sweet as pie.

So next time you set your course for a city that has exciting places to eat and plenty of natural trails for your feet, try Traverse City.

Story behind the name:
Three Point One Four

Pi. Pie. That should about tell you the extent of our math skills.

Chapter 74

Season 5, Episode 12

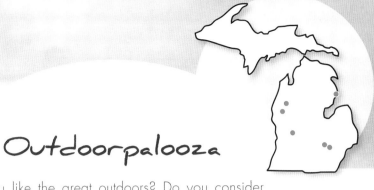

Outdoorpalooza

Do you like the great outdoors? Do you consider yourself an outdoors person? Are you outdoors right now? Well, if not, for gosh sake, get up off the couch, get outside and enjoy Michigan's great outdoors (after you finish reading this book, of course... let's not get carried away).

When it comes to natural surroundings, Michigan is the natural choice for your next outdoor adventure. So we proudly bring you UTR's first ever Outdoorpalooza. That's right, in this chapter I'm gonna take you outside and stay outside until we've had more fun than a true outdoorsmen can endure. So grab your virtual sunblock and compass, because here we go.

Pinckney State Recreation Area
(734) 426-4913
8555 Silver Hill Rd., Pinckney, MI 48169
www.michigan.org/property/pinckney-recreation-area

Did anyone ever tell you to go take a hike? It happens to me all the time. So I decided to do something about it. The Pinckney State Recreation Area is a hiker's paradise in southeast Lower Michigan that offers mile after mile of wonderful wilderness, cozy campsites and beautiful lakes. If you're looking for a place to get away from it all that's not all that far away, this is a state park you need to peruse.

Before we hit the trailhead to conquer the great unknown, we checked in with Park Manager Chuck Dennison to find out more about this awesome outdoor asset. He explained that a lot of people love this park because they don't have to sit in traffic and head up north to find a slice of wilderness. The park is 11,000 acres with twenty named glacial lakes and over forty miles of hiking trails to explore. They also have modern, rustic and even hike-in wilderness camping for those who like to really get away from it all. Heck, they even have an awesome yurt you can use that has lakefront property. This place is simply a boater's, hiker's or biker's dream.

With the sun sinking fast and a few hiking miles notched on our belts, we headed back to our camp site for brats, s'mores and a few of my famous super scary campfire ghost stories. And after a great meal, a good scare and a few hearty laughs, we turned in for the night.

The next day we woke refreshed, feeling alive and ready for another fun-filled day exploring this great state park. If you're wondering how far you have to go to find some awesome wilderness in southeastern Lower Michigan, just try Pinckney Recreation Area.

Hunt's Canoes
(989) 739-4408
711 Lake St., Au Sable Charter Twp., MI 48750
www.huntscanoes.com

When it comes to canoeing you'd probably expect me to get caught up the creek without a paddle, and you'd probably be right. So I went out and hired me an expert (one who has paddles!).

Every year thousands of people come to Michigan and canoe our beautiful rivers and streams. So I decided to give it the old UTR try myself. But for me to be a competent canoer, I needed to find someone who knew everything there was to know about canoeing. And for that, I went to **Hunt's Canoes** in Oscoda. This family-run business has been sending happy paddlers down the mighty Au Sable River for decades, and you won't find people friendlier or more passionate about this waterway or this part of Michigan.

On the way to where were we launched the canoes, they stopped to show us some incredible views from high above the river. We saw miles and miles of pristine forest and beautiful river bends. What a breathtaking place to be.

Anyway, back to my quest to conquer the canoe. With the boats in the water it was time to get this paddle party started. Here goes nothin'… and guess what? There was nothin' to it. Even I wasn't half bad.

My river guide for the day was Travis Boik. He's a great young guy with an even greater knowledge of this majestic river. Travis's great aunt and uncle started this business way back in the '70s, and after a few years in Colorado, Travis moved back for his love of this river.

There are so many great things about the awesome Au Sable. You can use it year round for fishing, and summers are perfect for canoeing, tubing and kayaking. Because of the warm water and countless sandy beaches, it's a great place to swim as well. The water is crystal clear and most of the river runs through a national forest, so natural beauty is pretty much all you'll see.

Trips can range from a full week to a single afternoon or even just a couple hours. Another great thing about this trip is that as you head downriver, the current quietly does most of the work for you. All you have to do is to steer a little, laugh a lot and enjoy the scenery and serenity. If you're hunting for your next Michigan adventure, Hunt's Canoes in Oscoda will put you up the creek with a paddle. The rest, my UTR friend, is up to you.

Bo Burke - Climb a Tree
(231) 835-1111
Cedar, MI 49623
www.boknowstrees.com/home/1324662

Let me ask you something. When was the last time you did something for the first time? Well, if you've never climbed a tree before, here's somebody who'll make sure your first time isn't your last time. His name is **Bo Burke** and he's all things trees. He's an Arborist, an expert, an enthusiast and, heck, he's even a certified tree surgeon. If you've always wondered what it's like way up there where the birds hang out, Bo runs a tree-climbing club just outside of Traverse City in Cedar (pun intended).

We went to see Bo so he could show us the ropes (literally) and get me up and into his world. Now with Bo, it's safety first, second and third. So after a thorough lesson in technique and how all the equipment worked, we got harnessed up and ready to rise to the occasion. Before I knew it, I actually got the hang of it and we were high above the forest floor. The harness you wear is solid and secure and you use certified mountain climbing ropes. Bo also goes out of his way to pick trees that are solid, safe and have great views. The day we climbed he picked a beautiful and massive Black Walnut.

The way Bo looks at it, mountains are far away but there are thousands of trees all around us, so why not climb them? This was one of the coolest things I've done in a long time (and let's face it, I get to do a lot of cool stuff). Bo even let me try out a tree hammock. That was very cool.

If you'd like a bird's-eye view of just how beautiful Michigan really is, look up Bo and his club, "Climb A Tree," and get up there. It was easy for me. After all, I am a bird brain.

Barothy Lodge
(231) 898-2340
7478 E. Barothy Rd., Walhalla, MI 49458
www.barothylodge.com

The final part of our UTR Outdoorpalooza adventure took us to a place that blew our collective minds when it comes to log cabin comfort. If you're looking for a luxury lodge for your next fishing trip, outdoor excursion or even family vacation, the **Barothy Lodge** in Walhalla will knock your waders off. It's a collection of classic lodges that are rustic enough to make you feel real, but comfortable enough to make you almost wanna stay inside the whole time. From pool tables and indoor Jacuzzis to incredible kitchens and fantastic fireplaces, every cabin is completely unique and surrounded by breathtaking natural beauty. Heck, the Pere Marquette River even runs right through the property. Bonus!

We hunkered down for the night at a cabin called Duffy's lodge, a perfect fit for the UTR crew, and rested up for the next day's doings.

Tommy Lynch - The Fish Whisperer
(231) 898-4832
PO Box 1102, Baldwin, MI 49304
www.thefishwhisperer.com

Well, I've heard of the Horse Whisperer, the Dog Whisperer and heck, I've even heard of a Whispering Willow, but a Fish Whisperer? Do fish even have ears?

Well, by now you've probably guessed two things. One, I'm going fishing. And B, I know absolutely nothing about fishing. That's why I secured the expert services of **Tommy Lynch**, the one and only Fish Whisperer. When it comes to any and all things fly fishing, this guy is the wizard of the water. He knows every fly, every fishing hole and he even knows some of the old fish in the river by name.

We met up with Tommy on the Pere Marquette River just south of Baldwin where I tried both fly-fishing and, given my general lack of skills and knowledge, probably Tommy's patience as well. Lucky for me he was a really nice guy.

Once we were boat bound and I was getting my casting down, Tommy and I commenced to relaxing, talking and fishing for hopefully the one that wouldn't get away. Well, the first fish I hooked turned out to be just that, the proverbial "one that got away." Tommy said it was a big one, but I guess we'll never know how big. So for story purposes, it was a whopper! My casting left something to be desired. I was catching mostly tree branches, bushes on the side of the river and I think I almost bagged a squirrel.

Tommy got hooked on fishing when he was just a little kid and got the nickname "Fish Whisperer" from an old college girlfriend. I didn't ask. Now he's so steeped in the sport that he spoke a whole different language I could hardly understand.

With Tommy's good humor and his great expertise and guidance on and under the water, it wasn't long before "it" happened. Fish on!

Well, I guess it's a tradition to kiss your first fly-fishing catch (at least that's what Tommy told me) so I puckered up and gave her a smooch. Turns out I caught a beautiful Wild Rose Brown Trout with the most incredible neon pink spots, and as Tommy explained, you don't keep it. You catch the fish, thank it for the experience and send it on its merry aquatic way. Quite simply put, this was a day I won't soon forget.

So if you're looking for someone to help you match the hatch, catch a ride with the one and only Fish Whisperer Tommy Lynch, because when you catch a beauty like the one I caught, I guarantee you won't be whispering!

And don't forget. If you love the great outdoors, there's no greater place to be than Michigan.

Story behind the name:
...and the Hook was Stuck in the Door!

Campfires always bring out scary stories. Tom tells a whopper of a tale that always ends with the ominous line: "...and the hook was stuck in the door!" Come to think of it, all his stories end that way...

Chapter 75

Season 5, Episode 13

Festival Special

Welcome to another patented UTR Festival Special
where we take you to some of Michigan's craziest, most
wonderful and most funnest fests. Michigan really does have
some of the best festivals you'll find in the entire US. Why? There
are tons of them here to be proud of. You name it and we've got a
festival for it. Because, let's face it, there's so much in our great state
to celebrate, we just can't help ourselves.

Tulip Time in Holland
(616) 396-4221
74 W. 8th St., Holland, MI 49423
www.tuliptime.com

Now here's a festival that's totally flower powered, and people go there from around the world to see it. But I didn't have to drive far, because I live in Michigan. Bonus!

Every spring, thousands of people travel from near and far to Holland, Michigan for one of the most colorful festivals of them all, Tulip Time. Back in the day, people from the Netherlands settled this town, so this week-long festival features a lot more than just these pretty perennials. You'll also experience more Dutch tradition, dancing and celebrating than you can shake a wooden shoe at.

The day we were there featured the Volksparade. It's the main "people's parade" of the festival, and it's made up of thousands of locals dressed in authentic Dutch costumes. But don't forget tradition. First things first, the town crier has to call out to the mayor and city council to inspect the streets and see if they're clean enough for the parade.

This ceremony is fascinating and a lot of fun to watch. All the city officials stand in a huge circle and inspect the street for cleanliness, and as tradition always seems to have it, the streets are never quite clean enough. So before the parade can start, the town crier calls out to the citizens of Holland to walk down the main street of town with buckets, brooms and brushes to scrub the street clean.

After proclaiming me an honorary Dutchman, the town crier said it was time for VanDerTom to VanderDon some real Dutch attire and hit the streets. After all, there was a lot of scrubbing to be done. So in the blink of an eye, and "wit da changin' of da clothes," we all got Dutch, got down and started scrubbing the streets for the big parade. They even put me in some authentic wooden shoes, which by the way were way more comfortable than I thought they'd be. If you try them, the secret is two pairs of socks.

It really is a wonderful experience to see this entire community come out to recreate time-honored Dutch traditions. Even the Governor stopped by to do his part as the parade commenced. In one afternoon we saw more beautiful flowers, more Dutch dancers and more friendly and happy people than we'd ever seen before. Tulip Time is a colorful, cultural experience that will have you clicking the heels of your wooden shoes together and saying, "There's no place like Michigan."

Mighty Uke Day
(517) 896-4025
Old Town Lansing, MI, 48906
www.mightyukeday.com

On Under the Radar we always try to bypass the ordinary and bring you the extraordinary. That's why we totally skipped regular Uke day to bring you to **Mighty Uke Day**.

You read right, every year in May tons of Ukesters from around the country converge on Lansing's Old Town to pluck, play and celebrate this diminutive (yet dynamic) little instrument. This funky festival features live shows, workshops, open-mic stages, children's activities and even helps raise money for local school music programs. I tracked down the main man, Ben Hassenger, to find out why this growing festival, inspired by such a little instrument, has such a big following. He told me that when Canadian film maker Tony Coleman brought his documentary about the ukulele to Lansing's Old Town for a showing, the town loved it so much that a festival was born. Tony explained that this fun and approachable instrument got its name when Portuguese workers brought their tiny guitars to Hawaii in the 1800s. The Portuguese players' fingers were so fast that the Hawaiians said they looked like jumping fleas, and in Hawaiian, jumping flea is pronounced ukulele. This really is a festival that celebrates Lansing's awesome Old Town and this portable little companion we all love. So if you like to have fun and you like happy music, come to Mighty Uke Day next year. You'll dig it the most.

Empire Asparagus Festival
(231) 331-3077
Empire, MI 49630
www.empirechamber.com

In our never-ending quest to bring you some of Michigan's most funnest festivals, we decided to feature one that actually revolves around a vegetable. Besides, my wife says asparagus is good for me.

If you love asparagus, you'll love the northwest part of Michigan's mitten. The sandy soil and climate in those parts makes it the perfect place to grow this delectable vegetable. But if you love it so much you wanna kick up your heels and celebrate it, the Annual Empire Asparagus Festival is exactly where you need to be. This tiny town has a big heart, a big personality and is big on this crunchy green vegetable.

Just as we pulled into town, the asparagus recipe contest was winding down, so I got in line as quick as I could to sample all the asparagus-laden entries. From asparagus soups and salads to salsas and soufflés, I tasted them all. Delicious!

This festival is compact, full of fun characters and all about the awesome flavor of this plentiful vegetable. From asparagus beer and asparagus brats to deep fried and even raw asparagus, the folks there really know how to celebrate those little green stalks. Yes, I did say asparagus beer. It's made by Right Brain Brewery and it was awesome.

One of the locals who truly personifies this festival is Paul Skinner. He owns Miser's Hoard, a great little old-and-new curiosity shop right in downtown Empire, and when it comes to asparagus-inspired fun, Paul's the guy to hang with. According to him, the town of Empire has a cool and quirky personality, which makes it the perfect place for this fun fest. Empire also happens to be one of my favorite little towns in Michigan. I asked Paul why the porta potties were placed a little farther away than they are at other festivals. He responded with a sly wink and genuine chuckle.

I'll be honest: even if you don't like asparagus, this little action packed festival will definitely fill your fun bucket. Heck, they even go highbrow with a legitimate asparagus-inspired poetry contest. I, of course, didn't win, but I did have an absolute blast reading my mediocre masterpiece aloud to the crowd.

My very favorite part of the festival is what has to be the tiniest parade on Planet Earth. In fact, it's so small, the parade actually circles the block and goes through town twice. That's awesome! It may have been small, but it was way big on enthusiasm and town pride!

If you're looking for a festival that's got a ton of energy, fun and flavor all wrapped up in a little stalk that will remind you later why you love it so much, check out the Asparagus Festival in Empire. When you tell your friends you went, they'll be green with envy.

Elvis Festival
(734) 483-1035
56 E. Cross St., Ypsilanti, MI 48198
www.mielvisfest.org

As I'm sure you know, at times I can get a little confused, so on the day we showed up at the Elvis Festival, I was wearing the finest "Elf" outfit money could buy. I had it all goin' on: the funny hat, the unflattering green tights and even the wacky shoes that curl up at the end. I was one awesome elf. But unfortunately, I had only glanced at the brochure, and it was actually the "Elvis" Festival. So after a brief bout with embarrassment, I retired to my luxurious UTR talent trailer, and in mere moments emerged in an outfit much more fitting to the occasion. That's right: I was impeccably and accurately dressed in full garb as the rare and elusive "mustached" Aloha Elvis. Thank you, thank you very much!

This is Michigan's official Elvis Festival that happens at Riverside Park for two days every July in Ypsilanti's Historic Depot Town. Thousands of Elvis lovers and people who love to be Elvis converge to shake rattle and roll out the red carpet for all things Elvis. There's music, food, fun stuff for the kids and some of the best Elvis impersonators and performers you'll ever see.

One of the extraordinary people who make this event such a huge rockin' success every year is Mary Decker. When she helped start it back in 2000 it was just a small gathering. Now it's bigger than most of Elvis's shirt collars. This fun musical festival has everything you need to Elvis out. They've even got a midway that features marvelous Elvis memorabilia and mouthwatering Elvis munchies. I didn't see any peanut butter and nanner sandwiches, though, so you might have to bring your own.

There are more folks here who love the king than you can shake your hips at. We saw Elvis, after Elvis, after Elvis, after Elvis, to the point where I totally lost control, jumped into the crowd and shared my inner Elvis all over everybody. I moved like Elvis, danced like Elvis, took photos and selfies as Elvis and even flirted with the ladies like Elvis. Heck, I did more shakin' than should be allowed by law. But when all was said and done, I did what I came to do: celebrate the King.

So no matter what period of Elvis you're into, you'll find him at the Annual Michigan Elvis Festival in Ypsilanti. Oh, and if you do see the infamous crazy mustached Elvis, don't be alarmed… that's just me!

Story behind the name:
…and the Hook was Stuck in the Door!

Campfires always bring out scary stories. Tom tells a whopper of a tale that always ends with the ominous line: "…and the hook was stuck in the door!" Come to think of it, all his stories end that way…

Chapter 76

Season 6, Episode 1

· UP Adventure

If you haven't been to Michigan's beautiful Upper Peninsula yet, what's your excuse this time? You're afraid of bridges? You don't like clean air? Your dog ate your driver's license? Well, for gosh sakes, cut it out.

Michigan's incredible UP is what I like to call "our own out west," and it's right in your backyard. From pristine forests and waterfalls to fabulous art and fantastic food finds, everything you need for a true Michigan adventure is all over the UP. Even if you're a city slicker, there's tons of energy, culture, history and architecture up there to keep you happily hopping from town to town. It truly is a treasure that more of us need to explore.

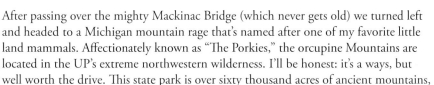

Porcupine Mountains Wilderness State Park
(906) 885-5275
33303 Headquarters Rd., Ontonagon, MI 49953
www.porcupineup.com/porcupine-mountains-wilderness-state-park

After passing over the mighty Mackinac Bridge (which never gets old) we turned left and headed to a Michigan mountain rage that's named after one of my favorite little land mammals. Affectionately known as "The Porkies," the orcupine Mountains are located in the UP's extreme northwestern wilderness. I'll be honest: it's a ways, but well worth the drive. This state park is over sixty thousand acres of ancient mountains, towering virgin timber, remote trails, wild rivers and secluded lakes.

And speaking of secluded lakes, there's one place at the Porkies I'd always wanted to see, and the short hike to it was even suitable for a low-plains flatlander like me. It's called Lake of the Clouds, and to make sure we found our way to and from it, I met up with Park Naturalist Bob Wild. Actually, it's only about a minute walk from your car.

When you first step onto the overlook high above the lake, I guarantee you'll have what I call a "Grand Canyon moment." I was speechless when I laid eyes on it. Bob said the number one comment he hears from people is that they never knew something like this existed in Michigan. To make our moment even more special, just as we came up to the railing, a pair of beautiful bald eagles riding the wind currents soared right up and over our heads. What an amazing sight.

Lake of the Clouds is nestled deep in a mountain canyon and sits about halfway up the park in elevation. Lake Superior is at about six hundred feet above sea level, but the highest peak in the park hits almost two thousand. There are tons of trails and backcountry camping sites around the lake. They even have rustic cabins where you can check in and check out of the modern world. There is so much beauty to take in at Porcupine Mountains Wilderness State Park that you might want to stay a few days, and for that, they've got you covered. This is a world-class camping destination for nature lovers far and wide, and with majestic views of the Lake Superior shoreline just steps away, you'd be hard-pressed to find a better place to get your camp on than right there.

On our way to what Bob called a "must see" part of the park, he even took us to see one of the yurts they have available. If you've never stayed in a yurt before, Google it. They're half tent, half cabin and all the way cool.

Now when I say that the UP is our own "out west," the next place Bob took us proved that to be absolutely 100% true. Even though it's about a forty-five minute drive and you actually change time zones getting there, the west end of the park is, in a word, awesome.

Once we got there Bob took us on a short walk and down a series of steps to see the majestic cascading waterfalls of the Presque Isle River. Talk about scenic; you'll see dozens of waterfalls, incredible pools, water slides and fantastic geology all surrounded by beautiful old-growth forest. Bob said it best when he said, "This place alone could be a park." The downriver hike Bob then took us on was spectacular. Around every bend was another view worth a long and lingering look. It's unbelievable how much beauty and extreme wilderness we have at this massive park. Be sure to plan for extra time when you get to this part of the Porkies, because you'll both need and want it.

All my life I wanted to see the Porcupine Mountains, and it took me getting a TV show to finally do it. Don't wait until you get your own TV show. Get up there and see these mountains soon. They're so beautiful, you'll think you're in Michigan.

Keweenaw Brewing Company
(906) 482-5596
408 Shelden Ave., Houghton, MI 49931
www.keweenawbrewing.com

The next morning we drove back east, turned left at the Keweenaw Peninsula and drove an hour north into copper country and to one of the UP's most historic, energetic and beautiful cities.

Winter, spring, summer and fall Houghton is alive with everything you need to satisfy your urban urges. There are plenty of great places to eat, stay, shop and play, all in beautiful natural surroundings. The city sits about halfway up the peninsula on the south side of the Keweenaw Waterway and right across from the city of Hancock. Houghton also happens to be home to one of Michigan's most prestigious universities.

Michigan Technical University is a great school that brings young people from around the world there to study science, technology, engineering and even forestry. Heck, some of them like it there so much they decide to stay and build their future there.

Case in point is Dick Grey at the Keweenaw Brewing Company. He's a former Michigan Tech student who graduated, went away, but came back to make some beer that I find pretty darn tasty. Originally a "middle-earther" from Midland, Dick wanted to be an engineer, so he hightailed it up to Michigan Tech. After graduation he went west, but the natural beauty of the Houghton area eventually brought him back. Now, he's making beer with so much character and flavor, he managed to make one of my new favorites, "Widow Maker Black." This dark and toasty treat was named after one of the menacing machines they used to use down in the copper mines.

Dick will tell you that he's got the greatest job in the world, and to share his wealth of knowledge he even hires tons of current and former Michigan Tech students to teach them about both business and beer. So not only does Dick create some mighty fine brews, he's also helping to create Michigan's future market makers. Bonus!

Well, I went, I saw, I drank and then I didn't see so well. So as always, I let Jim drive. But suffice it to say, if you're thirsting for a beer with a passion for this peninsula, The Keweenaw Brewing Company is a great place to start. Just remember to always enjoy your adult malted beverage responsibly.

The Quincy Mine Tour
(906) 482-3101
49750 US-41, Hancock, MI 49930
www.quincymine.com

With a belly full of brew, I was hankerin' for some history, so as my head cleared, we headed north over the Portage Lake Lift Bridge and through the historic town of Hancock. This is another unique town totally worth exploring. As you head north out of town the road winds up, up and out of the valley, giving you some incredible views of both cities. Once you get to the top, you'll want to stop at the historic Quincy Mine for a trip down and into this area's fascinating copper mining past.

Back in the day, this part of the Upper Peninsula was the copper mining capital of the world. It was known as "Copper Country," and many a penny came out of mines just like this one. The Quincy Mine Tour is one of the most fascinating things you'll ever do. From the incredible towering shaft house built by the same company that made the Mackinac Bridge to the world's largest steam hoist, there's as much history above ground as there is below it. To make sure we left no nugget unturned, we dug up and took a tour with Tom Wright. He was wonderful. He was so full of passion and information that we couldn't help but share his enthusiasm. After suiting up for our subterranean tour, we boarded the authentic cog railway car and let Tom's incredible knowledge take us down and into the mine. At the actual entrance of the mine, we all hopped off the cog railway and onto a steel wagon that transported us on tracks deep, deep into the earth. Even though you travel about two thousand feet back into the mine, you're only about 360 feet below the surface. You'll pass by some of the oldest rock strata in the world that was laid down by hundreds of ancient lava flows over 1.1 billion years ago. The temperature in the mine is a constant forty-three degrees.

In the mine's heyday, from 1910 to 1912, the miners would work as deep as nine thousand feet below the surface by candlelight in sweltering conditions. At that time it was the deepest incline shaft in the world. Many miners gave their lives to help build Michigan and America's Industrial Revolution.

Tom painted such an interesting and detailed picture of this mine's incredible history that not once on the tour did you feel anything but fun and fascination. At the Quincy Mine tour they dig deep to make sure you have an absolute blast. I'm normally a little claustrophobic, but I'll be honest: the tour was so fascinating and it's such a huge realm down there that it never even entered my mind. But I did find an actual copper nugget. Tommy gets a new pair of shoes!

The Douglas House Saloon
(906) 482-2003
517 Shelden Ave. #1, Hougahton, MI 49931
www.facebook.com/Armandos-Restaurant

After looking into the UP's captivating cultivation of copper, we looked into our future for the evening and saw that after all that traveling, tasting and touring, we were destined for some fun in downtown Houghton. After a long day in the mines there's nothing better than a trip to your favorite saloon for a cold beverage and some delicious pickled eggs. Wait, what did I just say?

You read right, I said pickled eggs, and at The Douglas House Saloon they serve those and a whole lot more. This place is not only famous for its pickled pleasures, it's also got tons of history and the locals love it. So, to get a better handle on my pickled predicament, I plopped down in front of the one and only Bob "Bubba" Macgowan. He takes a lot of pride in preserving not only eggs, but also this historic Houghton landmark.

Like so many others in Houghton, Bob attended Michigan Tech, left and eventually returned. What he loves most about the area are the people, and he's spent the last thirty years at The Douglas House Saloon helping to carry on all its traditions. Since 1890 this place has been an important part of the community. And speaking of community, generations continue to come back to enjoy these magical, mystical little pickled eggs. They even ship them all over the US. Well, after a bit of both coaxing and coaching, I tried my first pickled egg. I can now safely say that I've had one. Are they good enough for you to travel to Houghton, try one and perhaps never leave? There's only one way to find out!

Fitzgerald's Restaurant and Eagle River Inn
(888) 487-1700
5033 Front St., Eagle River, MI 49950
www.eagleriverinn.com

The next morning, we loaded up, fueled up and headed up the Keweenaw Peninsula to find a place we discovered completely by accident a couple years ago and were determined to find again. Imagine you're driving along, you're tired and weary, seemingly in the middle of nowhere and all you want is an incredible place to eat, drink and spend the night. Oh, and that has incredible views of Lake Superior. Well, guess what? We found it in Eagle River.

Behold The Fitz, one of the comfiest, funkiest, faraway places you'll ever wish you'd found before. Sure it's out of the way, and way up the Keweenaw Peninsula, but it's also way cool. In 2008, Mike LaMot and his buddy Marc Ray bought The Fitz, a.k.a. **Fitzgerald's Restaurant and Eagle River Inn**, and went on a mission… a mission to turn it into a foodie, drinkie and sleepy oasis that people from across the country are finding.

Mike and Marc are two guys who (as they say) bought the place when they were too young to know better. Now it's turned into the best thing they've ever done. These are guys who like to do things right, so after getting the inn in order, they started to nerd out. First they nerded out on fine whiskeys, then on Michigan craft beers and eventually on serious gourmet barbeque. The rest of the menu is varied and very, very good, and where else can you eat with Lake Superior lapping at your toes? It's also the kind of place where once you find it, you're family.

We may not have found it by accident this time, but The Fitz still turned out to be an incredible place to unwind, whet our whistles, fill our tummies and even get forty solid winks. Yeah, it's far away, but once you're there, it's not far at all.

Story behind the name:
Heart of Gold

In this episode we featured the Quincy mine tour in the UP, so we started thinking of mining songs. Neil Young's Heart of Gold came to mind for the lyric, "I've been a miner for Heart of Gold…" Seemed like a good one.

Chapter 77

Season 6, Episode 2

•Pentwater
•Manistee

I just fell in love with Pentwater about five minutes after we pulled into town. After reading this chapter, you will too. Pentwater is a West Michigan beach community that is absolutely perfect for worshiping the water. It's got a world-class marina with some boats that could probably sail around the world, a beautiful Michigan white sand beach with plenty of soft sand to take home in your shoes and lots of happy, friendly folks who'll be thrilled when you get there.

The Hexagon House
(231) 869-4102
760 6th St., Pentwater, MI 49449
www.hexagonhouse.com

Well, you know us on UTR, we thrive on the awesome and unusual, so using a simple form of geometry, we found a place like no other. You've heard the old expression, "Six ways to Sunday." Well, I have no idea what that means, but we found a six-sided bed and breakfast that will amaze you.

Just a short ways from downtown (on, of all things, 6th street) is The Hexagon House, and it's one of the most unique and beautiful places you can stay in all of Michigan. This stately six-sided structure is a true tribute to Victorian architecture. And it has more grace, elegance and charm than you can shake a doily at.

Matt and Sandy Werner are the heart and soul of this graceful place and have owned and operated the inn since way back in the 1900s. This beautiful bed and breakfast was built back in 1896 and is nearly as old as the town. Legend has it that the original owner built a six-sided home so the devil couldn't catch him in a corner. I don't know if it worked, but I do know that you'll see quite a few octagon structures, but six-sided buildings are very rare indeed. Everything about The Hexagon House is frilly, fun, fascinating and full of history. It's a must-stay place if B&B's are your bag. Our time at The Hexagon house was so memorable, it's an experience I'll remember to never forget. Oh, and if you do go, ask them to show you Harry Potter's room. It's pretty unique, and who knows, he may even be there. :-)

Pentwater Artisan Learning Center
(231) 869-5323
780 Park St., Pentwater, MI 49449
www.pentwaterartisan.org

The next day we mustered up two goals: to learn something and then to eat something. We always get hungry when we think. So we headed over to the **Pentwater Artisan Learning Center** on East Park Street for a lesson in… well, just about everything.

This place is eleven thousand square feet of how-to that will turn you into an expert in no time at all. No matter what craft or skill you're craving to conquer, the Artisan Learning Center can help you get there. From painting and pottery to woodworking, jewelry making and even welding, if you're hankering to learn how to make or do something, this is something you should definitely do.

To help me learn more about this awesome learning center, I checked in with Sue Hop. She and I had an absolute blast making the rounds to find out what inspired all these people to expand their horizons and learn a new skill or craft. Every town should have a place like the Artisan Learning Center. That way we could all learn new things and even how to do some things better. I checked to see if they offered a class in how to host a TV show. No such luck.

Gull Landing
(231) 869-4215
438 S. Hancock St., Pentwater, MI 49449
www.gulllanding.com

This next portion of the Pentwater program brought us to the part where we ate. No surprise there, but this time we picked a place that would entertain all of our senses.

At **Gull Landing** you can get plates of great food, plenty of awesome atmosphere and even live jazz to munch to. The place has a laid-back summer resort feel and is the perfect place to meet and eat with the locals. Owner Diana Russell practically grew up there. Decades ago, her parents started it as a hotdog and root beer stand, when one day a local chef proclaimed, "Hey, I can make prime rib." The rest, as they say, is history, and that very chef is still there today. Gull Landing really is a Pentwater summer tradition and generations return every year to reconnect and kick back. The evenings there are magic. As you wine, dine and listen to live music, the setting sun silhouettes the sailboats as they return to the harbor. Perfect!

Our philosophy on UTR is to go where the locals go and you'll find your happy place. And you won't find a place to eat and party happier than Gull Landing. You also won't find a place that fits your getaway plans better than Pentwater, where you can stay, learn and even play in classic mitten-state style. Well, did you fall in love with Pentwater?

When you drive into **Manistee** you'll probably have the same reaction I had, "Wow… what a cool downtown!" This is a classic Michigan city with incredible architecture that was built with lumber money back in the 1800s. In the year 1900, Manistee actually had more millionaires per capita than any other city in the entire US, and the Victorian homes and churches there will inspire you to walk through its beautiful neighborhoods.

Today the city is preserving its illustrious past and moving into a fascinating future with young and daring entrepreneurs who are helping shape Michigan's bright and prosperous future.

Manistee is also a great beach and boating community that has all the aquatic accouterments you need to enjoy the great Lake Michigan. So you can soak your soul in the sand and surf or tie up your vessel and still enjoy some great city life. If you're high on classic Michigan living, you might even want to live there.

Orchard Beach Aviation Scenic Air Tours
(231) 723-8095
2323 Airport Rd., Manistee, MI 49660
www.orchardbeachaviation.com

Guess what? I know some folks who can get you so high on Manistee, you'll see the whole place in about an hour. **Orchard Beach Aviation** is just north of town and the perfect way to see how beautiful this part of Michigan truly is. They offer fun and affordable scenic air tours of the area that will have you looking down and feeling up about where you chose to be.

Our experienced pilot and captain for the day was Gayle Sonefeld. She loves what she does and where she lives and was genuinely excited to share it with us. Once we got our cameras and crew on board, we took off into the "mild" blue yonder for a ton of flying fun. As we climbed higher and higher above Lake Michigan and Manistee, I knew this was going to be very cool. Aerial views are the best and this is a great, fun and affordable family activity. The tour lasts about an hour and the incredible Lake Michigan shoreline views are spectacular. A fall color flight would be amazing.

We loved every minute of it, landed and instantly started making plans to bring our families back. The Orchard Beach Aviation scenic air tour really is a great way to see everything you don't want to miss in Manistee.

Iron Works Café
(231) 655-9845
254 River St., Manistee, MI 49660
www.manisteekitchen.org

And speaking of missing something, there's one thing on UTR we never, ever miss, and that's a good meal. So we decided to break bread at a place that not only serves healthy, locally sourced food, it's also part of a grassroots movement that's helping this entire community eat better. The **Iron Works Café** is part of a new non-profit organization called The Manistee Community Kitchen, and they've organized and energized this entire community to help end hunger and obesity in Manistee County. Local chef Brandon Seng helped take the concept one step farther by purchasing the old Iron Works Building in town and turning it into a café that brings local vegetables, fruits and this philosophy to fruition. The old Iron Works Building is a very cool, funky old structure that was the birthplace for industry in Manistee. In the early 1900s they built pumps and steam engines there. Now this striking structure is helping to develop a sense of place through community gardens, a farmer's market and an awesome and creative cafe. The sign on the outside of the building says it all: "Cultivating the past and planting the future." This building might not be an iron works anymore, but they are working on making all of us in Michigan a lot healthier, and that works for me. Next time you're near Manistee, manage to get yourself over to the Iron Works Café. They'll serve you information, inspiration and a great meal… bonus!

The Ramsdell Inn
(231) 398-7901
399 River St., Manistee, MI 49660
www.ramsdellinn.net

The Ramsdell Inn is the gem of downtown Manistee. This incredible structure was built in 1891 for a cost of only $35,000. Now it serves as the anchor to this great city, and it's as much fun to look at as it is to walk into. If you want to stay at a place with fascinating history, you should make some history of your own at the Ramsdell. But wait, there's more. Down the stairs and around a huge and impressive granite pillar is TJ's Pub, a great place to meet, greet and eat with friends and family. It's a classic, cozy pub with everything you need to feel good again.

The two people who personify this pub and the passion it takes to move a monument like the Ramsdell into the future are Lindsey and Matt Swidorski. They've taken this gem and shined it up for all of us to enjoy. Lindsey and Matt love Manistee, and it was their dream to own a business downtown and be a part of the city's continued success. Acquiring the Ramsdell was a dream come true. This young couple has done wonders and turned the Ramsdell into a wonderful place to stay. Every room is decorated differently and the suites are sweet. They will never, ever make buildings like this again, so if you get the chance, stop by the Ramsdell for a room or just a Reuben and a round of your favorite beverages at TJ's Pub. You'll end up loving history as much as we do.

Story behind the name:
I Wanna Take You Higher

Song titles provide most of the names of shows to our brains. When we get a chance to go airborne, we're taking some Sly Stone with us.

Chapter 78

Season 6, Episode 3

Restaurant Roundup

Now be honest, you watch UTR just for the restaurant segments, don't you? Go ahead, you can tell me. I thought so. Well, that's awesome because food is half the reason we make the darn show. Every episode we try to put in at least a couple great places to eat, because we know that's what you guys love. And believe me, eating all that good food is no piece of cake. Actually, it's easy as pie. So strap on your favorite bib and belly up to the buffet, because here comes another one of our patented UTR restaurant specials where we take you to some of our favorite eateries from episodes gone by.

Hoffman's Deco Deli & Café
(810) 238-0074
503 Garland St., Flint, MI 48503
www.hoffmansdecodeli.com

Some things just naturally go together, like peanut butter and jelly and liver and onions. Oh, and those little fish shaped crackers with that yellow cheese that comes out of a can (mmmmmm…). But when we were in Flint, we found a place that blew our minds. How about this combination: antiques and deli food. I know; it hurts just thinking about it. But at Hoffman's Deco Deli & Café… it hurts real good!

Hoffman's is the creative conglomeration of Mark Hoffman, his brother Heath and their father Nick. Upfront, it's a first-class, funky art deco deli that serves awesome sandwiches, salads and wraps. And in the back is an explosion of antiques the likes of which I've never seen before. It's crazy. It's wonderfully weird, and it totally works!

I have to say that this really is one of the funkiest, coolest places I've ever been to. And Nick, Mark and Heath are three of the coolest dudes you'll ever meet. Hoffman's has become the place for Flint's urbanites to eat, kick back and connect. The day we were there they even had an "Under the Radar" wrap on the menu. Nice!

As for Nick's Antique Emporium in the back, my wife Cathy is an antique aficionado and a classic clothing connoisseur. I took her to Hoffman's and her exact words were, "This place is to die for." The collection of collectables there is first class.

This is two generations working hard and thinking outside the box to make Flint a better place for the next generation. If you like good people, positive energy, great food and awesome antiques all smershed together, there's only one place I know of: Hoffmann's Deco Deli & Café.

Legs Inn
(231) 526-2281
6425 N. Lake Shore Dr., Cross Village, MI 49723
www.legsinn.com

If you're just like me and you've heard of **Legs Inn** your whole life and never been there, well, you're just like me. But now that I've been there, we're just a little bit different.

The historic Legs Inn is like something you'd see in a fairy tale, but a fairytale where they serve great Polish food and Michigan draft beers… bonus! It's stone on the outside, hand-crafted wood on the inside and probably one of the coolest places you'll ever walk into. The inn is located at the end of the Tunnel of Trees Drive in Cross Village, once a thriving fishing and lumber town.

George and Kathy Smolak, along with their two sons Mark and Chris, make up two of the four generations who continue to care for this great Michigan landmark. George's Uncle Stanley, who was born in 1887, emigrated from Poland and built Legs Inn. Now people go there from around the world to see the incredible wood carvings inside. It's called Legs Inn because of the inverted stove legs Stanley decided to use on the roof in the front of the building. Wonderfully weird!

Legs Inn is so much more than just a great restaurant; it's a pure Michigan destination. People who go there describe it as a unique museum, art gallery and monument to nature. If you're lucky enough to get a table out on the patio, the views of the sunset over Lake Michigan are breathtaking. Great atmosphere, great food and great beer, all smothered in Smolak hospitality.

The Legs Inn was a great way to top off our trip to Harbor Springs. It was a one-of-a-kind experience, and even if you do it two and three times, it will still feel special. Michigan truly is a special place, and that's why it's the place I always return to.

The Maple Grille
(989) 233-2895
13105 Gratiot Rd., Hemlock, MI 48626
www.themaplegrille.net

Most restaurants bring food into their kitchen to cook for you. Well, here's a guy who took his kitchen outside to where the food is. It's called The Maple Grille, and it's a modern twist on the way things were done way back when. No freezers, no microwaves and no ovens, just fresh, local food cooked over a wood fire, right in front of you.

Josh Schaeding is the young chef who's turning heads and filling stomachs right by the side of the road. This truly is one of the most unique dining experiences we've ever had doing the show and one of the best. Josh depends on local farms and ranchers for the flora and fauna he serves up, and he even grows a lot of it himself. Imagine food so fresh that the chef just went right out back and picked it for your meal.

Even though the menu changes daily depending on what's available, one thing stays constant at The Maple Grille, and that's family. With their help, Josh built the modern yet earthy structure that makes up both his outdoor kitchen and the dining area. It's funky, cool and right out in fresh air… perfect!

We dined on rib eye with secret sauce, lake trout, rabbit confit, coulotte steak, tri tip, grilled redskins, spaghetti squash and homemade cornbread. Hard to believe, but I was speechless.

So if you're looking for a unique dining experience with fresh local food and great people, The Maple Grille is only a drive away.

Note: since our first visit, The Maple Grille has also opened an indoor dining area. Great news for those days Mother Nature is having one of her moods.

The Cooks' House
(231) 946-8700
115 Wellington St., Traverse City, MI 49686
www.cookshousetc.com

Have you ever had a meal that was so good, you felt like you went to a cook's house for dinner? Well, guess what? We did! That's because it's a restaurant called **The Cooks' House**, and not only is it actually in a house, this funky restaurant is serving some of the best food you'll find this side of the Milky Way. Chef Eric Patterson, his wife Teresa and Chef Jennifer Blakeslee have created an intimate dining experience that will make you feel like you're part of their foodie family. And when I say intimate, I mean intimate. This cozy little eatery only seats about twenty-five, so it really is like you're sitting in someone's hip little home having supper. It's casual, comfortable and the perfect place to meet other people who appreciate great food.

In all the conversations I've had with chefs and restaurant owners across the state, I don't think I've ever met people more passionate and dedicated to their craft, their staff or their patrons. Every single person we encountered there was genuine and the real deal. They source locally, cook seasonally and have a great philosophy about how they create their meals. They don't just think up a dish and then try to find ingredients for it. They take whatever fresh ingredients are available and create something around them. It really is art in the kitchen.

Well one dish and glass led to another, and before we knew it, we were full, filled with great stories and already planning our return. If you want a great Michigan-made meal, just walk right into The Cook's House. You don't even have to knock!

La Taqueria San Jose
(616) 284-2297
1338 Division Ave. S., Grand Rapids, MI 49507
www.facebook.com/Taqueria-Sanjose

Well, if you're paying close attention, you might notice **La Taqueria San Jose** is listed twice in this book. It's not an error… we just like it so much, we put it in this special episode, too. Turn to page 96 to read about our first time there.

Story behind the name:
Chow Hound

We eat a lot. And you seem to like it when we do.

Sit On It
Detroit

Chapter 79

Season 6 Episode 4

Sit On It
Detroit

182

• Detroit

Detroit: the new frontier. These are the adventures of the TV Show Under the Radar. Our mission? To explore cool new businesses, seek out fun stuff to do and eat at great restaurants. To boldly go places you may have never been before. Sound familiar, my Trekkie friends?

Well, thank goodness Detroit isn't a million light years away, because right now it's lighting up with so many awesome things to see, do and eat, you just might need a Star Trek transporter to get yourself home. So dial in your coordinates for the Motor City, put your vehicle in drive and set your phaser to fun. Because we're landing in Detroit in three… two… one…

By the way, for you amateur astronomers, Detroit is located in Southeast Lower Michigan on Planet Earth in the Orion Arm of the Milky Way Galaxy and part of the Virgo Supercluster. Nice to know!

Sit on it Detroit
(313) 680 5733
www.facebook.com/Sit-On-It-Detroit

Sometimes you just have to sit down and think about it to realize there's a problem. Well, here are two young guys who sat down, thought about it and then stood up and did something about it!

Kyle Bartell and Charlie Molnar are two enterprising young guys who noticed a lack of seating at bus stops around the city. People were standing, sitting on the ground or just making do with what they had. So they started what's called **Sit on it Detroit**, took responsibility, took some reclaimed wood and are making a real difference all around town.

Kyle and Charlie started revamping parks and public spaces when they were at Wayne State University. Some people accept what they see and others make change. These guys make change. They love Detroit and wanted to make a difference and bring back a sense of place and community. Let's be honest, most people their age are trying hard just to figure themselves out, but here are two young guys who are also trying to figure out ways to make life better for the people around them. That's pretty cool.

These benches are comfortable, funky, functional, organic and add a real artistic touch to the urban landscape. Every bench is decked out with different, dynamic art and they even built little libraries underneath so folks would have something to read while they wait. I dropped in a couple UTR books. It's the least I could do.

Next time you're in Detroit and you see some of Kyle and Charlie's handy work, give 'em a nod, because they're helping make Detroit a little bit better for all of us.

Louisiana Creole Gumbo
(313) 446-9639
2051 Gratiot Ave., Detroit, MI 48207
www.detroitgumbo.com

If you're hankerin' for a heapin' helpin' of some authentic Louisiana Creole Gumbo, hop in your car and start driving… to Gratiot Avenue in Detroit, that is. Because I know a place that will not disappoint. I guarantee!

Way back in 1970 Joseph Stafford founded **Louisiana Creole Gumbo** and brought real, genuine Creole cooking to the Motor City. It's a tiny eatery that serves up huge amounts of savory southern selections. Now, mind you, this place ain't nothin' fancy. The atmosphere is earthy, urban and real, and the food is the real deal, too. Through Detroit's good times and bad, this authentic eatery has stood the test of time because people keep coming back.

Today, Joe Spencer and his family are keeping Joseph Stafford's recipes, legacy and love for this great city alive and well. In 1982 Joe was in radio and looking for a change when he fell in love with this little Creole cookery. It turned out the original owner, Joseph Stafford, was ready to retire, and before Joe Spencer knew it, he owned the place lock, chicken stock and barrel. Creole cooking is a combination of French and African cuisine that is often misunderstood. It's not always hot and spicy like a lot of folks think, but it is always very flavorful. If it's Creole, they serve it. Heck, they even serve five different types of gumbo.

Joe and his family are some of the nicest and most genuine people you will ever meet, and they do more than just serve food. They also serve the community where they live. They support local churches, help feed the hungry and even mentor young people. It's not hard to understand why this place has been an icon in the city for so many years, especially when you taste the food. If you like a little spice and a sense of place on your plate, I think you'll agree: Louisiana Creole Gumbo is a must stop in the Motor City. You know us at UTR… if the food ain't good, we ain't goin'!

John's Carpet House & Big Pete's Place
(313) 995-8715
2133 Frederick St., Detroit, MI 48211
www.johnscarpethouse.com

Now we all know that some communities in Detroit are still singing the blues. Well, here's a little-known neighborhood that's using the blues to put a smile on the entire town.

It's called **John's Carpet House & Big Pete's Place**. It's a lively social gathering and jam session that happens every summer Sunday afternoon to pay tribute to a man who loved his neighbors and loved to play the blues. And even though there's no carpet, the house is gone and John is no longer with us, Albert "Big Pete" Barrow keeps these soulful sessions alive to honor his friend's name.

John Estes was a junk man and a drummer by trade who loved the blues so much that, back in the day, he carpeted his big front porch, and on Sundays would invite musician friends over to put on a show for the neighborhood. Well, the good music and good will he created has spread so far that today people come from as far away as Alaska, Japan and Germany to bask in this bluesy hullabaloo. You'll see everything from local cats to some pretty serious celebrity players perform, and the crowd that gathers is just as much fun. People from all walks walk in, set down their chairs and blankets and enjoy this fantastic free for all.

When it comes to having a good time in Detroit, I can always use people who love The Blues. And if you think the music is soulful, the food you'll find there is some of the best down-home BBQ you'll ever taste anywhere. I think I gained about ten soulful pounds as I sampled all the down-home cooking.

Then it happened. With a little bit of sun, soul and social lubrication, I managed to muster up some courage, get up on stage and get down with some funky blues. I, too, am a drummer by trade.

Next time you're in need of a funky good time, on any given summer Sunday afternoon, just head for the corner of Frederick and St. Aubin in Detroit. That's where you'll find John's Carpet House and a lot of happy Detroiters. John would be very proud of what this has become.

Kyle and Charlie started revamping parks and public spaces when they were at Wayne State University. Some people accept what they see and others make change. These guys make change. They love Detroit and wanted to make a difference and bring back a sense of place and community. Let's be honest, most people their age are trying hard just to figure themselves out, but here are two young guys who are also trying to figure out ways to make life better for the people around them. That's pretty cool.

These benches are comfortable, funky, functional, organic and add a real artistic touch to the urban landscape. Every bench is decked out with different, dynamic art and they even built little libraries underneath so folks would have something to read while they wait. I dropped in a couple UTR books. It's the least I could do.

Next time you're in Detroit and you see some of Kyle and Charlie's handy work, give 'em a nod, because they're helping make Detroit a little bit better for all of us.

Detroit Vegan Soul
(313) 649-2759
8029 Agnes St., Detroit, MI 48214
www.detroitvegansoul.com

What if I told you there was a vegan restaurant in Detroit where the food was so good, you wouldn't even miss the meat? I know, I thought the same thing until I went to **Detroit Vegan Soul**.

Okay meat lovers: stop shrugging your shoulders, because right in the heart of Detroit's historic West Village is a place that just might make you a believer. Sure, it may be minus the meat, but it's plusses when it comes to flavors and textures will enlighten your meat-muddled mind.

Detroit Vegan Soul is exactly what it says it is: a meat-free restaurant that's taken a savory and soulful approach to their meatless menu. Erika Boyd and Kirsten Ussery create what they call cruelty-free food, and the rest is relatively recent history.

Vegan simply means "no animal products whatsoever," a.k.a. "all flora and no fauna."

So how do they make soul food? Erika explained that pleasing your palate is really all about flavors and textures, and they've got it down to a soulful science. Originally the two of them got into the vegan lifestyle for family health reasons and it turned into a mouthwatering movement. This comfort food is so good and so healthy you'll feel better even before you leave. To be honest, I was dying to find out who was there to miss the meat and who was there just because the food is such a taste tempting treat. What I found was that even though this place is totally vegan, carnivores, omnivores, pescatarians, vegans and vegetarians were all dining simultaneously in soulful and decadent delight. No matter the preference of their palate, they all loved the food. If you're tired of being a meathead like me, head to Detroit Vegan Soul and savor the flavor of their meatless menu. Because even if you "love" meat, with this food you won't miss it for a moment.

Read this next paragraph like you're Spock from Star Trek: So be logical, my UTR friends. Do a little traveling of your own and transport yourself to Detroit's new frontier. Where else can you sit in style, get great gumbo to go, sport a smile from the blues, eat without meat and fowl with new friends? Just take it from this wise and logical space traveler. Detroit is where people with a vision are coming to live long and prosper. (Now, make the sign of the Vulcan and go explore Michigan). :-)

Story behind the name:
Sit on It!

We are huge fans of Happy Days and really like the polite ways they dished out burns.

Chapter 80

Season 6, Episode 5

• Flint
• Eaton Rapids

If you haven't been to Flint, you'll see why I love it right
when you drive downtown. This is a city with an illustrious
past, a vibrant present and a promising future. There are tons
of new up-and-coming businesses, awesome establishments and
enough creative cuisine there to keep you coming back again and
again. And thanks to UM Flint and Michigan State University, it's
another one of those cities where young people are reconnecting
and pumping up the energy.

Yep, Flint has everything a modern urban dweller could want or need to survive
and thrive in our new city centric society, except one. And guess what? They
fixed that in a really big way.

Flint Farmers' Market
(810) 232-1399
300 E. 1st St., Flint, MI 48502
www.flintfarmersmarket.com

Flint's fantastically cool new Farmers' Market is a multi-use, multipurpose, state-of-
the-art food facility that's designed to do one very important thing: reconnect us with
real food. When we were there I took some table time with Karianne Martus and Sean
Gartland. They're two of the market makers who keep this downtown market alive
and full of fresh food.

This place is a fantastic foodie destination. From the wide variety of vendors to the
cooking classes and demonstrations, the market has become the culinary centerpiece
of the community. They have restaurants, special events, incubator kitchens and even
host parties and weddings there. The cool building alone makes the trip worthwhile.
This market really is an incredible edible endeavor, and the people who live in Flint
have a powerful passion for this place. Not only does this market add a sense of place
to the community, it turned what was once a fresh-food desert into an awesome edible
oasis for urban dwellers to devour. Wanna see a city market done right? Well, right
now would be a great time to come forage for fresh food at the Flint Farmers' Market.

Freakin' Unbelievable Burgers
(810) 422-5428
5100 Corunna Rd., Flint, MI 48532
www.freakinburgers.com

All that being around food at the market gave me a powerful hunger, and what I felt like was a freakin' unbelievable burger. Lucky for us, we were in Flint and the folks at **Freakin' Unbelievable Burgers** took great care of us. This brazen burger joint was the brainchild of Brent Skaggs, a restaurateur who decided it was time to build a better burger.

It all started when Brent and his wife felt like a great hamburger. They looked and tasted far and wide and couldn't find one they loved. So they set out to satisfy themselves and ended up satisfying an entire community. As for the borderline provocative name, the Skaggs family was experimenting and cooking different burgers at home in their kitchen when his wife suddenly yelled out, "Now that's a freakin' unbelievable burger!" Brent's eyes lit up, the name stuck and the rest is a real tasty history. Another one of their secrets are Brent's buns, so to speak. He uses only locally baked brioche buns and has forty-four different toppings to adorn your dinner.

So if you're in the mood for a really good burger, just go to Flint for a Freakin' Unbelievable Burger… and tell 'em Tom sent ya.

The Mounds Off Road Vehicle Park
(810) 736-7100
6145 E. Mt. Morris Rd., Mt Morris, MI 48458
www.themounds.org

The best way to drive your vehicle off the road is when you do it on purpose. I've tried the other way and it's not a lot of fun.

If you're ready for some serious off-roading, head over to **The Mounds Off Road Vehicle Park** in Genesee County. This is one of the greatest off-road playgrounds you'll find anywhere. There are over two hundred acres of hills, dunes, mud pits, trails and rock climbs, all designed to test your head and your tread. They've got all types of terrain, they're open year round and you'll see all kinds of vehicles getting down and dirty in the mud. Moments after we got there a jovial jamboree of Jeepsters showed up, showed off and got off-road ready. Park Manager Garry Pringle and I hitched a ride with the one and only Stephanie Ambabo, a.k.a. Super Steph. When it comes to kicking up some soil, the boys ain't got nothing on that girl!

With quite a few bumps under our belt, Super Steph decided to take on one of the most formidable rock climbs in the park. And I was blown away. This takes skill, nerves and a lot of practice, and she nailed it. After the climb, Steph took us on a wild and crazy ride through the mud pits. This was awesome! We were all making waves, slinging mud and hoping like heck we'd make it through. I don't think I've ever had this much fun getting this dirty before in my entire life.

For some good clean fun and a filthy vehicle when you're done, get your off-road vehicle to The Mounds just north of Flint. Your local car wash will be glad you did.

Oh, and next time you feel like visiting a city with great energy that's getting better every day, take a day trip to Flint. Who knows? That one day may make you wanna stay!

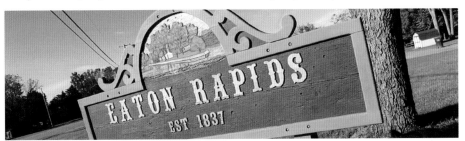

Eaton Rapids is the only city of the same name on the entire planet. Which means if you go there, you've probably never been there before. And even though the city sits smack dab in the middle of Michigan's lower mitten, the entire downtown is actually on an island. That's right; the only way to get downtown is by bridge, hence the nickname "The Island City." If you're looking for Main Street America with a hometown atmosphere, this is a place where you should plop yourself down and make yourself right at home.

Urban Air
urbanair@wakeupdowntown.com
www.urbanairwakeupdowntown.com

And speaking of making yourself at home, every year Eaton Rapids is home to a fantastic phenomenon called **Urban Air**. For four days every fall, over one hundred classic and vintage Airstream travel trailers converge on the town, park up and down the main street, set up camp and become a cozy cash mob like no other. This event is meant to wake up, shake up and economically fortify downtown, and when these Silver Twinkies arrive, the town comes alive. It's quite a sight to see.

Now, if you're wondering who's responsible for this wonderfully wacky event, Kirk MacKeller is one of the fellers. He explained that folks sign up online, come into town and have a good time. They wine, dine, shop and hold special events that support local charities. They even have a trailer decoration contest affectionately called "Pimp Your Blimp." Kirk went on to proclaim that Airstream owners are, by nature, some of the most creative, generous and hospitable nomads you'll ever meet… and we met them all. Trust me, you'll get invited in and see some of the coolest and most creatively decorated digs ever to be driven around. I honestly can't remember the last time I had this much fun with strangers. And then it hit me: this is a UTR episode… and we haven't eaten anything in Eaton Rapids yet! Not good.

Mark's Gourmet Dogs & Hot Diggity Dog Hotdog Stand
(517) 580-3404
5330 W. Saginaw Hwy., Lansing, MI 48917

All that hobnobbing with the locals made me and the guys hungry, so we set out in search of the perfect hotdog. And suddenly, there he was: Eaton Rapids' one and only Hotdog Man!

Mark McGee is loved by this entire community for two reasons: 1. He and his wife Krysta and their son Christian are absolutely wonderful people, and 2. They own **Mark's Hot Diggity Dog Hotdog Stand**, where they serve up tasty gourmet hotdogs for all (including us) to enjoy.

Mark and Krysta got their start when they won a Food Network contest that gave them enough to get started. Krysta had the idea to start with a cart and they were off and grilling. These aren't just regular hot dogs. They've gone way out of their way to put a creative and gourmet twist on the traditional dog. You can get yours plain if you want, but what these two do with this classic American meal is amazing.

If you're looking to rediscover your love for hot dogs, Mark and Krysta have taught the old dog some new tricks that will tickle your taste buds. And speaking of looking for something, keep an eye out for their new permanent location right downtown. That way you'll be able to bring your dog in out of the cold!

The English Inn
(517) 663-2500
677 S. Michigan Rd., Eaton Rapids, MI 48827
www.englishinn.com

It turned out that Eaton Rapids and Urban Air had everything we needed to have fun, and at the same time help this great hometown thrive. So we packed up and headed out for… well, you guessed it… yet another incredible meal (remember, we eat a lot on UTR).

We headed just a short ways north of town to a grand and fancy place where we could eat and even stay the night in classic style. **The English Inn** is where you go when you want to celebrate, impress, fall in love, relax or just treat yourself to some four-star food in a warm and friendly atmosphere. This historic inn and restaurant definitely needs to be on your Michigan bucket list. Erik Nelson and his fine family have owned this incredible property for more than twenty years, and they invited us in and made us feel right at home.

The home was originally built in 1927 for the general manager of Oldsmobile, Irving Reuter, and his wife Janet. Now it's a wonderful place to simply soak in. From the amazing classic cuisine to the beautifully appointed rooms and immaculate grounds, Eric and his family have gone above and beyond to preserve this wonderful piece of Michigan history for all of us to enjoy. The ambience in the main dining room upstairs is absolutely perfect. It's refined, elegant and sophisticated, everything you'd expect in a fine-dining experience. What we didn't expect were the fun folks we encountered in the inn's basement pub. That place was a party and totally worth a visit.

If you're longing for luxury that you don't have to create or clean up after, consider the English Inn. It may be how the other half lives, but if they let me live in it for a while, you're a shoo in! And if you think we picked Eaton Rapids just because the word "eat" is in the name, you're right. But, let's face it: it's still a really cool place to be!

Story behind the name:
Silver Twinkies—Yum!

The iconic Airstream camper is affectionately known as a Silver Twinkie. You know us. We are always thinking food…

Chapter 81

Season 6, Episode 6

•Middle of the Mitten

Even if you're not a palm reader, your life line should
tell you that Michigan's Middle is a great place to be. So
Jim closed his palms around the steering wheel and we headed
for Michigan's Middle Earth. Then we merrily meandered down the
mitten and found the kind of stuff that will totally make you wanna high-
five this great state.

Dawson & Stevens Classic Diner and Bottle Cap Museum
(989) 348-2111
231 Michigan Ave., Grayling, MI 49738
www.bottlecapmuseum.com

To make things easy (that's how we like it on UTR) we started high and headed
low. First up we hit the awesome town of Grayling for a marvelous museum
where they also happen to serve malts… bonus!

Do you ever wish you'd saved all your bottle caps? Well, welcome to **Dawson &
Stevens Classic Diner and Bottle Cap Museum**, where you'll find over ten thousand
Coca Cola collectibles on display. Now, make no mistake; this is a fully functional
vintage diner with all the classic comfort cuisine you're accustomed to. But at this
diner, your dinner comes with some pretty classic eye candy.

Where did all this incredible Coke memorabilia come from? And how did it all end
up in this delightful diner? To find out, I sat down with collector Bill Hicks and diner
owner Bill Gannon. They're the Bills behind the bottles beneath all the caps.

Almost forty years ago a neighbor told Bill Hicks that a couple old coke bottles he found might be worth some money. That little bit of information got him started collecting. His casual collecting eventually turned into a powerful passion and painstaking pursuit, so he traveled far and wide, amassing one of the most impressive collections in the world. Meanwhile, Bill Gannon was looking for some Coke collectibles to adorn a classic fifties-style diner he had just purchased. Well, the two met, Bill was amazed, a conversation ensued, a friendship blossomed and Bill Gannon bought the entire collection for two very important reasons: Bill Hicks wanted the collection to go to someone who would truly appreciate it and never break it up, and he also wanted it to be somewhere where he could still go and enjoy it. Mission accomplished! Walking into this Grayling landmark is like taking a step back to a time when things were a little simpler and when a business deal between two total strangers could turn into a lifelong friendship.

You can't help but feel good here. So if you think things go better with Coke, stop by the Dawson and Stevens Classic Diner in Grayling. Because there's enough Coca Cola stuff here to make "everything" better... even this book.

The Ziibiwing Center
(989) 775-4750
6650 E. Broadway Rd., Mt Pleasant, MI 48858
www.sagchip.org/ziibiwing

A lot of us in Michigan know very little about the Native Americans who live right here among us, which is kinda sad since they were here first. **The Ziibiwing Center** in Mt. Pleasant is an absolute treasure for those who believe in celebrating and perpetuating the great culture of these First Nations people. This place offers an absolutely fascinating educational experience that will bring you up close and personal with the Saginaw Chippewa Indian Tribe as well as other great Michigan tribes.

William Johnson is the curator at the center, and his passion for this precious preservation is amazing. He made the entire experience seem so very real for us.

This place is so much more than a museum. It's a cultural center that truly lets you participate in the history. For more than ten thousand years, these indigenous people developed a beautiful, rich and complex culture that is all around you at the center. The incredibly lifelike and life-size dioramas alone will amaze you. You'll experience and learn about all the great tribes of the Great Lakes region. Once you tour this awesome facility, you really gain a deep sense of respect and understanding for these great people. After all, their American history really is the first American history. So stop by the Ziibiwing Center in Mt. Pleasant and get a real feel for these first Americans.

Uncle John's Cider Mill
(989) 224-3686
8614 US-127, St. Johns, MI 48879
www.ujcidermill.com

How'd you like to visit a cider mill that's so big and has so much cool stuff you can see it from space? Behold Uncle John's Cider Mill, a colossal place that's so full of fruit and fun you just might wanna move in. If you're looking for classic family fall activities and edibles, everything you need for an awesome autumn is there.

To make sure we left no apple unturned, I met up with Mike Beck. He's a fifth generation family farmer who helps keep Uncle John's jumpin'. It all started as a roadside fruit stand decades ago, and now they grow over thirty-five different varieties of apple and turn them into everything from pies to potent potables. Uncles John's is like a one-day vacation destination with tons of outdoor activities for the kids that will send them home full, happy, healthy and plum tuckered out.

After a great conversation and a couple sips of Mike's special cider, I decided to take the tractor ride and follow some folks out to see if my massive memory could master the classic twelve-acre corn maze. Well, with a little help from my friends Jim and Eric, I found my way out. Uncle John's may be giant, but if you're in the mood for some down-on-the-farm fun and food, you may as well have a lot of it. Wanna make some classic Michigan fall family memories? Take them to Uncle John's Cider Mill. You'll be a-MAZED. Get it? Maze? Hoo boy.

Michigan Princess Riverboat
(517) 627-2154
3001 Lansing Rd., Lansing, MI 48197
www.michiganprincess.com

Next, we headed south to a place in Lansing where I could take a real princess out to lunch. Only this one floats on a river. It's called the **Michigan Princess** and it's an old-fashioned, triple-deck, stern-wheel riverboat that cruises up and down the Grand River. They do special events, fall color cruises, a blues cruise, weddings, proms and even a lunch cruise. That one had our name written all over it.

Once I gained permission to come aboard, I headed to the ship's wheelhouse for some pre-cuisine conversation with Captain Chris Chamberlain. Chris came from a long line of sailors, and twenty-five years ago his dad decided to wrangle up and run a riverboat. The rest, as they say, is water under the bridge. This is a big boat. It's 110-feet long, forty-four feet wide and pretty darn tall. As the boat steamed lazily down the river, I couldn't help but ask if I could steer the boat for a while. Captain Chris actually let me do it. Don't worry, we all survived.

This trip is an absolute ball, especially in the fall when the colors are so awesome. If you're anywhere near Lansing and you're not afraid to get full while you float, check out the Michigan Princess River Cruise. It's our own royalty right here on the Grand River.

Spector Beatles Museum
(517) 648-2043
6700 Aberdeen Dr., Dimondale, MI 48821

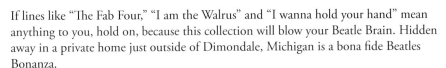

If lines like "The Fab Four," "I am the Walrus" and "I wanna hold your hand" mean anything to you, hold on, because this collection will blow your Beatle Brain. Hidden away in a private home just outside of Dimondale, Michigan is a bona fide Beatles Bonanza.

In the home of Viki Spector is probably the most incredible, complete and comprehensive private Beatles memorabilia collection, called **Spector Beatles Museum**, ever amassed. Viki started this collection years ago, and she continues to buy more of everything that has anything to do with the four lads from Liverpool. Everywhere you look, John, Paul, George and Ringo appear in every kind of mold, medium and manner imaginable. To say I was impressed is a huge understatement. From comic books and Beatles bubblegum to one-of-a-kind metal molds and precious paintings, you'll see the rarest of the rare. Viki estimates that she has well over five thousand Beatles things to talk to you about. Believe me, she has some fascinating stories. Again, this is a private collection and tours of no more than four at a time are available by appointment only. But if you're a Beatles fan, I would make it a point to make an appointment promptly. I love meeting people like Viki who have such a genuine and powerful passion for what they do. I'd heard of this incredible collection, but seeing is believing. And believe me, if you're a Beatles fan, you'll find Viki and her volumes of rare Beatles stuff to be absolutely awesome.

Story behind the name:
Three Little Kittens...

On UIR shoots, it seems like we're always leaving something behind. Lenses, tripods, monopods, pod-pods, camera cases, microphones. You name it, we forgot it. We're just like those three little kittens…

Chapter 82

Season 6, Episode 7

• Romeo

When it comes to genuine Americana, Romeo is right out of the pages of history, and they've preserved it beautifully. From an actual working Nineteenth Century blacksmith shop to countless rare and authentic artifacts, the folks in Romeo have a true passion for the past.

And talk about a "home" town, when it comes to classically restored historic homes, Romeo makes for a wonderful walking tour through time. Every type of classic American domicile is done up right. From Greek and Gothic to Victorian and one of my favorite, Italianate, the collection of historic homes there will blow your mind. They may look like museum pieces, but the people there actually live in them and love them.

And if you're hankering for even more history, Henry Ford's first engine foundry was even in Romeo. They've got three museums, an opulent Opera house, an art center, two libraries and more antiques than you can shop for in a month of Sundays. Not bad for a town of just over 3,500 folks.

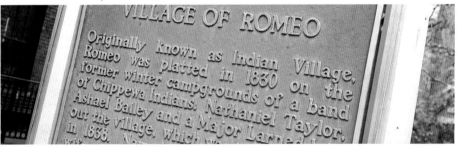

The Clyde Craig Blacksmith Museum
(586) 752-4111
301 N. Bailey St., Romeo, MI 48065
www.romeohistoricalsociety.org

If you want a great historical experience while visiting Romeo, check out the **Clyde Craig Blacksmith Museum**. We stopped by for a chat with town history guru and museum curator Richard Beringer. This is a very cool and authentic place to find out who and how the town was founded. For more than thirty years, Richard has researched and relived much of Romeo's illustrious past. He took us through almost two hundred years of fascinating Romeo history. This was the first time I had even been in a real working blacksmith shop.

Yorokobi Sushi
(586) 752-7010
117 S. Main St., Romeo, MI 48065
www.yorokobisushi.com

Another thing Romeo has is a great downtown with cool shops and plenty of places to stroll, relax and unwind. They also have some great places if you crave classic cuisine. In Romeo, amidst all the authentic Americana, is the kind of food you'd expect to find. Except for the next place we went. Sushi, anyone? You heard right. It's a sushi restaurant that's right downtown in the middle of this classic country-side community. How'd this happen, and who's responsible?

Meet Dimitri Bonnville, a young guy who had a love for this fine foreign food, traveled almost to the orient (actually, California) and brought it all the way back to Romeo and opened **Yorokobi Sushi**.

Sushi in Romeo is kind of like "When Worlds Collide," but Dimitri's fascination with fresh fish took hold of him and he couldn't hold back. So this local guy found his calling, took a leap of faith and opened the farthest thing from American comfort food you can find. But the people of Romeo are finding it to be fantastic.

Don't let the name Dimitri fool you. This young and inspired chef went all the way to California and studied at the Sushi Institute of America under a guy whose name I can't even pronounce, so this is the real deal. His presentation is perfect, the flavor profiles are profound and the place has a cool and funky atmosphere that will make you melt into your meal. If you've never had sushi before or you're just plain "ascared" of it, this is a comfortable American place to make your move.

Is there really room in Romeo for this cuisine from another continent? Well, after our conversation we sat down, dug in and came up with a resounding YES! It just goes to show you that America really is a melting pot of all things edible. Even in this abundance of Americana, you'll definitely wanna try the sushi at Yorokobi. By the way, Yorokobi means "peace and joy," so I recommend you enjoy a piece of sushi there soon.

Romeo Historical Society's Barn Tour
(586) 752-4111
290 N. Main St., Romeo, MI 48065
www.romeohistoricalsociety.org

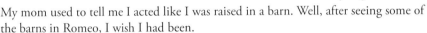

My mom used to tell me I acted like I was raised in a barn. Well, after seeing some of the barns in Romeo, I wish I had been.

When it comes to good old-fashioned barns, America has had a love affair with these classic structures for more than two hundred years. There's just something legendary and romantic about these utilitarian yet majestic structures. We all love them, and we all love to look at them.

Then there are those rare individuals who love them so much, they take these historic structures, get creative and make them a part of who they are. And every year on the Romeo Historical Society's Barn Tour, you get to meet these people and experience their unique barns. This fun and fascinating tour took us all around Romeo. And not only did we see some incredibly creative barns, we met some absolutely awesome and proud people.

You'll see everything from barns people live in to barns people turned into auto shops, museums, nightclubs, theaters and even giant man caves. The tour only happens once a year and the barns are constantly changing, so call ahead to make your plans. Who knows, someday you might want to buy a barn, and you're gonna need some ideas. There's no better way to see what you might do than on The Romeo Historical Society's yearly Barn Tour. Believe me, after the tour you'll want to live in a barn, too.

Terror on Tillson Street
info@terrorontillson.com
www.terrorontillson.com

When it comes to the spookiest of all holidays, there's Halloween and then there's HALLOWEEN, if you know what I mean. And if you'd like to experience the latter of the two, trick or treat yourself to **Terror on Tillson Street**. This is Halloween in hyper drive and people come from all over the Midwest to see it. Believe me, you won't believe it either, until you do see it with your own ascared eyes.

Every year Tillson Street in Romeo is full of some of the biggest and most elaborate Halloween displays you'll ever see. It's also full of people with some of the biggest hearts you'll ever know, and that's because they use the power of Halloween to give back to this great community.

Before we got started, I took some time to talk with the heart and soul of this spooky street, Vicki Lee. Vicki grew up with Halloween on her birthday, so it's always been a special day for her. And now with the phenomenon of Tillson Street, she loves to joke that thousands of people come to see her on her birthday. Usually Halloween is simply fun and good cheer, but like I said, these folks are giving back in a big way. The Buzz Lee Memorial Scholarship Fund was started by Vicki Lee's Family in honor of their husband and father, William "Buzz" Lee. They even help sponsor The Wounded Warrior Project, Kids Kicking Cancer Organization and a food drive. It really is scary how much the people of this neighborhood care about others.

Tillson Street is also a safe place to take your kids. When Vicki's sons got too old to trick or treat, they started what's called "The Bulldog Security Patrol." The entire street is blocked off to traffic and the Bulldogs make sure everyone has a safe and fun Halloween. If you want to "treat" yourself to a spectacular (and charitable) Halloween next year, the "trick" is to get your family to Tillson Street in Romeo.

And speaking of Romeo, if you want to step way back in time and even sample some sensational sushi, spend a day in this historic town. Who knows, in a couple hundred years, they may be talking about how much fun you had there.

Story behind the name:
Where For Art Thou... Romeo?

We're in Romeo, and the PBS Rule Book states in paragraph four, subchapter two, line 2,458: Whenever a Shakespeare quote can be used, the shot shall be executed. (Consider it executed.)

Chapter 83

Season 6, Episode 8

•Lake Orion
•Gaylord

Do you suffer from boring-townatosis? Need a
new place to live, work or play that'll lift your spirits
and lower your blood pressure? Well, Doctor Daldin has a
prescription for you that's real easy to swallow.

Lake Orion is one of those towns where the sum of all its parts makes it one of
the best places to live in Michigan. From life on the lake to time on the trails,
everything you need to increase your quality of life is right there. And at the center
of it all is a quaint little downtown with tons of interesting places to shop and cool eateries
with awesome edibles. Heck, it's so nice there, the car wash even has a waterfall!

Orion Marine Center - Historic Boat Tour
(248) 693-2400
10 N. Park Blvd., Lake Orion, MI 48362
www.orionmarine.com

Since so much of the Lake Orion experience is Lake Orion itself, I thought I'd spend
some quality time smack dab in the middle of it. So we contacted the great folks
at **Orion Marine Center** and took a boat tour with local historian Riva Campbell
and DDA President Suzanne Perreault. Riva runs the tour, which is creatively called
"History, Folklore and Lies."

This lake is big and beautiful, and the historic boat tour is a fascinating blast. You'll hear
fables, stories, legends, rumors and awesome anecdotes that will amaze and fascinate you.
Just one of the things we learned was that Lake Orion is actually listed in Ripley's Believe It
or Not for being the first inland lake to have a marine postal service. So many people live
around the lake in little canals and nooks and crannies that from 1905 to 1951 there were
thirteen mail boats delivering mail around the lake. I'd tell you more, but I don't want to
ruin the tour. Riva was riveting, so I'll let her tell you the rest.

This was a great watery way to find out more about this awesome aquatic community. Every
town should have a lake attached to it. So if your town doesn't, ya best start digging. :-)

Palazzo di Bocce
(248) 371-9987
4291 S. Lapeer Rd., Lake Orion, MI 48359
www.palazzodibocce.com

Speaking of digging something, if you're Italian, you know an Italian or you've always wanted to be Italian, here's a place you'll really dig.

Palazzo di Bocce is like a crash course in being an Italian aristocrat. From fine dining and fantastic surroundings to the fun and ancient sport of bocce ball, this place will turn you Italian in no time at all. It all started when Anthony Battaglia retired, got bored and started building. What he built was a world-class facility where you can have an incredible Italian dinner, play a few rounds of bocce ball, or both. At first Anthony just wanted to build a little club where he and his friends could play some bocce, but you know Italians… they love to eat. I can say that because I am one. So, 32,000 square feet, ten courts and a ridiculously good restaurant later, a destination was born. Anthony's heart is as big as this place, and after only a few minutes with him, I could feel his passion and pride.

Well, since I already know how to eat Italian, I figured that with the expert tutelage of Bocce champs Jason Wisnewski and Jose Barro, I'd be rollin' 'em like a pro in no time. Bocce ball is kind of like a combination of bowling and curling. The goal is to roll your balls down the court and try to get them closest to a smaller ball called the pallino. This game is definitely tougher than it looks, but also a whole lot of fun and a great way to work up an appetite.

So we bocced… well, sort of. They did. I, at least, tried. We had an absolute blast. Then we sat down to some awesome Italian and ate, drank and laughed, and if we could have stood up after we were done, we would have done it all over again. Palazzo di Bocce will make you feel so Italian, you'll leave with an extra vowel on the end of your name. So let me make you an offer you can't refuse: go to Palazzo di Bocce, have dinner, play some bocce ball, and if you don't have a great time… what's a madda you!

Orion Art Center - Dragon on the Lake
(248) 693-4986
115 S. Anderson St., PO Box 674, Lake Orion, MI 48361
www.dragononthelake.com

There may not really be a Loch Ness Monster. And Bigfoot? That's a bit of a stretch. But believe it or not, out in Lake Orion there really is a Dragon on the Lake!

Actually, there are a ton of them in all shapes and sizes, and they're all there for a very good cause. It's called Dragon on the Lake, and it happens every August to celebrate this great town and to help support the Orion Art Center. This community festival celebrates art, music and, of course, the legend of the dragon.

Dozens of teams in boats decked out like big colorful dragons compete to help raise money for the arts. And, of course, for bragging rights. Not only is James Jenkins the Orion Art Center director, he's also the man who breathes fire into this great festival. James explained that there really is a legend of an actual dragon on Lake Orion. There are several colorful stories, with one being that over one hundred years ago, some boys built a big wooden dragon and pulled it across the lake to scare some old ladies. If you want to hear a few more stories, you'll have to frequent this fun festival. This floating festival has a little bit of everything. You'll see dragon dancers, drummers and a community that really wants to give back. If you're not ascared of dragons, check out Dragon on the Lake in Lake Orion, because Nessie and Bigfoot ain't got nothing on this event.

And if you love living the good life, you'll like Lake Orion a lot. It's a town, a lake and everything in between.

Hey UTR adventure lovers, here's a trivia question you can try to stump a friend with sometime. What Michigan city in the Lower Peninsula sits on the 45th parallel, has the highest elevation, is surrounded by rolling hills and unspoiled forest, has over one hundred lakes and five blue ribbon trout streams? If you already knew the answer, **Gaylord**, you must be a golfer!

Gaylord is the self-described golf Mecca of the Midwest. It's got seventeen championship courses that are nestled deep in some of Michigan's most scenic surroundings. Golfers flock to this place like… well, golfers to golf. Even though golf is a great game, on this trip to Gaylord we were looking for fur, food and a fun place to shop, and we found all three.

Call of the Wild Museum
(989) 732-4336
850 S. Wisconsin Ave., Gaylord, MI 49735
www.callofthewildgaylord.com

Remember when you were a kid and your whole family would pile into the car and head off on one of those classic Michigan summer vacations? Then on the way up north, your parents would pull off I-75 at exit 282 and take you to Call of the Wild Museum. Remember how much fun that was? Well, guess what? My mom never stopped. But, lucky for me, the crew didn't mind at all.

Call of the Wild Museum has been creating fun and educational vacation memories for more than fifty years now. Talk about a blast from the past. When it comes to old-school family vacation cool, Call of the Wild is a fur-filled flashback that will take you back to a time when the family wagon was your primary portal to adventure.

This fascinating place is exhibit after exhibit of taxidermied terrestrials all in dioramas depicting their natural habitats. I didn't want to wander into the wild alone, so I arranged a personal tour with the museum's number one woman, Janis Vollmer. Her parents started Call of the Wild back in 1957, and her family has been tending to these former fauna ever since. You'll see everything from bears and bald eagles to turkeys and timber wolves, all in natural surroundings. It's a great way to learn about animals and their natural balance.

This retro animal roundup really is a fun place to take the entire family. But just remember, there's no need to feed these exhibits. That is, of course, unless you come upon the endangered and elusive TV Show Host exhibit. He'll eat anything.

The Bearded Dogg Lounge & Old Spud Warehouse
(989) 731-0330
314 S. Otsego Ave., Gaylord, MI 49735
www.beardeddogglounge.com

Well, after a walk on the wild side, we decided to head into downtown Gaylord and check back in with modern civilization. Also known as The Alpine Village, Gaylord has a great main street with tons of places to get lost and then find yourself again. It's a classic Northern Michigan town with everything you need for fun and to fill your tummy. And this Tommy's tummy was on empty.

What do you do when you see a sign that says "Old Spud Warehouse" and "The Bearded Dogg Lounge"? Well, you do exactly what we did. Turn around, pull in and see what the heck is up.

What are these two places? What do their names mean? And why are they stuck together? Well, there's only one (or maybe two) ways to find out. So I flipped a coin and headed on into **The Old Spud Warehouse** for an explanation and hopefully, eventually a good meal.

Once inside, my look of confusion inspired a spontaneous game of Twenty Questions with Jenny Sopper. Apparently a hundred years ago, this place was a potato warehouse where farmers would store their spuds. Now it's a store that features the coolest array of anything and everything you can think of for you and your home. To say this place has character is a huge understatement. You can feel the history with every step you take on its old pine plank floors, and everything offered is unique and far from ordinary. There's a sense of humor and a cool, creative twist to all the items you'll see, and every one of them seems to have a story. From funky furniture and fixtures to jewelry and art, it's all good.

The Spud Warehouse is so wonderful and weird, you're bound to find something fun and unique around every corner, and the best part is, around one of them, you'll even find **The Bearded Dogg Lounge**.

A beloved furry family friend inspired the name of this cool and comfortable eatery. And the love of great food and drink inspired the rest. Chris Newburry explained that the lounge started as a place where the men could hang out while their wives shopped at The Old Spud Warehouse. Now apparently both genders enjoy The Bearded Dogg's casual sophistication (and the store is not reserved for wives anymore). It's a hip and happening hangout for those who enjoy gourmet food, signature cocktails, microbrews and creative cuisine. No fryers or microwaves here, and the pasta is all made in house. The people, atmosphere and our meals were all perfect and we made a ton of new friends. Well, I did my part by telling you about both The Old Spud Warehouse and The Bearded Dogg Lounge. The only question left for you is which one do you go in first? Either way, I think you'll be happy!

Gaylord City Elk Park
(800) 345-8621
Grandview Blvd., Gaylord, MI 49735
www.gaylordmichigan.net/elk-viewing-40

Have you heard of the herd they have in Gaylord? Well, now that I've heard of them, I have to tell you about them.

The Pigeon River State Forest just northeast of Gaylord is home to the only free-range elk herd in the entire Midwest. And part of that herd is maintained and cared for at the **Gaylord City Elk Park** just south of town. This is a great place to get out of your car and get up close and personal with these massive and majestic mammals.

To find out more about these mighty creatures, I spent some time with a mammal who's a lot more like me, Ed Tholl. Elks are huge, with the males topping off at around nine hundred pounds. When you see them up close like this, you can see just how beautiful they really are. The herd is visible year round. We were there during feeding, so all the elk were present and putting on quite a show. This is something kids will love.

Now that you've heard of this herd, you should really head to the Gaylord City Elk Park and have a look. So take our advice at UTR: get in your car, get to Gaylord and get started having fun. It really is one of best places to learn, eat, shop and connect with nature… haven't you HERD? Hoo boy!

Story behind the name:
I Wanna Take You Higher
Song titles provide most of the names of shows to our brains. When we get a chance to go airborne, we're taking some Sly Stone with us.

Chapter 84

Season 6, Episode 9

Detroit

The new Detroit is a place you just have to see to believe… and I believe that once you see it, you'll see that seeing is believing, because believe me, what you'll see is unbelievable.

Well, if you made any sense of that at all, you're smart enough to know that Detroit's comeback isn't coming back; it's here right now. And it's exploding with great flavors, fun things to do and plenty of positive people to help you get the most out of your experience. There's also a ton of new inspiration, education and innovation happening right now. So activate your sense of adventure, because we're back for more of the Motor City.

DIME - The Detroit Institute of Music Education
(313) 223-1600
1265 Griswold St., Detroit, MI 48226
www.dime-detroit.com

Wouldn't it be great to have a dime for every talented young person out there hoping to make music their life? Well, guess what? Detroit does!

DIME is the Detroit Institute of Music Education, a brand new college right downtown that's giving aspiring musicians a great place to get a real education in the music business. Sure, this place is a college, but when you step through the door, it feels like you're walking right into the music industry.

Kevin Nixon and Sarah Clayman are two accomplished and award-winning music producers from the UK who came to Detroit, saw what they liked, heard what they liked and opened their doors to all who love music.

Kevin and Sarah have worked with some of the rock and roll greats. They put together a curriculum that polishes the students' talents and then lets them explore the business of the music industry. The atmosphere is like a giant music studio, and the sense of excitement in the students is contagious. The room we filmed in that day had a giant mural of Jimi Hendrix recording in his studio. Classic!

As they say, "a collision of coincidences" brought them to Detroit, but once they were here, Kevin and Sarah fell in love with the history, talent and passion of the Motor City music scene. From the churches to the clubs, they were blown away with what they saw and what they heard. If you're serious about making it in the music industry, this is the place to register. So if someone offers you a dime for every musician changing the future of Detroit's music industry, take them up on it. Because with all the talent we have here, that kind of change will go a long way.

The Fowling Warehouse
(313) 264-1288
3901 Christopher St., Detroit, MI 48211
www.fowlingwarehouse.com

Do you like football? Do you like bowling? Do you like to make up strange new words? Well, have I got a fun-filled new sport for you. It's called Fowling. That's right, a combination of football and bowling, and in Detroit at the **Fowling Warehouse** they have everything you need to turn this crazy sport into your new favorite pastime.

Chris Hutt is Detroit's founding father of Fowling. He actually invented this crazy game about fifteen years ago while tailgating at the Indy 500. He and his buddies thought, "Hey, wouldn't it be cool if we built a bowling alley for our tailgate?" Well, they did and the ball ended up everywhere it wasn't supposed to be. Not good if you're tailgating next to these guys. That's when it happened: while picking up the pins and calling it quits, Chris noticed some guys next to them throwing a football. He put the two together in his mind, and a silly sport was born.

The game is simple. It's just like bowling, only you throw a football at the pins. The fun part is that you never know what the football is going to do. The ball ends up everywhere, so this is a great way to meet fellow fowlers. The game is also more about accuracy than strength, so guys… get ready to hand over your man card. The Fowling Warehouse features frequent fowlers, frosty-cold adult beverages and even live bands. It's a righteous, raucous good time!

After a quick lesson from Chris and a few feeble fowls, I suddenly decided I was fantastic! So I had a hilarious time fowling with about a hundred of my new best friends. There is no way you can not have fun doing this (if that even makes sense). It's great exercise and a great way to meet new people. Fowling may be two sports in one, but if you count the beer it's three, and I seriously suggest you give it a try.

Story behind the name:
Somebody Loan Me a Dime

Chicago Bluesman Fenton Robinson wrote the song and Boz Scaggs made it soulful, but it's clearly "about dime" we started to make more musical references in the show-naming department. Oh, and the man's name is Fenton. Coincidence? I think not.

Chapter 85

Season 6, Episode 10

•Woodward Road Trip

Welcome to another one of our special edition
UTR "Road Trip" adventures where we pick a Michigan
road, drive down it and see what cool stuff we uncover.
This time we're gonna cruise Woodward Avenue. Why? Well,
because for gosh sakes, it's Woodward!

Woodward Avenue is one of the most iconic drives in all of America. It's been designated an Automotive Heritage Trail, an All American Road and a Pure Michigan Byway and has had a rich and romantic love affair with the car and all the towns it touches for well over one hundred years. Almost anything you want, need or even crave you'll find along its twenty-one and a half mile stretch. This is one of the few roads with a rep, and you instantly become cooler just by driving on it.

The Detroit Historical Museum
(313) 833-7935
5401 Woodward Ave., Detroit, MI 48202
www.detroithistorical.org

The Detroit Historical Museum is one of the best places you can go to learn about this great city. For eighty-five years, this fascinating place has chronicled the life and times of this entire region. And it's right in Detroit and right on Woodward for you to explore.

I met up with Senior Curator Joel Stone who took me way back in Detroit time. Joel personifies the passion for Detroit's illustrious past. The DHM is far from sleepy; it's a fun, colorful and interactive place where you can actually walk through time. If you head downstairs, you'll come upon "The Streets of Old Detroit," an actual cobblestone street complete with shops where you can stroll from the early 1800s to the early 1900s.

At the museum you'll also learn about Detroit's role in the Underground Railroad, World War II and how we became the automobile capital of the world. You'll even see a real working auto assembly line. This great place has fascinating

exhibit after exhibit, and after spending some quality time there, I started to feel pretty proud about where I'm from. The Detroit Historical Museum is a way-back building you should definitely build into your schedule. Just do yourself a favor. Try to remember not to forget it.

La Dolce Vita Restaurant
(313) 865-0331
17546 Woodward Ave., Detroit, MI 48203
www.ldvrestaurant.net

We all have an inner Italian just waiting to get out, enjoy life and celebrate great food. Well, mine got out and brought me straight up Woodward to this place. He's a real good boy!

Just north of Six Mile on the east side of Woodward, tucked away in Palmer Park, is what Italians would call "a little slice of heaven." Now, you may drive by it a few times before you see it, but once you find it, you'll never forget it. **La Dolce Vita** is the real deal when it comes to genuine Italian cuisine. And if you want atmosphere, this place is more romantic than red sauce and offers something Italians perfected: garden dining.

Before I started repeatedly uttering the phrase, "Please pass the pasta," I thought it best to find out how this slice of Italy has eluded my personal pizza for so long. So my inner Italian and I sat down with owner Enrico Rosselli.

La Dolce Vita means "the sweet life," and that's exactly what Enrico set out to do when he opened his doors twenty-two years ago: share some of the sweet life of Italy with his guests. He claims he made the restaurant a little hard to find on purpose, making it a true hidden gem. No advertising here, just word of mouth and mouths full of magnificent Italian cuisine. Check out the Sunday brunch. It

will become a new tradition for your family. Rico was one of the most genuine and gracious hosts we've ever encountered on UTR. He sat us down, filled us up and shared story after story about his fascinating life and love for people. Both he and this place are one hundred percent old school, and that's perfect! So, next time your inner Italian gets out, don't worry. Just hop in the car and head to La Dolce Vita, because that's where he or she will probably be. And who knows, maybe it's even their turn to buy. Bonus!

The Rust Belt Market
(810) 441-0956
22801 Woodward Ave., Ferndale, MI 48220
www.rustbeltmarket.com

A few miles up Woodward in Fabulous Ferndale is a place known as **The Rust Belt Market**. It sits proudly on the northwest corner of Creativity and Business, also known as Woodward & Nine Mile. But, what exactly is The Rust Belt Market?

It's an eclectic mixed market of talented local merchants. If you're into supporting and purchasing local, The Rust Belt Market is a must stop on Woodward Avenue. From art and edibles to wearables and collectibles, you'll find tons of locally made products, services and even events all in one very cool space. It's a great concept that does great things for this community.

There's so much to see and explore there, I thought it'd be best to secure the services of the man who had the original plan, Chris Best. Chris and his wife Tiffany made and continue to make this place happen. Chris calls The Rust Belt a "living market" because it reflects the people of this community. I'd call it a village of very passionate and talented people who are doing and selling some extraordinary stuff. This place has its own energy and atmosphere and the unique shop owners there create and collect some of the most unusual items you'll ever encounter. Even if you don't buy anything at the market, just being there is a blast. The market is so overwhelmingly packed with cool people and their products you'll probably need to walk through it few times to make sure you see everything.

If you wanna to do your part to help small business survive and thrive in Southeast Michigan, stop by The Rust Belt Market and lay down a little cash. Not only will you get something really cool for it, your small investment will do big things to help change our future.

Primi Piatti Gourmet Italian Market
(248) 566-3353
550 N. Old Woodward Ave., Birmingham, MI 48009
www.primipiattimarket.com

Well, we're back in Italy, only this time it's on old Woodward Ave. in Birmingham at Primi Piatti Gourmet Italian Market. This is a place where you can take a little bit of Italy home with you whenever you want. Owner Monica Bizinya'no Zamler's love for Italian art, culture and, of course, cuisine is instantly evident when you walk into this place. And you can taste the passion in everything she prepares.

When it comes to plates of perfectly prepared pastas, meats and cheeses, Monica has a profound passion. A few years ago she decided to change her life and do what she loves, and what she loves is food, Italy and meeting people. Perfect! In Italian, "primi piatti" means "first course," and that's exactly what she specializes in. She makes fresh pastas everyday and puts together meat and cheese platters that are so beautiful, they look Hollywood art directed. At the shop you'll also find authentic Italian candies, canned goods and even art and accessories.

Lucky for us we were there for one of Monica's Tasting Tuesdays, and as the store filled with pleasant patrons who are passionate about pasta, we all shared, laughed and tasted great food. Even if you can't find your inner Italian, go try the awesome edibles at Primi Piatti Gourmet Italian Market in Birmingham.

The Bat Zone
(248) 294-7370
75 W. Huron St., Pontiac, MI 48342
www.batconservation.org

Of all the animals in the animal kingdom, the one species that really needs a better PR person is the bat. But after you meet this guy, you'll see they totally got it!

Rob Miles is the REAL Batman and he's changing the way we all think, feel and interact with bats at **The Bat Zone** in Pontiac (astute viewers will remember that when we featured it on the show, The Bat Zone was located at Cranbrook Science Center in Bloomfield Hills). It's the headquarters of The Organization for Bat Conservation, and their main mission is to keep bats alive and thriving all around the world.

Rob explained that bats are becoming endangered and that they are sadly misunderstood by most people. Bats are actually pretty harmless and extremely important to our environment. Michigan bats, for example, only eat insects, and a single bat will ingest up to 5,000 bugs a night. Bats also provide the US farming industry with 50 billion dollars a year in pest control. They simply have them for dinner.

At The Bat Zone you'll see everything from creepy little vampire bats to the giant, gentle fruit bats. You'll experience fifteen different species and learn about everything from where they live to how they echolocate. Actually, up close and personal... they're kinda cute.

This is an experience your entire family will enjoy. So go to the Bat Zone and meet some of your new best friends. Oh, and if you think you've got bats in your belfry, good. Leave 'em there; they do great things for the ecosystem.

And if you think a road trip is in your future, cruise up or down Woodward Avenue. It's a road where you can learn, eat, shop and even show your support for the planet.

Story behind the name:
Thunder Road

It's our Road Trip show, and Woodward is such an iconic stretch of highway that we needed an iconic name. Bruce Springsteen's Thunder Road is an epic journey of a song and so is this episode. Turn it up then roll down the window and let the wind blow back your hair.

Chapter 86

Season 6, Episode 11

Sunrise Side Adventure

Now, when it comes to exploring Michigan, we've all heard the "West Side Story." But if you head east you'll feast on flavorful food, find friendly folks and tons of fantastic family fun stuff to do. And in this chapter, we've got four instances for you! If I counted right.

Michigan's **Sunrise Side** continues to be the place to go when you want to stretch out, get real and revel in some of the best of everything our great state has to offer. You'll find miles of beautiful Lake Huron shoreline, tons of classic towns to explore and gobs of great activities for the sportsman in all of us. Honestly, if you want to rediscover your sense of adventure, you need to venture up Michigan's Sunrise Side.

The Fireside Inn
(989) 595-6369
18730 Fireside Hwy., Presque Isle, MI 49777
www.firesideinngrandlake.com

On this special sunrise sortie, we decided to work our way south, so we headed down the coast on M-23 in search of our first awesome adventure. And you know us, it didn't take long before we hit the brakes and dropped UTR anchor.

On this show we're always looking for cool places to stop, stay, eat and play. Well, up in Presque Isle we found a family-owned place that's been making great vacation memories for over a century.

On the eastern shores of beautiful Grand Lake and only a stone's throw from Lake Huron sits the **Fireside Inn**. And when you drive into this place, you instantly become one with the natural surroundings. From its classic rustic main lodge to the comfy, cozy cabins, everything you need to kick back, unwind and have some serious fun is at your disposal.

Terry and Allen are two of the McConnells who keep the tradition of this great inn intact. They invited me to sit and chat on the inn's 165-foot open air front porch that overlooks the lake. Incredible. When they were kids, their folks bought the inn and brought them up here to get away from the rat race. Now they'll both tell you it's the best thing that ever happened to them.

The Fireside Inn is where you go to tune out, turn off, unplug and relax. There are no phones and no TVs. What you will find are tons of great outdoor activities for the kids and plenty of time to reacquaint yourself with the lost art of conversation. The best part of this old school vacation destination is that when you hear them ring the bell, breakfast or dinner is served. It was just then the dinner bell rang. Well, you don't have to tell the UTR crew twice, so we hightailed it to the dining room for a prime rib roundup fit for a king. I even enjoyed my queen cut. And after dinner, me and the fellers commandeered some canoes and launched onto the lake for some floating frivolities. Heck, we didn't even tip over. There's a first.

Need to get away? Well, a great way to do it is with earth, wind and the Fireside Inn in Presque Isle. It's got all the elements you need to create some awesome Michigan memories.

Tom Moran & Moran Iron Works
(989) 733-2011
11739 M-68, Onaway, MI 49765
www.moraniron.com

Next, we headed inland on our way to Onaway for an inspirational story of art, iron and one man's movement to keep Michigan great.

Tom Moran created, owns and operates **Moran Iron Works**, a Michigan company that's known around the world for custom fabricating huge modular industrial parts for the power industry. The company's also known for creating a culture of innovation and education in the fiery field of welding.

But Tom is equally known for something else: taking his tremendous talents with metal and making artful Michigan monuments for all to enjoy. You'll see his giant metal sculptures all across Michigan, and he's even put together a walking art exhibit at the Awakon Park Sculpture Trail in Onaway. There you'll encounter everything from giant former president heads to mythical dragons and even the world's Largest Steering wheel. Tom sees this as a way to strengthen his community. I see it as a way to bring attention to the tremendous talent we have here in Michigan.

These giant metal sculptures are scattered across the state, with the largest concentration in the Northeast Lower Peninsula. You'll have to do a little research to find them all, but that's what we did and it was a blast. Other than the Awakon Park in Onaway, Rogers City is a good place to start.

So next time you're traveling across our Great Lake state and you see something that's large, made of iron and awesome to look at, you can bet it was probably made by Michigan's own Iron Man, Tom Moran.

The Gailes @ Lakewood Shores Resort
(989) 739-2073
7751 Cedar Lake Rd., Oscoda Twp., MI 48750
www.lakewoodshores.com

If you want to play a round of golf the way the Scottish and Old Tom Morris intend, go to **Lakewood Shores Resort** in Oscoda and play a course there called **The Gailes**. They have three great courses at Lakewood, but The Gailes gives you an experience that recreates the look and feel of the famed seaside courses of Scotland. You'll see double greens, sod face bunkers on the fairways and tall grass surrounding it all. Craig Peters is the general manager at Lakewood Shores, and after calculating my handicap for an hour on an abacus, we commandeered a cart and got things started. Little did he know that when it comes to golf, I'm a great tennis player.

Craig said golfers come from far and wide to play this authentic and award-winning course. There's really nothing else like it in Michigan, and playing this course saves you an expensive airline ticket to Scotland. Unfortunately, not even the liquid scotch could save my golf game.

Golf at The Gailes and the Lakewood Shores Resort was an absolute classic blast. Craig was cordial. The weather was wonderful and it proved two very important things: 1. We have hidden treasures around every corner on Michigan's Sunrise Side, and B. I'm a bad golfer no matter what continent I play on.

Walleye Fishing with Captain Mike Veine at Trophy Specialists
(734) 475-9146
15555 Cassidy Rd., Chelsea, MI 48118
www.trophyspecialists.co

After hours of trying to hit a little white ball, it was time to see if we could get something else to hit. Only this time, not with a club, but with a fishing pole. That's right, we went back out on the water to see if, once again, I could be taught to fish. The fish seem to have their part down.

If you're a Michigan angler and Walleye is your water breather of choice, you probably already know that Saginaw Bay is a Mecca for catching this mighty (and, from what I hear, tasty) fish. So, with the help of Captain Mike Veine at Trophy Specialists we grabbed some bait, boarded his boat and set out to bring back some big ones.

Mike's been running a charter in these waters for over fifteen years, and he both knows and loves what he's doing. He's had folks from as far away as China fish on his boat, because he knows where the fish are. Apparently the Walleye grow fat and happy in Saginaw Bay because of the warm water and weed beds. What everyone failed to tell me is that they also have teeth. Yikes!

Once we got about four miles out onto Lake Huron, Captain Mike did what he does best: set all the lures. And I did what I do best: absolutely nothing. With all the lines in, I was ready to sit back, relax and enjoy a cold beverage, when suddenly it happened! Fish on!

And it happened and happened and happened and happened. You see, that's the trouble with fishing with someone who actually knows what they're doing. You spend all your time catching fish. Heck, I got so tired we all took turns. Jim caught some fish, Eric caught some fish and Matt reeled in the biggest walleye of 'em all: a mammoth twenty-eight incher. You should have seen the teeth on that one. By the end, pretty much all our biceps were burning big time.

Thanks to Captain Mike we had a fun and fish-full day on Saginaw Bay. When we were back on solid ground, Mike even completely cleaned and prepped our fish for future frying. Now that's what I call service. It truly was a "great lake" day.

So if you like your Michigan morning sunny side up, spend a little time on the Sunrise Side. With all the great places to stay, play and get away from it all, you'll have everything you need to make great Michigan memories.

Story behind the name:

Walking on Sunshine

Yup. Now that song is stuck in your head, too. Good luck getting rid of it.

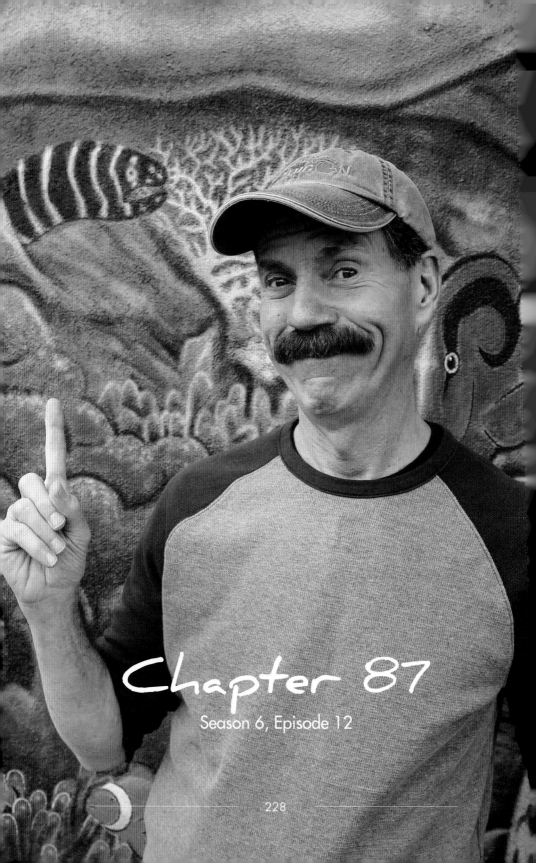

Chapter 87

Season 6, Episode 12

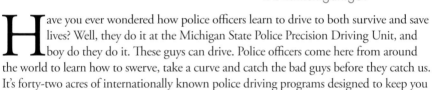

•Lansing
•Grand Rapids

Lansing continues to be one of Michigan's greatest cities to live, work and play in. As our state capital, it leads us. As a great food destination it feeds us, and with tons of new businesses and young people choosing to make their future here it breeds a sense of excitement and forward motion that's helping to move Michigan forward. It's full of opportunity for people who want to make their mark on the mighty mitten.

Michigan State Police Precision Driving Unit
(517) 332-2521
7426 N. Canal Rd., Dimondale, MI 48821
www.michigan.gov

Have you ever wondered how police officers learn to drive to both survive and save lives? Well, they do it at the Michigan State Police Precision Driving Unit, and boy do they do it. These guys can drive. Police officers come here from around the world to learn how to swerve, take a curve and catch the bad guys before they catch us. It's forty-two acres of internationally known police driving programs designed to keep you and the officers safe and sound.

Sgt. Mike McCarthy is an instructor at the academy, and when he's not behind the wheel, he's behind the success of many of Michigan's finest. But since being behind the wheel is so much more fun, he put me in a patrol car and put me and the car through some paces. This was the first time I ever got to sit in the front seat of a cop car… sweet!

First we hit the high speed pursuit track… oh boy. Sgt. McCarthy both amazed me and scrambled my brains with his skills. It was amazing how deliberate and calm he was through some very hair-raising maneuvers. Must be the training. Next up Sgt. Mike checked my hand-eye coordination with a basic maneuvering exercise using standard traffic cones. That's right; he actually let me drive this time. How did I do? Well, if you haven't seen this episode, I was amazing. If you've seen it, you can stop laughing now.

Finally, Sgt. McCarthy decided to take my skills to the limit on the infamous skid pad. This is where officers learn to control their car if it goes out of control. What happens is they wet down the pavement and you head toward it at a good rate of speed. As soon as you hit the wet road, you jerk the wheel to the right and see how long it takes you to regain control of the car. Sgt. Mike was amazing. I, however, am still spinning from the experience. I think I hit a new school record for rotations.

So next time you see a police officer expertly maneuvering safely through Michigan, you'll know exactly where they learned it: at the Michigan State Police Precision Driving Unit in Lansing. Just remember, when it comes to making a getaway, you'll never outrun one of these guys. Unless, of course, I'm driving.

Preuss Pets
(517) 339-1762
1127 N. Cedar St., Lansing, MI 48906
www.preusspets.com

If you're looking for a zoological paradise where you can purchase some pretty cool pets, Preuss Pets in Lansing's Old Town is the perfect place to peruse.

Not only is it one of Michigan's largest family-owned pet stores, it's probably one of the most awesome places you'll ever go to find your next new best friend. Preuss Pets is a destination for all things animal. From fish to fur and even feathered friends, Preuss has almost any fauna you might wanna find. And this place is so cool and colorful, just going there to ponder the purchase of a pet can be an absolute blast.

Rick Preuss is the creative higher primate who made this store what it is today, and he and his entire staff genuinely respect animals. The creative displays purposefully prompt you toward the proper pet for you, because they want to make sure that the experience between owner and new-found friend is a loving and lasting one. They've really created a community of animal lovers that goes far beyond the store. Preuss Pets is also a place where you really get to experience the animals and spend quality time with them. They also conduct in-store classes and offer educational outreach programs. Heck, you can even have a birthday party in the midst of all these animals. It is so much more than a store.

If you want to turn your happy home into a wild kingdom, bring your inner animal to Preuss Pets in Lansing. Whether it cheeps, chirps, barks or even burps, Rick and his awesome team of animal experts will help make it happen in a big or even little way.

Harry's Place
(517) 484-9661
404 N. Verlinden Ave., Lansing, MI 48915
www.facebook.com/HarrysPlaceLansing

When it comes to a great neighborhood watering hole where you can rub elbows with the locals, I'm all about that. And for three generations, Harry's has been holding down a friendly fort and serving up liberal libations and awesome edibles in this classic Lansing neighborhood.

Harea Bates and her father Art have spent decades turning this place into the place everyone wants to be, and the entire community loves them for it. Being at Harry's is more like being at a big family gathering where everyone knows and loves you. There's no quiet time here, just happy, hungry people sharing and caring for each other.

Harry's really is a great place to go for friendly folks, fantastic food and sensational spirits. You may show up a customer, but you'll leave as a close friend. Just don't be surprised if the next time you go everyone knows your name.

And don't be surprised if you fall in love with Lansing. After all, where else can you go for a spirited spin with Michigan's finest and have this much fun finding a new furry friend. I love Lansing more every time I go.

If you like cities that have incredible and diverse dining, endless shopping, fascinating history and architecture, cool museums, great green spaces and bountiful micro breweries all wrapped up in a vibrant cosmopolitan community, let's face it: **Grand Rapids** is your kind of town. We come to Grand Rapids for all these reasons, and I'm about to tell you about three more.

Odom Reuse
(616) 784-8733
1029 4 Mile Rd. NW, Grand Rapids, MI 49544
www.odomreuse.com

If you're looking to build future stuff with pieces from the past, have I got a great place for you. Odom Reuse is a reusable building material provider that helps turn old pieces and parts into new, commercial and residential digs. They select, salvage and sell to people who are looking for something classic, cool or unusual or just looking to help the environment by reusing. Bruce Odom is the man whose name is on this building, and when he's not searching for sensational salvageables, he's talking about them. This is a do-it-yourselfer's dream store where you can get some great old reusable stuff that has character you just don't see any more. From floors and doors to fixtures and fun crazy stuff, it's a gold mine of things that are still good to go. They even had tons of reclaimed barn wood in bountiful colors.

I had so much fun meandering through the store with Bruce, because everything in there had an interesting history or cool back story. There was even a table there that was made from an old high school gym basketball court. The top was inch-thick maple flooring with part of the three-point circle cutting through its middle. Very cool. This place is chock full of cool, rare and unusual stuff. And, you've heard me say a hundred times on UTR that they just don't build things like they used to. Well, if you go to Odom Reuse, you can. And it helps save time, money and the environment. Bonus!

Chris Freemen & Eat GR
chris@eatgr.comwww.eatgr.com

Now let's say you're in Grand Rapids and you want to find a cool, new restaurant to try. Wouldn't it be great if you had thousands of friends to help you find one? Well, thanks to this guy, you do.

Chris Freemen is a man on a mouthwatering mission, and that mission is to tell the whole world about the great food they have in GR. So he started a Facebook group and website called **EatGR!** It's a community of people who love to explore local restaurants and share their positive experiences with others. And when Chris isn't at work, he's working hard digging up some of Grand Rapids' most "under the radar" food finds.

Chris is actually a realtor by trade, but he also loves to trade great restaurant finds with fellow foodies. Because he would travel around all day showing houses, he began discovering tons of little out-of-the-way places to grab a bite. He also found that the best way to meet people is over an interesting meal, so he started searching and sampling. Now, Chris has become the Pied Piper for food enthusiasts all around Grand Rapids. He loves discovering the little mom and pop places that make meals from the heart. That's exactly why we hit it off so well with Chris. We have that same philosophy on UTR.

If you enjoy great food and making new friends, join your fellow foragers on Facebook and check out EatGR.com. Oh, and if you see Chris out there, tell him thanks for a job well done. Or medium rare, if that's how you like it. Get it? D'oh!

GR Bagel
(616) 259-9699
423 Norwood Ave. SE, Grand Rapids, MI 49506
www.grbagel.com

On UTR, when it comes to awesome edibles, we'll do almost anything, even if it means getting up at three a.m. So the next morning we set out all bright eyed and bushy tailed (NOT) in search of sustenance.

Some men quest for fame and fortune. Other men quest for discovery and adventure. But you're about to meet a man whose quest was to build a better bagel. Rene Pascal Kalter is a man who believes a bagel isn't bona fide unless you boil it first. And at GR Bagel, he and Lisa Barhydt are determined to show the entire world why.

These bagels are old school. Real old school, like how they made them back in the 1600s. A lot of places steam their bagels before baking them, but in order to get what Rene calls "the chew," they gotta be boiled. There's a real science to making a great bagel and the entire process takes about two days, so these things are definitely not fast food. But what they are is mmm-mmmm-more please! Rene came to Grand Rapids looking to be a baker, but when he couldn't find work, Lisa lovingly said, "You make a great bagel. Go for it." Well they did, and now thousands of folks from near and far are going for **GR Bagel**. Have you ever had a bagel that's just ten minutes out of the oven? OMG!

Bagels may have been the beginning of this popular place, but now they even serve up cookies, rolls, scones and some of the best breakfast sandwiches this side of lunch. Everything is awesome and it's all organic. A lot of people miss their calling in life, but not Rene; he found it, boiled it, baked it and made a better bagel out of it. And all you have to do is go to GR Bagel and eat it! So if Grand Rapids sounds like your kinda town, what are you waiting for, some TV show host to tell you to go there? That'll never work! :-)

Story behind the name:

RUN!

Everyone running in high speed looks funny.

Chapter 88

Season 6, Episode 13

•Pontiac
•Howell

Pontiac is a city with a long and illustrious past. But like a lot of American cities, it went through some pretty tough times. I say went, because right now, Pontiac is alive with new development, revolutionary ideas and energized young people reconnecting with its core. If you're looking for a Michigan renaissance on a fast track, take a lap around old Wide Track Drive. You'll see the future right before your very eyes.

The Menagerie
(248) 648-1505
154 N. Saginaw St., Pontiac, MI 48342
www.menageriekitchen.com

At **The Menagerie** they say they're a diverse collection, and in their case it's food. Well, if you've seen UTR, you know that food is our favorite thing to collect.

The Menagerie is one of the best food finds you'll ever, well, find. And you'll find it in downtown Pontiac. It's a lot of different things that all add up to a place enlightened foodies are flocking to. From great Sunday brunches and celebrity chef gourmet pop-up dinners to an incubator kitchen and even cooking classes, The Menagerie really is a collection of all things food.

James and April Forbes created a cupcake contest a few years back and turned that sweet success into something that's so much more. They're now helping enlighten this entire community when it comes to real food. So many of their friends were chefs that they decided to give them a place to explore their creative cuisines, and the people of Pontiac approve. Their Sunday brunch is, in a word, sensational.

These pop-up dining experiences really are a unique way to meet fellow foodies, and at the same time taste some of the newest creations being made by Michigan's most adventurous chefs. I had a great time making new friends, sharing awesome stories and renewing my love for this great city. If you're looking to elevate your edible endeavors, make your way to The Menagerie in Pontiac. They'll make you into a fourth degree foodie in no time at all.

Mayor Deirdre Waterman
(248) 758-3133
47450 Woodward Ave., Pontiac, MI 48342
www.pontiac.mi.us

Well, they say when you wanna get something done, go directly to the person in charge. So when I wanted to know more about all the cool stuff happening in Pontiac, I called the Mayor's office, and guess what? They said she'd actually talk to me.

Mayor Deirdre Waterman is the dynamic woman in charge when it comes to Pontiac's new energy and identity. Just a few minutes with her and you're ready to move there. She was originally trained as an ophthalmologist, which is probably why she has such great vision for the city. She's also one of those people who never considered running for public office, not until she felt the calling to give back to this incredible community.

Boy, when it comes to being a driving force behind Pontiac's comeback, Mayor Waterman is all that. And speaking of driving…

M1 Concourse
(866) 618-7225
1 Concourse Dr., Pontiac, MI 48341
www.m1concourse.com

If you're a car person, get ready to make a pilgrimage to Pontiac because the ultimate place to press your pedal to the metal just got made.

Proudly named after America's first highway, **M1 Concourse** is a brand new world-class motorsport facility and destination that's the ultimate place to drive, store, maintain, collect, eat and even live with your cars. And it's right in Pontiac. This place is a dream come true for auto heads who've been looking for a way to take their love of high performance cars to the next level.

The person who leveled eighty-seven acres to make this dream track a reality is daredevil developer Brad Oleshansky. Six years ago Brad simply set out to give Detroit's car community a place to gather. Now he's got a complex and track that's internationally known. He calls it an auto enthusiast destination where you can bring your car or your club and collaborate with fellow lovers of the fast and the furious. If you're so inclined, there's also a private garage community where you can purchase your own garage and deck it out as your office, condo or even man cave. They also have tons of special auto events there.

This place gets more exciting with every lap. Heck, I got so excited I talked them into letting me wave the checkered flag, and after a brief lesson in Tom-flaggery, I think I waved it wonderfully.

If cars are truly your thing, I think you better hit the gas and head to M1 Concourse. It's a world-class, Michigan-made motor Mecca that's helping put Pontiac back on a fast track.

On this show we're always talking about how Michigan towns are great places to live, work and play. Well, when it comes to **Howell**, it knocks all three out of the park. It's a city with great people, personality and plenty of places to stop, eat and shop. The downtown is classic pure Michigan and the homes and neighborhoods are some of the most beautiful you'll find anywhere. If you're looking for a place to live, you'll love it. And as Goldilocks would say, "It's not too big and not too small… it's just right." For a great way of life, that is.

Mike & Jon in the Morning on WHMI
(517) 546-0860
1277 Pkwy., Howell, MI 48843
www.whmi.com

How'd you like to have your own radio station? Well, in Howell and Livingston County they totally do.

WHMI FM is in, on and all about this great part of Michigan. It's a home-grown product that produces great quality radio for people they actually call friends and neighbors. They may not be a giant when it comes to their broadcast area, but when it comes to Howell and the surrounding communities, what they offer is huge!

Mornings on WHMI you'll find Mike Marino and Jon King (a.k.a. **Mike and Jon in the Morning**) and what they do is help locals launch their day by breathing life, laughs and a genuine love for their hometown of Howell. And if you like hit songs that'll help you get up and go, these guys will rock your morning routine.

In the day and age of satellite and huge corporate radio, these guys are an anomaly because they broadcast almost exclusively to the people right in their community. It may be a smaller broadcast, but these two guys are big on this town and all the people in it. So next time you land in Livingston County, check out how WHMI is helping this great community thrive. Who knows, you might even hear your favorite song at the same time… bonus!

2FOG's Pub
(517) 518-8056
118 W. Grand River Ave., Howell, MI 48843
www.fogspub.com

Have you ever heard the old expression, "Speak softly and carry a big stick"? Well, here's a place in Howell where you can speak easy and carry a big drink. That's because this speakeasy is real easy to like, but I'll be honest, the entrance can be a little hard to find (as I found out). But thanks to my deductive reasoning and keen sense of direction, oh, and a sign on a wall in the back alley, I finally found it.

This is 2Fogs, one of Howell's favorite places to find great food, meet new and old friends and partake in a potpourri of potent potables. And once you find your way in, you're in for an evening of fabulous frivolities. After hobnobbing with some of 2Fogs' friendliest folks I pulled up a pint with Joe Parker and Brian Atkinson. These are the two guys who actually spawned this speakeasy. This place is underground in more ways than one because they built it down in a basement. That's what gives it that real speakeasy kind of feel. After Joe and Brian acquired the building, so many people said to them, "Hey, the atmosphere down here is really cool. You should make it a bar." So after hearing that about eleventy billion times, they did just that. Now it's the place in Howell where the community connects with each other, great food and awesome beverages.

If good food and friends all wrapped up in a place that's a little hard to find is for you, go to Howell and find 2Fogs. Oh, and if you want to know what 2FOGs stands for, just stop by anytime. These two friendly old guys'll be happy to tell ya. Oops!

Michigan Challenge Balloonfest
(517) 546-3920
1200 W. Grand River Ave., Howell MI, 48843
www.michiganchallenge.com

What's full of hot air and high on the great state of Michigan? You guessed it, the **Michigan Challenge Balloonfest** in Howell. If you guessed me, don't worry... you're still right. :-)

If you're looking for an up, up and a way cool event the entire family will love, the Michigan Challenge Balloonfest gets high marks... literally. It happens every June in Howell, attracts over one hundred thousand bona fide balloon lovers and is probably the most colorful collection of anything you'll ever see. Before the balloons began their awesome ascent, I spent some time with Michelle Token. She's the director of Balloonfest and has the perfect attitude for an event with this much altitude. She told me how over fifty balloons come to Howell from across the Midwest to fly their colors. Balloonfest has been going for thirty-plus years and has created a huge ballooning family in the area.

I couldn't wait for the big inflate. Then suddenly they announced that the weather conditions were just right for flight. So after the pilots assembled for a pre-float photo, I met with my balloonist for some instructions. Then the infield became a surreal sight of these majestic monsters coming to life. It was so astoundingly cool to be in the middle of the launch field, surrounded by these gentle giants as they took shape and readied for flight.

We got the go-ahead, hopped in the basket, took a deep breath and suddenly we were airborne and headed for the heavens. This truly is the moment you realize you're doing something very special.

Once we got sufficiently high enough (so to speak), my capable and accomplished captain Rick Kerber and I got comfortable and commenced conversing. Rick is an absolutely awesome guy who made me feel completely comfortable at 1,200 feet. Life really is beautiful up there. You lazily ride the wind and take in all the incredible scenery. This was never even on my bucket list, but the experience was so cool, I got to drop it in and take it out on the same day. Convenient!

Well, now it was time to come down and look for a place to land, and we, along with about a dozen other balloons, landed in a field behind someone's house. Oh boy, this wasn't going to be good. But the reaction wasn't at all what I was expecting. Before I knew it, we were all safely on the ground toasting with champagne and making tons of new friends. This was a wonderful and bubbly way to end an absolutely incredible experience. If you do make it to Balloonfest, another very cool thing they do happens on Saturday night. At dusk, all the pilots inflate their flying machines and perform what they call the "evening glow." It's quite a sight to see: dozens and dozens of balloons lighting up the night sky in a fiery collage of colors. This is something the kids absolutely love, almost as much as we adults. So if you're looking for a festival the entire family will be fond of, come watch these fantastic balloons fly into the sky at The Michigan Challenge Balloonfest. It's a great, big, cool and colorful reminder of why we all love where we live.

Story behind the name:
I'm Full of Hot Air

Balloons are full of hot air... so are hosts.

Chapter 89

Season 7, Episode 1

Island
Adventure

If you watch UTR, you know that we have a long and illustrious island anthology. We've been to South Manitou Island, Mackinac Island, Charity Island, Harsens Island, Windmill Island, Belle Isle and even the island city of Eaton Rapids. You might say we have an affinity for islands. Hey, I just did!

Fresh Air Aviation
(231) 237-9482
6918 Old Norwood Rd., Charlevoix, MI 49720
www.freshairaviation.net

So on this, our newest island adventure, we stopped by **Fresh Air Aviation** in Charlevoix (really nice people), boarded a Beechcraft Queen Air (really nice plane) and our pilot Keith Teague got us in, up and on our way over Lake Michigan to beautiful Beaver Island.

Aside from being a great pilot, Keith is one of the nicest guys you'll ever meet and he's been taking people on this year-round, ten-minute flight to and from the island for twenty-eight years. Beaver Island is about fourteen miles long, seven miles wide and is the most remote inhabited island in Lake Michigan. The water is so clear and clean that, from the air, it and the surrounding archipelago of islands almost look tropical.

Flying to, around and over the island gave us some absolutely incredible views of its natural beauty. This is actually the first time I ever flew to an island in Michigan, and I have to tell you, it was such a cool experience I almost didn't want to land. But heck, we've got an island to explore. So we landed, unloaded and hit the ground running (well, driving) with our official guide and awesome island enthusiast, Steve West.

Steve West
chamber@beaverisland.org

On the way to our first stop Steve proclaimed that, "Beaver Island is a lot different than Mackinac Island. There's no such thing as Beaver Island Fudge, and they keep their horses in the field where they belong." After a good chuckle, he gave us more great island info. Beaver Island is nicknamed "The Emerald Isle" because of all the Irish immigrants who settled there. The island gets about fifty thousand visitors a year, and there's every kind of accommodation you need, from hotels and motels to vacation homes and cozy cottages for rent. The main town is Paradise Bay on the north end of the island, and don't be surprised when people wave as you drive into town. On Beaver Island, everyone is a friend.

This is a laid back, relaxed and trusting community. People actually leave the keys in their car, because hey, you're on an island. Where ya gonna go? You'll see tons of Irish influence everywhere, and aside from plentiful Irish eatables, you'll find lots of fun things to do. There's beautiful beaches, boating, biking and hiking. You'll also probably run into some proud Native Americans whose ancestors were the original inhabitants of these islands. This was and still is a very special and sacred place to them, and they deserve our acknowledgement and respect.

Stoney Acre Grill & Donegal Danny's Pub
(231) 448-2560
26420 Carlisle Rd., Beaver Island, MI 49782
www.stoneyacre-donegaldannys.com

Well, thanks to Steve we got our bearings straight and our land legs back. So, we set out in search of something we always seem to seek on our segments. That's right, sustenance (a.k.a. food). We found that and a whole lot more at a cool yet curious place. On the outside it looks like a good old-fashioned dairy barn, which it used to be, but once you enter, the tables turn... and they turn with awesome edibles, wonderful whistle wetters and islanders enjoying a delightful dose of Irish enthusiasm. That's right, you're at **Stoney Acre Grill & Donegal Danny's Pub**, where the locals meet, take a seat, get something to eat and occasionally even stomp their feet to live music.

To find out what was what, I sat down for a candid conversation and a couple pints with the proud proprietor, Eric Hodgson.

This place still looks so much like a dairy farm, you may just drive by it a couple times. It's half watering hole, half restaurant and a complete blast of a place to be. Eric explained that this is where you go if you want to become an island insider. You'll find tall drinks and taller tales, and the restaurant has heaping helpings of food for the famished. It's a ways south of town, but it's totally worth the trip. This is the perfect place to live it up and let down your Irish locks.

The Brothers Place Lodge
(231) 448-2204
27380 Pine Chip Rd., Beaver Island, MI 49782
www.beaverisland.org/hotels-motels-lodges-bbs/the-brothers-place

After some bona fide Beaver Island hospitality and a bevy of fortified beverages, we said goodnight to our newfound friends at Stoney Acre Grill & Donegal Danny's Pub and made our way over for a bath and a soft bed at **The Brothers Place Lodge**. Not my brother's place; this place was really nice.

The Brothers Place is a rustic, north-woods lodge that for seventy years served as a retreat house for the Christian Brothers Religious Order. Now it's a summer stop for people who like things simple and nostalgic. And take it from a genuine character: this place has genuine character. A great breakfast is part of your package, but not heat, so make sure you go when it's warm. The bathrooms are also down the hall, so if you find my toothbrush, please let me know. We loved our experience there.

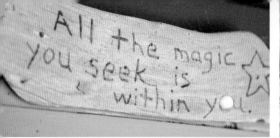

The Beaver Island Toy Museum
(231) 448-2480
37970 Michigan Ave., Beaver Island, MI 49782
www.beaverisland.net/People/Toy_Museum

The next morning we set out rested and renewed with clear island air and an urge to explore more, and that brought us to a place that was like something I'd read about in a fairytale. Let's face it; no matter how old you are, you're still a kid inside. If you wanna let that kid out for a while, I've got just the place.

When you walk into **The Beaver Island Toy Museum**, you'll think you're dreaming… dreaming back to when toys and times were much simpler and your imagination had to be bigger. Batteries not included here, because with these toys, they're just not necessary. Now, if you're wondering whose happy place this is, meet Mary Scholl, a wonderful woman who continues to collect and coddle her inner kid. Way back in 1979, Mary came to Beaver Island on her honeymoon and fell in love with what she calls "this magical place." So she packed up and brought her piles of playthings to the island. This toy store and museum is almost as fascinating as Mary. She really personifies the inner kid in all of us. Everywhere you look are nostalgic toys of the past, and plenty of toys kids still want today. Kids have beaten a path to the front door of this little house that can be a bit hard to see from the road. Just drive slowly and look for the stream of kids coming and going. This really is a special place. If you think you've lost touch with your inner kid, all you have to do is hop in your car… then on a plane… then a car… and get yourself to The Beaver island Toy Museum. Your inner young 'un will thank you for it.

Central Michigan University Institute for Great Lakes Research
(231) 448-2325
33850 East Side Dr., Beaver Island, MI 49782
www.cmich.edu/colleges/cst/iglr/Pages/default.aspx

I don't mean to scare your inner kid, but right now it's time for some science, and on Beaver Island, Central Michigan University does a lot of it. At CMU's Institute for Great Lakes Research, students are learning a ton about the natural water world and what makes it work. The day we stopped by, Dr. Don Uzarski was there to help me sift through the science. Don is the program director, and when it comes to connecting kids with our Great Lakes, he's the captain. For over fifty years CMU has been giving students the chance to study the complex science of the lakes at this biological station. It's the perfect place for research because Beaver Island is right in the middle of Lake Michigan. Dr. Uzarski also showed me how they're now using underwater drones to help find some pretty cool subsurface stuff. The students are studying everything from the impact of invasive species to the everyday fish and aquatic flora they find.

I was really glad to see that Central Michigan University is doing such a great job letting these young people explore our natural world on this incredible island. I was also glad there wasn't a pop quiz when we were done. When you look out across Paradise Bay, it's the little building with the red roof at the tip of the peninsula. You can't miss it.

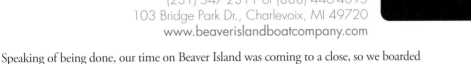

Emerald Isle Ferry
Beaver Island Boat Company
(231) 547-2311 or (888) 446-4095
103 Bridge Park Dr., Charlevoix, MI 49720
www.beaverislandboatcompany.com

Speaking of being done, our time on Beaver Island was coming to a close, so we boarded the historic **Emerald Isle Ferry** and headed back to the Michigan mainland for yet another UTR adventure.

This 130-foot ferry is literally the lifeline for the island. Heck it holds almost three hundred people, carries cars and can even squeeze in a semi. It's how most people get to and from the island. The two-hour trip was a blast and the captain even let me try my hand at the wheel for a while (actually, he made me use two hands).If you're looking for a fun and fascinating memory-making Michigan island adventure, float or fly yourself over to beautiful Beaver Island. Who knows, if you go you just might have as much fun as we did. Any more, and you might move there.

Story behind the name:

I'm on Island Time Now

As far as islands go, Beaver Island is remote. Granted, not as remote as Isle Royle, but it still takes some thought to get out there. But once you're out there, you're on island time, and it's time for a nap.

Chapter 90

Season 7, Episode 2

• UP Adventure

Are you getting tired of our awesome UP adventures? Well, if you are... TOUGH! If you haven't been to Michigan's incredible Upper Peninsula yet, I'm gonna show you four more reasons why you need to get UP there right now. I've said it before and I'll say it again, the UP is our own "out west." It's a whole different world up there with incredible people, fantastic food, tremendous towns to try and nature that's like nothing you've ever seen before. There are so many things for your bucket list up there that you might wanna buy a bigger bucket. Now on this UP adventure, we decided to do something we've never done before. Cross the bridge and take a hard right. About fifteen miles north on I-75, we headed due east on 134 through the Les Cheneaux Island Area.

This is a beautiful shoreline drive that takes you past an archipelago of islands formed by that wild and crazy ice age. It's an incredible and historic harbor area for boaters and explorers. But first things first.

After about an hour's drive, we hit a little town called De Tour Village at the tip of the peninsula. Then we boarded a boat and took the twenty-minute Drummond Island Ferry ride to an island of the same name. This pristine island is large (250 square miles) and largely uninhabited, yet home to one of the nicest resorts you'll ever kick back at.

The Drummond Island Resort
(906) 493-1000
33494 S. Maxton Rd., Drummond, MI 49726
www.drummondisland.com

The Drummond Island Resort has everything you and your family need to regroup, refresh and rejuvenate yourself in Michigan's awesome outdoors. There's great golf, fabulous dining and some of the most breathtaking views of this island-infested area. There's also every kind of accommodation and tons of terrain to explore. It's simply a classic UP place.

As for us? Well, you know the crew; they always seem to like it when I'm a little out of my comfort zone, so we headed over to The Cedars Sporting Clays Course to see me with a shotgun. Tim Higgins is the Cedars' main marksman and he was there to make sure I shot straight, true and not at you. After a quick lesson in gun safety (and which was the dangerous end) we commenced to rootin', tootin' and shootin'. This is a huge forty-acre course where you follow a trail and test your marksmanship in a variety of semi-real situations. From flying fowl to simulated rabbits running across the ground, your timing and targeting will be tested. We were actually shooting the dangerous and elusive skeet, which I understand are indigenous to just about anywhere you'll find a shotgun. We stalked our clay prey and had a fun day in the forest. Believe it or not, I actually did pretty well.

Even though I'm really not much of a gun guy, I have to say I had a ballistic blast dispatching all these inanimate, imitation animals. No one got hurt and it really does give you a true appreciation for how hard hunting can be. And the Drummond Island Resort gave me a true appreciation for just how comfortable you can be on this cool island. Tommy likey!

Island Charters
(906) 484-3776
64 N. Greenwood Dr., Cedarville, MI 49719
www.islandchartersmi.com

The next morning we de-islanded on the ferry and hightailed it back west on 134 to the tiny town of Hessel. There we met up with Greg and Jeff Lipple of **Island Charters**. And after boarding their boat, we set out on a four-hour float that would get us up close and personal with this awesome archipelago.

First of all, these are two of the greatest guys you'll ever wrangle a boat ride with, and they know these waters like we know food on UTR. Whether you need a fishing charter, a ride to one of the islands or a tour like we took, Greg and Jeff at Island Charters are experts on everything that has anything to do with these waters. For generations their family has been working and playing amongst these islands, and their genuine passion for Les Cheneaux shows. From houseboats and boathouses to beautiful coves and secluded beaches, we saw it all. "Les Cheneaux," by the way, is French for "the channels." Makes sense.

When it comes to this beautiful island area, you've really got to get out and around them to appreciate them, and Greg and Jeff were great guides to have. We learned a lot, laughed a lot and got to spend some quality time in a place few people peruse. Whether you're looking to find some fish or just a fantastic tour of these waters, check out Island Charters. You'll be chatting about it for years to come.

P.S. We never did see the Les Cheneauxness Monster… check out the episode to see what I'm talking about. :-)

Les Cheneaux Culinary School
(906) 484-4800
186 S. Pickford Ave., Hessel, MI 49745
www.lcculinary.org

You were probably wondering when we'd get around to food. Well, fear not, my UTR food enthusiasts. Here we go.

The Les Cheneaux Culinary School in Hessel is a relatively new place that's making waves on land with its fresh, unique and tasty approach to the art and education of food. It's part school, part restaurant and all things edible. Zach Schroeder is the program director and executive chef, and he's dedicated his life to the love of learning about food. Zack is a young guy who grew up in the area and his passion for the preparation of food is unparalleled.

When you first walk in, you won't even know that it's a school. The place looks more like a very cool and contemporary restaurant, which it really is. In the front you'll find folks from all over enjoying great views and incredible food. In the back are aspiring young chefs from across the US honing their culinary skills with fresh, local and natural ingredients. From a fine Bolognese to a bona fide business plan, these students learn all aspects of running a successful restaurant. Almost everything is sourced from local farmers or gardens the students are in charge of caring for. They also go out of their way to give dishes the unique flavors of this island area by foraging herbs and ingredients from nearby forests. Great care is taken to make sure this great food reflects this great area.

It fills my heart when I see motivated young people who are passionate about their pursuit. It's even better when that pursuit is something that also fills my stomach. Bonus! So next time you enjoy an exceptional meal out think about the great work they're doing up in the UP. Who knows, a Les Cheneaux chef may have prepared your meal.

Les Cheneaux Islands Antique Wooden Boat Show
(906) 484-2821
www.lciboatshow.com

If you love wood, water and a wonderfully nostalgic time, have I got a happening in Hessel Harbor for you. It's called the Les Cheneaux Islands Antique Wooden Boat Show, and it happens every summer in August. Classic boat enthusiasts and onlookers come from far and wide to witness these little floating yachts of yesteryear.

Shirley Jewell is a committee co-chair for this great event, and when it comes to making this classic happening happen, she's a real gem. It's hard to explain, but when you see these classic wooden boats, you instantly fall in love with them. These are cruisers from a bygone era and the owners are so proud to put them on display. Almost every boat I saw I wanted. Many of these boats are from the 1930s, '40s and '50s, but some date way back to the late 1800s and early 1900s. These woodies are wonderful and you'll see well over 150 of them in this small harbor. You'll also meet tons of friendly folks from across the country. The boat owners love to tell their stories; all you have to do is ask.

This fantastic flotilla featured some of the coolest classic and vintage boats I've ever seen. If you want to do some aquatic time travel, treat yourself to the Les Cheneaux Islands Antique Wooden Boat Show in Hessel. Oh, and when you're done picking out all the boats you wish were yours, back on dry land this awesome event also features a fantastic local art festival, so be sure to check that out as well.

Honestly, if you want to have as much fun as we do on UTR, plan your own UP adventure soon. All you have to lose is your lack of love for the UP. After that it's a wild and wonderful ride… yee haw!

Story behind the name:
UP Done Right

Usually when we've featured the Upper Peninsula on the show, we've crossed the bridge and headed north or hit a hard left and ventured west. This time, we crossed the Mighty Mac and turned right!

Chapter 91

Season 7, Episode 3

Ann Arbor
Ypsilanti

Have you ever wanted to go to a part of Michigan
that's so cool you become cooler just by being there? Well,
I know exactly where you should go. I just hope it works on me.

Ann Arbor and Ypsilanti are two great cities connected by their
urge to educate, innovate and give us restaurants where we're glad
we ate. The locals call them A Squared and Ypsi. I call them two
great places to plant your person and explore all the great things they
have to offer. If you're looking for interesting people doing awesome
things, you've come to the right region.

From the University of Michigan in Ann Arbor to Eastern Michigan University in Ypsilanti, this part of Michigan has almost too much to offer. There's enough cerebral energy there to make Michigan's future very bright. And the natural beauty of these two towns will give your sense of place great places to play. But enough talking about these two terrific towns; let's start traversing them.

First up, we hit awesome Ann Arbor, an enlightened landscape of cool places, green spaces and plenty of people who love where they live. And the food scene there will melt your mouth-watering mind. And speaking of food, we found a guy who put his dream in a jar.

The Brinery
734) 780-7140
www.thebrinery.com

You remember Peter Piper, right? He was the guy who picked a peck of pickled peppers. Well, here's a guy who's pickled more peppers than Peter Piper could ever even possibly pick. And I'm about to prove it. (Jim gave me a dollar when I finally said this right for the show.)

At The Brinery, they go way beyond just packaging peppers. David Klingenberger and his mighty crew of brazen briners bottle everything from hot sauce and sauerkraut to traditional tempeh and even an award-winning kimchi. David is definitely the man with brine on his mind, and he likes to say that eating brined foods stimulates your inner economy. Apparently our insides are a complex ecosystem of good bacteria that these foods totally help support. Way, way back in the day when there was no refrigeration, they would brine things to preserve them. Now we do it because it's a healthy tradition.

With David, it all started with a bumper cabbage crop at a farm where he used to work. He started brining, got hooked and a business was born. At The Brinery they don't add vinegar to the food; they use a natural bacterial fermentation that tastes really good and is good for you. Just like milk turns to yogurt, this process cultivates a beneficial bacteria that eats the sugars and releases acids that preserve the produce. In the process it also creates a biologically rich food that's good for your digestion. It's complicated, but completely natural. David is yet another example of someone who followed their heart, listened to their gut and found their calling (and in a jar, no less). So, if your inner economy is in recession, stimulate it with a boost of good bacteria from the Brinery. You'll earn interest in some awesome new foods.

Downtown Home and Garden & Mark's Carts
(734) 662-8122
210 S. Ashley St., Ann Arbor, MI 48104
www.downtownhomeandgarden.com

What do you do when you want to grab a bite to eat with friends, but one guy wants a sandwich, another guy wants Thai food and the third guy is not hungry but wants some gardening supplies? Well, here's a different place you can go.

Mark Hodesh had an idea. He already ran a classic business called Downtown Home and Garden. But he wanted to create a communal place downtown where Ann Arborites could come and connect. So in an empty lot lingering behind his store he created Mark's Carts, a casual collection of cuisine-carrying caravans that offer people a place to congregate and celebrate Ann Arbor's awesome edibles.

Even though this segment was supposed to be all about the great eats at Mark's Carts, I have to tell you that Downtown Home and Garden is one of the most awesome and unique open-air stores you'll ever saunter through. It's earthy, old school, eclectic and has stuff you didn't even know you needed. It's become a destination in downtown Ann Arbor, and just to make your shopping experience more enjoyable, there's even a beer garden attached. Mark is so much more than a shop owner; he's a social scientist who has created a sense of place for folks who want to eat, drink, connect, share and shop.

Getting back to the food carts out back: you'll find all kinds of casual and convenient cuisine from multiple continents cooked by passionate proprietors who love what they do. It really is a great place to grab a bite, and the atmosphere is fun and festive. As always, call ahead to find out what's cooking, brewing and doing.

Ann Arbor Rowing Club
(734) 930-6462
1325 Lake Shore Dr., Ann Arbor, MI 48108
www.a2crew.com

The Ann Arbor Rowing Club is a community rowing association that offers everyone and anyone the chance to race down the river in amazing speed and style. They're located on the Huron River and they offer a complete range of rowing programs. "Row, row, row, your boat gently down the stream" is definitely not what these guys do, because if you've ever seen or been on a crew boat, you know that it's all about how fast you go.

Before we got started, Lisa Psarouthakis got me saddled up in a simulator to learn proper rowing technique. With one solid semi-lesson under my UTR belt, Lisa corralled a crew and we headed down to the dock to hit the H2O. I quickly discovered that even though everyone's passion for this sport was the same, the rowers come in all ages, shapes, sizes and abilities. Mine just happened to be old, skinny, wimpy and talentless. Oh well, it's a start.

Well, not only did I do a lot better than I thought I'd do, I had an absolute blast. The Ann Arbor Rowing Club is a great way to meet people, stay healthy, have fun and work up a big appetite, which comes in handy on UTR. If you're looking for a new hobby that will help you connect with Michigan's great outdoors, this is a watery one you'll wanna try. Yea, you may get a little wet, but that's half the fun.

Now we head east to Ypsilanti, where "hip" has a hold on the entire town. This is an awesome place with classic architecture, a cool, funky vibe and tons of people who are passionate about being there. Our first stop was in Ypsi's Historic Depot Town. It's a part of the city where you can relax, be who you are and totally let your hair down. And speaking of letting your hair down...

Original Moxie Natural Hair Care
(734) 340-4022
306 N. River St. C, Ypsilanti, MI 48198
www.originalmoxie.com

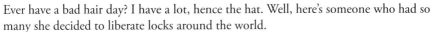

Ever have a bad hair day? I have a lot, hence the hat. Well, here's someone who had so many she decided to liberate locks around the world.

Rachel Blistein used to hate her hair, and like a lot of people, for years she tried to make it what it wasn't. Then a light went on, she started Original Moxie and her hair-raising ride began.

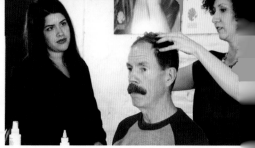

Rachel was convinced that my UTR hat was hiding my true potential, so she subtracted my chapeau and set out to fix my follicles with her patented seven-point assessment. I think with my lack of locks, she only made it up to four. But it sure felt good to be pampered.

It all started when Rachel finally rid herself of all the conventional concepts of beauty. After years of coloring, straightening and beating her hair into submission, she let her hair go, cultivated her curls and became the beautiful and confident person she is today. She started by developing hair care products for herself in her kitchen at home. The next thing she knew, family members were asking, friends came calling and retailers were reaching out to her. Through tedious trial and error she experimented and discovered what made all the different hair types tick. Her products smell as good as they work and she uses only all natural, hair-healthy ingredients. With Original Moxie, Rachel Blistein is helping women across the country be who they are by finally letting their hair have its way. If you're tired of trying to be something you're not, contact Original Moxie and just be you. After all, that's who you are!

Cre Fuller & Tin Angry Men
tinangrymen@gmail.com
www.tinangrymen.com

Believe it or not, in Ypsilanti there's a man who's creating an entire invasion of mighty metal men. But don't worry. You'll like these little guys.

Cre Fuller is part artist, part junk collector, part inventor and one of the most likable and creative minds you'll ever manage to meet. He takes stuff you and I throw away and turns it into some of the most menacing and at the same time charming little robots you'll ever encounter. His home is even a perfectly decorated and colorfully coordinated cartoon of retro treasures. You've got to have an eye for this kind of creativity, and I think Cre has three.

He calls his collection of work Tin Angry Men, and if you like cool, you'll be captivated. These little men are made with everything from lamps and toasters to clocks and coffee pots, and they're some of the coolest collectables you'll ever carry home. You really have to see these things up close and personal to get a real feel for how funny and fascinating they are. When it comes to the Ypsi art scene, Cre is a big contributing force. He helps head up a local indie art fair there creatively called DIYpsi (dip-see). It's a curated indie art fair that takes place both summer and winter. Vendors represent some of the finest handmade goods on a local, regional and national level. Each show also includes a variety of hand crafted food and drink and occasionally an eclectic mix of live music. If you want to see and feel what helps give Ypsilanti its mojo, this is an event you need to experience.

I don't think I've ever seen a more charismatic collection of little metal men in my entire life or met a cooler cat than Cre. Even his hairless dog, Chickens, is way cool. If you find robots riveting or maybe want an ironclad clown around your house, reach out to Cre Fuller at Tin Angry Men and he'll fabricate you a freaky friend in no time at all.

Go Ice Cream
(734) 219-7484
10 N. Washington St., Ypsilanti, MI 48197
www.goicecreamgo.com

Now, we all know that ice cream is pretty much the best thing ever invented. Well, here's a guy who loved it so much he made his own, got on his bike and started sharing it with the world.

If there's one thing Rob Hess likes more than ice cream, it's people. So, when he invented his own brand of frozen fun, he hopped on his bike and started delivering frosty-cold creamy goodness to all of Ypsi. Hence the name, Go Ice Cream. Well, both Rob and his ice cream became so loved by this community that he cast his fate to the wind, poured a couple more cups of cream into the kettle and a brick and mortar was born.

In his new ice cream parlor, Rob makes real ice cream the old fashioned way and he's making more people happier than ever. Rob was originally a film maker who would relieve the stress of the day by making ice cream in his kitchen at night. Well, one thing led to another, he fell in love with the science of it all and scooped himself a new future.

As fun as ice cream is, Rob takes his craft seriously. He reads books, attends seminars and even studied ice cream at the world's most prestigious ice cream school at Penn State University. For seven days, twelve hours a day they actually study ice cream on the molecular level with some of the world's foremost ice cream scientists. But even after all the science, Rob loves ice cream because it brings people together.

Story behind the name:
Ro-Ro-Ro Your Bot...
(Get it? RO-BOT? Ugh.)

There are robots and rowing in this show. If this isn't an appropriate time to make a "Row-Row-Row Your Boat" reference, then I'm not sure when it is.

Chapter 92

Season 7, Episode 4

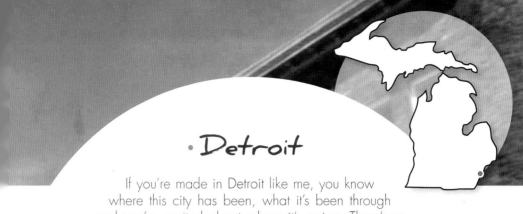

·Detroit

If you're made in Detroit like me, you know where this city has been, what it's been through and you're excited about where it's going. There's so much happening right here, right now in the Motor City that the right thing to do is show you! And luckily, that's what this book is all about.

Detroit is on track, coming back and one of the greatest places to explore more of the best Michigan has to offer. When it comes to art, edibles, architecture and awesome things to do, do yourself a favor: have an urban adventure and rediscover this dynamic downtown. Not only is it our biggest city, it's also one of the best places to find motivated people doing their thing and making their mark. So mark a day on your calendar and get down to Motown.

Sister Pie Bakery
(313) 447-5550
8066 Kercheval Ave., Detroit, MI 48214
www.sisterpie.com

Now, if you really want to taste of some of the new life that's moving into Detroit, here's some pie I think you should try. Lisa Ludwinski is a mad scientist of both sweet and savory. Actually, she and her whole crew are pretty happy, and she came up with a delicious way to help herself, help the entire community and serve up a heapin' helpin' of happiness for all those who love pie. **At Sister Pie** in Detroit's West Village, Lisa is making a big difference one slice at a time.

At Sister Pie, they believe in pure and simple ingredients. They also believe in high-fat French butter... bonus! They serve seasonal, so if cherries are available, you'll get the freshest. Bon Appétit magazine even said they would come to Detroit just to get a Sister Pie. From sweet treats to their savory breakfast creations, the flavor combinations there will amaze you. Every time I go back, I find my new favorite.

As for mankind, Lisa is doing her part to help this neighborhood thrive by creating a place where the community can connect. Her philosophy is to do right by people and the planet, and profits will come. She pays a living wage and even developed a "Sister Pie it Forward" program where folks can throw down a little extra coin when they make their purchase to help feed those less fortunate. Sister Pie genuinely is the kind of place you wish was in your neighborhood. But who knows? The way Detroit's West Village is growing, glowing and attracting new folks, maybe someday it will be.

Ask the Professor
(313) 993-3250
www.liberalarts.udmercy.edu/ask-the-professor/index.php

Do you ever think you know more than you know? It's not usually a problem with me, but if you like the occasional cerebral challenge and you'd like to be part of radio history, have I got a game show for you!

Ask the Professor is a fun and quirky radio quiz show that's been broadcast continuously out of University of Detroit Mercy since way back in the 1950s. The concept is fun and simple. Just send in your questions and see if you can stump the panel. Matt Mio is the host of the show and he, along with his muscular-minded panel of pondering professors, stand ready to answer all oncomers' questions. Well, at least they hope!

Matt was awesome. Not only did he give me some great tips before going on the air, he reassured me that the number one goal of the show is to simply have fun. So as the panel of professors took their place, we let the games begin. In honor of our visit, all the questions pertained to Michigan and the Great Lakes and I actually got a couple right. (Well, I'd better!) As the show went on, this enthusiastic group of academics made it real obvious why Ask the Professor has survived for so many years. Believe me, it was a ton of fun and makes for a fun and fascinating listen. If you occasionally like to nudge your noggin with knowledge, stimulate your cerebrum with a rousing round of Ask the Professor at Detroit Mercy. Who knows, I might be on again, and that way you'll win for sure.

Shakespeare In Detroit
PO Box 2642, Dearborn, MI 48123
www.shakespeareindetroit.com

One of my favorite Shakespeare quotes is, "Though this be madness, yet there is method in it." Wow, he must have seen UTR.

William Shakespeare lived way back in the Sixteenth Century, but even though he's been gone for a long time now, almost everything he wrote is completely relevant today. Shakespeare was a master when it came to understanding and expressing the human condition. He wrote all about life, love, struggle, conquest, victory, defeat and all the things in life that make us human. And that's why we can all totally relate to Shakespeare's prolific prose right here in the now.

Speaking of the here and now, here in Michigan, his spirit and genius are being kept alive by **Shakespeare In Detroit**, a troupe of talented and dedicated young performers who bring his timeless messages to the masses. The troupe performs throughout the summer at a variety of locations all around the city. The changing venues make every encounter a delightful surprise. All you have to do is check the schedule on their website, show up, throw down your blanket and capture some culture.

The person who personifies the passion for these performances is Artistic Director and founder Samantha White. She said it best when she said, "At the end of the day, when the costumes come off, it's the humanity of it all that really matters. If you've ever been cold, in love, jealous, betrayed, wished to make your life better, seen someone in pain or lost a family member… Shakespeare matters."

What is amazing to me is that four hundred years after his passing, so many Shakespeare quotes are used daily by people who probably don't even realize they're quoting Shakespeare. Here are just a few examples:

"In my mind's eye."

"Be true to yourself."

"Forever and a day."

"Love is blind."

"Won't budge an inch."

"What's done is done."

"Haven't slept a wink."

If connecting with a little culture in a big city sounds like a horizon you'd like to expand, sample a season of Shakespeare in Detroit. You'll be shocked how much Shakespeare you didn't know you already knew.

Marche du Nain Rouge
(313) 717-4298
Canfield St. near Cass Ave, Detroit, MI 48201
www.marchedunainrouge.com

The **Marche du Nain Rouge** is a wonderful, wild and crazy parade that happens every spring in downtown Detroit. It's like Mardi Gras on a mission, and the mission is to chase a 300-year-old little troublemaker out of the city. All shapes and sizes of Detroit defenders don their self-prepared parade apparel to participate in this fun event. Before the parade pushed off that day, Nain Rouge guru Francis Grunow filled me in on the legend of this creepy character. He explained that "Nain Rouge" translates in English to "red dwarf" and that he's a fabled and infamous spirit who cursed the city way, way back in the day. Today this mythical marauder symbolizes anything bad that has come to Detroit, so in good spirit, folks gather to rid the Motor City of this menace. It's purely symbolic, but a whole heck of a lot of fun.

Once I knew what the heck was going on, I got in the spirit, got in the parade and we all started running this little red rascal out of town. The costumes and character you'll see on the parade route will have you smiling for days after. We danced, we laughed, we cheered and we rock 'n' rolled our way all the way down to Detroit's Masonic Temple. This is where, every year, a huge crowd confronts the evil Nain Rouge with… well, let's just say a less-than-enthusiastic reception. As the Nasty Nain addressed the crowd, he was booed, heckled, jeered and told to just plain leave Detroit (all in good fun, of course). And just as he finished his sassy and sardonic speech, somebody must have made a call, because the famous Ghostbusters came to the rescue with their patented "Nain Be Gone" gooey green slime guns. It was quite a sight to see, and the kids loved it.

What's also interesting is that it's a closely guarded secret who is inside the Nain Rouge costume playing the part. Whoever it is, he or she does a great job of getting the crowd fired up. When all was said and done, and the Nain Rouge was finally on the run, I have to admit this really is a great way to meet some fellow Detroiters and make some fun Motown memories. Let's face it; nothing creates a sense of community better than banishing a bad guy, even if he doesn't really exist. Shhhh… but don't tell him I said that.

Story behind the name:
Nain Rouge, The New Co-Host of UTR

The Nain is the anti-Tom. He's vile, nasty, probably has bad breath (if we got close enough to smell). So he'd be a perfect co-host of UTR. You have to be tired of hearing all these great stories about Michigan by now… you're probably ready for some Nain-inspired stories.

Chapter 93

Season 7, Episode 5

• Battle Creek
• Bay City

Are you one of those torn individuals who loves
the beauty and serenity of nature but also likes the
excitement and energy of urban living? Well, here's a
Michigan city that balances both beautifully. Over the years
Battle Creek has done a commendable job of blending its
green spaces and business places. The river runs right through
the center of the city, and it's lined with plenty of popular pocket
parks where people can connect, relax and play. It's a big city
that's softened with beautiful natural surroundings.

Battle Creek is also going through a bit of a renaissance right now with tons of
unique new restaurants and stores surfacing. People are moving downtown, calling
it their own and making it a great place to put down roots, set up shop and create
an awesome future. It's also a great place to just come and explore for a day or three.

John Hart & Battle Creek's Bcycle Program
(800) 841-9494
200 Michigan Ave W., Battle Creek, MI 49017
www.battlecreek.bcycle.com

If you want to explore a city a great and fun way to do it is by bicycle, and in Battle
Creek, they've made it easy with their handy dandy Bcycle share stations. There are
currently four stations strategically located around town, and if you need some fun
and quick transportation, for a small fee you can just grab a bike and go. These bike-
sharing stations are catching on all across the country, and in Battle Creek they're
helping folks catch everything that's going on in this great town.

When we were there I grabbed a bike and a ride with John Hart. He's a bona fide Battle Creek expert, and he helped me wrap my head around their cool downtown. Urbanites there have it made. The town is extremely walkable and the river trail we rode winds right through the entire city. This is a place where the community stepped up to redefine and realign its downtown, and it's totally working. People of all ages are connecting with Battle Creek's core and making it the place they want to live, work and play. And when you live in a place this cool, it kind of all blends together.

My time with John wheeling around town gave me a great perspective and some genuine motivation to visit Battle Creek again. Heck, I hadn't even left yet. Good job, John!

Umami Ramen Restaurant
(269) 224-3264
78 Calhoun St., Battle Creek, MI 49017
www.umamiramenbc.com

You've heard the old lyric, "Life is but a dream." Well, some people take their dreams and turn them into a whole new reality, and they end up doing what they were meant to do. Now that I think about it, I wonder what I was meant to do?

Peecoon Allen traveled across the world and turned her dream into a reality that's tantalizing the taste buds of an entire town. Along with her husband Lance, she's taken her culinary roots from Thailand and transplanted them in Battle Creek. And the fans of her flavorful food are growing so fast she even opened her very own restaurant called Umami Ramen.

I caught up with Peecoon at the Farmers Market at Festival Market Square downtown where she practiced for her permanent location. Peecoon went to what she calls the "mom and grandma" culinary college and brought family recipes to this continent. Even though she was raised on classic Thai food, her menu is truly international. From Cuban to Korean and everything in between, Peecoon's main focus is flavor, and she's got it down to an art. Everything we sampled that day was a first-time taste sensation. Some people just have it, and she's definitely got it. Take it from a bona fide food lover, Peecoon cooks up a veritable "Ramen" empire of savory selections. If you want to try some tasty Thai (and beyond), take a trip to Umami Ramen in Battle Creek. I guarantee; you'll be back to Thai one on again and again!

Southern Exposure Herb Farm
(269) 962-1255
11269-N Dr. N., Battle Creek, MI 49015
www.southernmoon.com

When you hear the name Southern Exposure Herb Farm, you probably think, "Oh goody, Tom's taking us to a nice little farm where they grow herbs." Well, hold onto your Martha Stewart handbook and decoder ring, because this place takes elegance, dining and entertainment to a whole new level.

Sure, they grow herbs there, but it's also a place people come for incredible specialty dinners, entertaining and decorating workshops, cooking classes, fun and educational excursions around the world and even to get married. Scott Stoke and Curtis Whitaker are two ex-military men who got out of the service and then got started working harder than they ever did before. This place is as far from the military as you can imagine.

These two true gentlemen have created a home and garden seasonal paradise you just have to experience to believe. I'm not even much of a garden guy, but I was so amazed I wanted to work there. Scott and Curtis are so genuine and the staff are some of the friendliest and hardest working folks in the whole hospitality business. The entire place looks as though it was meticulously Hollywood art directed. If I ever get married again, I'm for sure having my wedding there. Just don't tell my wife I said that. :-)

The day we visited, they were having a specialty dinner entitled "Starry, Starry Night" featuring an incredible array of gourmet edibles. And without missing a beat, Scott and Curtis graciously extended an invitation for us to attend and partake. And of course, in typical UTR fashion, we responded with a polite and resounding, "YOU BETCHA!"

The night was, in a word, fabulous. Scott and Curtis welcomed all the guests, described the evening's food and frivolities and a fun and fulfilling evening was had by all… and I do mean full and filling!

So if you want to up your entertainment game, come expand your hospitality horizons at the Southern Exposure Herb Farm. And if you don't wanna get caught up a creek without a battle, visit Battle Creek and find out why this great, fun and vibrant city is such a natural place for you to be. It sure was the right place for me.

Fantasy Forest at Leila Arboretum
(269) 969-0270
928 W. Michigan Ave., Battle Creek, MI 49037
www.lasgarden.org

Hey UTR friends and family, here's a quick Battle Creek Tom Travel Tip for you: next time you're there, check out the **Fantasy Forest at Leila Arboretum**. They took a bunch of ancient ash trees that were killed by the awful Emerald Ash Borer, and instead of cutting them down they had some very talented artists carve them into an awesome array of cool castles, critters and characters. It really is an entertaining way to enrich this great community, and it's also a cool and colorful stop for tourists. If you get a chance, carve out some time to frolic through this fairytale forest. It truly is a fantastic fantasy.

On UTR we love cities that are moving forward, staying connected to their past and constantly rediscovering themselves. And in **Bay City**, you've got a trifecta of talented people, taste-tempting treats and a town turning its incredible history into a vibrant and exciting future. From its award-winning waterfront and exploding food scene to the countless people reconnecting with its core, Bay City was and is again a great place to live, work, play and make our mark. Even if your name isn't Mark!

Retro Attics
(989) 327-2213
1123 Saginaw St., Bay City, MI 48708
www.retroattics.com

Now, there's old furniture (like the stuff I have at my house) and then there's the stuff they have at Retro Attics. What's the difference? Well, for starters, the furniture at this place is ultra retro and captivatingly cool, and they carry way more than just furniture. Dena Pawlecki and Mike Bermuda are two hard working pickers who live for the hunt of a great find, and you'll find all their finds to be fantastic. From funky classic clocks and clothes to unusual art and cool collectables, it's all there. Mike and Dena truly are collectors extraordinaire, and everything in their place said, "Tom take me home." They specialize in mid-century modern, atomic era stuff, and if that has you scratching your head, just think "The Jetsons."

I think the reason these two are so good at what they do is because they have so much fun doing it. They hunt hard to find the kind of kitsch that'll keep you coming back for more, until your life is so cool someone might collect you. Seriously, I've been to a lot of places that had a lot I wanted, but this is the first place I ever went where I wanted almost everything in the place. If you want to have a cool and funky blast perusing stuff from the past, then don't drive past Retro Attics, because who knows, you might just find that certain special something. I found tons of them!

St. Laurent Brothers Candy Store
(800) 289-7688
1101 N. Water St., Bay City, MI 48708
www.stlaurentbrothers.com

Handmade chocolates, fresh-roasted nuts, candy, caramel corn and ice cream. Well, now that I've got your attention, it's time to talk about some Bay City history and just how sweet it is.

For generations folks have counted on the **St. Laurent Brothers Candy Store** to satisfy every sweet tooth in town. They've been a candy-covered icon there for over one hundred years, and when Steve Frye and Keith Whitney bought the place in the 80s they decided to carry on the tradition. And as Steve will tell you, their sweet success is something he lives for.

This candy store has been on the same corner in downtown Bay City since 1904. That's back when the street was known as "Hell's Half Mile" and was full of lumberjacks, saloons and houses of… well… not candy. While everything else has become ancient history, their incredible candies continue on. This is an old-school candy store that will put a smile on your face the moment you walk in.

After conversing about candy for quite a while, it was time to get my hands dirty (so to speak), so Steve took us way back in time and up in the old original elevator to where his number one candy creator works. This is where Dana Sporman makes her magic and some pretty awesome chocolates too. Our mission that day was to hand dip chocolate peanut clusters, and we had an absolute blast. Mine may not have looked as good as Dana's, but I guarantee they tasted as good. And, for that matter, so did my fingers.

If you're looking for a good confection connection in Bay City, St. Laurent Brothers has everything you, your kids and probably your grandkids will ever need. As we all know, candy is timeless.

Bay City's annual "Wine Walk"
(989) 893-3573
Downtown Bay City
www.downtownbaycity.com/winewalk.htm

A lot of cities have special events and gatherings for the people who live there because it helps create a sense of place and community. And the one we went to in Bay City had the word "wine" in it... sold!

This is Bay City's annual Wine Walk, where downtown eateries open their arms, open their bottles and celebrate life in this awesome town. Now, you may walk a little funny after a while, but that's okay because you're "walking." You're also walking with good friends, great food and the world's oldest social lubricant, and I'm not finding anything wrong with that.

To help me get the lay of the land and my hand around my first glass of vino I took some time with one of Bay City's principal food pioneers, Dave Dittenber. Dave loves this city so much that he's invested a great deal in its success. Heck, he even opened a restaurant or three right downtown to help attract folks back to the city center. This awesome event has been going on for almost twenty years now, and on this evening they were expecting almost two thousand wine walkers to converge on fifteen of Bay City's finest bars and restaurants.

It's simple; for a very modest price you get tickets that afford you samples of wine and savory snacks at each establishment. Even I figured it out. Whether your wine-walk is a skip, a saunter, a strut or a sashay, this is a wonderful way to create community. And as I could see (and also taste) Bay City is a wonderful place to find yourself. Heck, it's even good for finding funky furniture and classic candy. So spend some time in this exciting city by the bay. Who knows, you could like it so much you may decide to stay. Hey, that rhymed... bonus!

Story behind the name:

Up a Creek... With a Bicycle

You expected us to be up a creek without a paddle,
but we used a bike.

Chapter 94

Season 7, Episode 6

Grand Rapids

Have you ever talked to somebody who really
loves where they live? Well, if you'd like to have
that conversation over and over and over again, you
need to visit Grand Rapids, because the people over there
are over the moon about it.

That's right, Grand Rapidians absolutely love their town for a whole lotta reasons, and
in this chapter I'm going to tell you about four more. But first, let's review the top ten
things people truly love about this terrific town. Drum roll, please:

10. Great green spaces and gathering places

9. Incredible museums and a fascinating history

8. Innovative, creative and caring people

7. It's close to Lake Michigan

6. A food scene fit for a culinary king

5. Heck… it's Beer City USA… bonus!

4. A booming business community

3. Incredible architecture

2. A wonderful and walkable downtown

And the number one reason people love Grand Rapids? I'll just let you go there and
figure that one out for yourself.

Mercy Supply
(616) 780-0350
634 Wealthy St. SE, Grand Rapids, MI
www.mercysupply.com

Anvil Goods
(815) 343-3646
www.anvilgoodsdesign.com

It really does my heart good when I see old people doing young things. But when young people do old things, that's old-school cool.

In this day and age where so many things have become virtual, digital, impersonal and mass produced, it's great to see young people moving forward by taking a huge step back. And the artistry and authenticity of handcrafted local artisan offerings is making an awesome comeback.

Meet Rusty Zylstra, a local leather worker who started **Mercy Supply** and turned his hobby into a nationally known brand. Also, meet William Campbell, founder of **Anvil Goods**, where he and his wife Megan handcraft wood and metal to make one-of-a-kind furniture and fixtures. This is youth reenergizing a lost art.

The four of us hunkered down for a casual conversation, and I have to say, I was impressed. Rusty started working with leather out of necessity to make the things he wanted. Now at Mercy Supply he's hand crafting everything from leather wallets, belts and saddlebags to some pretty cool waxed denim wearables. His stuff is made to last and at the same time make a very cool statement. You will dig it the most.

William and Megan, on the other hand, are making furniture fixtures and even some kitchen utensils that are so cool and unique, you won't see them anywhere else. When we were there they were handcrafting a coffee table with an actual bullet lodged in it. I guess way back in the day, someone shot the tree, and the rest is, as they say, a great conversation piece.

From cutting boards to conference tables, when you purchase something from Anvil Goods, you're the only one who has it, because it's a one of a kind. Heck, these three throwback entrepreneurs even brought back the barter system. William and Megan helped build a lot of the interior of Rusty's store, and Rusty supplied William and Megan with some cool threads to create in.

If you like a personal touch given to the things you buy, buy them from the local artisans who actually touch them. There's nothing more satisfying than knowing who actually made them and knowing that you just did something good for your community.

The Spoke Folks
(616) 438-6674
221 Logan St. SW, Grand Rapids, MI 49503
www.thespokefolks.org

Now bicycles are normally just used for transportation, but here's an organization in Grand Rapids that's using the bike to build a better world for all of us.

The Spoke Folks are a non-profit of people who are trying to create a more just and inclusive community, and they're using the bicycle to move their message down the road. Jay Niewiek and his socially conscious crew will tell you they're changing lives and the world, one bike at a time.

On the surface this place looks like a cool and funky bike shop, but what this awesome organization does is give anyone and everyone access to a bike. Let's face it; we all want the same basic things in life, and by providing an entire community with reliable transportation, we all have access to opportunity. The bikes mostly come in as donations and some even go out with IOUs, but everyone who participates is helping make a difference. There's no racism, sexism or even classism going on here, just a lot of motivated people with their heads and hearts in the right place. Unfortunately, social change comes slowly and it's never easy work. So all of us here at UTR salute The Spoke Folks for their awesome efforts in Grand Rapids. Keep peddling, my friends, because with your help we can and will make it happen.

Lost & Found
(616) 732-3401
445 Century Ave. SW, Grand Rapids, MI 49503
www.treasuresoflostandfound.com

Ever lose something then find it? Well, I found a place where you can get lost finding stuff other people lost, and it's easy to find. Wait, I'm lost. Truth is, we all feel a bit lost sometimes, but eventually we find our way. Well, Mark Miller did exactly that. He lost his job, found his calling and opened **Lost & Found**, a super cool antique and second hand store that has something unique for just about everyone.

The first thing you need to know is that this place is huge. There's more cool stuff there than your brain can probably comprehend in a single visit. The other thing you need to know is that Mark is a great guy who really went out of his way to make this place a unique experience. From a single table-top item to entire rooms of fantastic and funky furniture, you will love just hanging out at Lost & Found. It really is more of a vintage store than an antique place, because everything there is designed for you to take home and use. This giant classic warehouse was once a fully functional furniture factory. Now it's a place you go to give your home some personality. If you wanna get lost and at the same time have fun finding something cool and unique for your house, come find Lost & Found in Grand Rapids. You'll find it to be pretty fascinating!

Brewery Vivant
(616) 719-1604
925 Cherry St. SE, Grand Rapids, MI 49506
www.breweryvivant.com

Way back when, people were actually dying to get into this place. Now, they're just dying to get in and drink the beer. You read right; this incredibly cool place used to be an actual funeral home chapel. Now it's home to **Brewery Vivant**, a place for great Belgian- and French-inspired beers, fantastic food and comfortable conversation. And speaking of conversation, I felt it wise to participate in just that with the man who had the original malted plan, Jason Spaulding.

Jason was a beer lover back in college (weren't we all?) and he was looking for a fun and unusual way to expand his hoppy horizons. When he first informed his folks he was forgoing grad school to brew beer they were none too happy. Now the entire community couldn't be prouder because of the cool culture he's created.

When you first walk in, the incredible stained glass windows and heavenly vaulted ceilings give away the fact that from 1915 until 1980 this was the largest funeral home in all of Grand Rapids. After that, for a while it even became a childcare center. Now it's my favorite kind of adult care center: a brew pub that also serves great food.

The word Vivant means "to be alive," which is actually my favorite way to be when I'm enjoying French and Belgian countryside-inspired ales. So, if you're "dying" for an unusually cool experience while you enjoy some tasty brew, great food and good friends, do it with the living at Brewery Vivant. Oh, and if you're counting, I think we're up to about eleven billion reasons why Grand Rapids is a place you need to be.

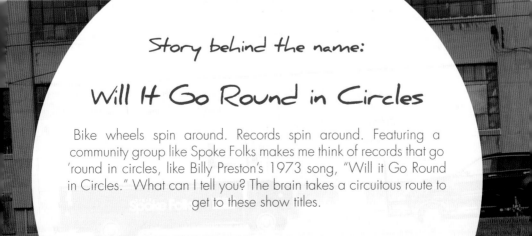

Story behind the name:

Will It Go Round in Circles

Bike wheels spin around. Records spin around. Featuring a community group like Spoke Folks makes me think of records that go 'round in circles, like Billy Preston's 1973 song, "Will it Go Round in Circles." What can I tell you? The brain takes a circuitous route to get to these show titles.

Chapter 95

Season 7, Episode 7

Restaurant Special

Grab your bib and your butter knife, because this chapter
is full of some fantastic food. We picked six of our favorites
from former shows that are guaranteed to make you wanna munch
your way across Michigan. Because this is a "best of" show and some
of these places are fully featured in other chapters, below you will find info
on where to find them in this book (with the exception of Hansen Foods, La
Becasse and Schuler's... those three were in our first book, so we included
their descriptions again in this book. Bonus!)

So, read on, or jump around for some of our favorite foods. Either way,
we're gonna make you hungry!

After 26 Depot
(231) 468-3526
127 W. Cass St., Cadillac, MI 49601
www.after26project.org

After 26 Depot is a place in Cadillac where you'll probably need both a napkin and a hanky. Check out page 128 for the full details.

Hansen Foods
(231) 873-2826
3750 W. Polk Rd., Hart, MI 49420
www.hansenfoodshart.com

We heard a strange tale about an awesome specialty grocery store called **Hansen Foods** in a cool little town called Hart. The owner of this store was said to be a sausage-making mad man, and people told us that if you ask him nicely, he'll even cook up the sausage for you right there on the spot. Well, at UTR, we love food fables like this, so we found the store and met this mythical man of meat.

Around those parts, they call Dave Hansen the "Homemade Sausage King." They also call him Dave (go figure). If you like gourmet, handmade, artisan sausage, Dave is your royal highness. Sure, he and his family own a great grocery store, but in his spare time, Dave's in the back coming up with some of the most unusual and tasty tube treats you'll find anywhere. From his signature asparagus sausage to his beer-filled "meat and potato" brats, I guarantee you'll find at least a half dozen to love. He makes over thirty different kinds.

We came, we saw, we helped make some sausages, we helped eat some sausages and King Dave sent us on our way with more brats than you could shake a mustard bottle at. You know us; those brats never made it home.

La Becasse
(231) 334-3944
9001 S. Dunn's Farm Rd., Maple City, MI 49664
www.restaurantlabecasse.com

What do France, the West Indies and Michigan's Leelanau Peninsula all have in common? Guillaume Hazaël-Massieux is the owner and chef at La Becasse, an intimate restaurant in Maple City that serves what he likes to call authentic French country cuisine.

Guillaume grew up in France eating the honest and rustic country foods his mother would prepare. After being bitten by that elusive culinary bug, he became classically trained, spent time sharpening his palate in the West Indies and is now loving living in the Leelanau Peninsula. As he so eloquently put it, "The wonderful people, beautiful surroundings and the rich agricultural environment make it the perfect place to be."

As with all enlightened chefs, Guillaume sources locally and creates seasonally. He also goes out of his way to help you match the perfect local wine to go with your meal. The atmosphere is quaint, casual and sophisticated and the food is simply awesome.

Guillaume and I have two out of three very important things in common: we've both been around the world, we both call Michigan our home… but this guy? He can cook!

Muldoons Pasties
(906) 387-5880
1246 M-28, Munising, MI 49862
www.muldoonspasties.com

You can't go to the UP without getting a pasty… check out page 117 to read about these!

Schuler's
(269) 781-0600
115 S. Eagle St., Marshall, MI 49068
www.schulersrestaurant.com

In the restaurant business, they say you're only as good as your last meal. Well at Schuler's, they've been saying it right here in Michigan for over one hundred years. And from what people told us, they haven't been wrong yet.

When it comes to fine restaurants, Schuler's is an institution here in Michigan. They also pride themselves in being a benchmark for quality, with an emphasis on local and fresh. Hans Schuler comes from a long line of people who understand what a meal out really means to most people.

In 1909 his grandfather started with a small sandwich shop, and over the years, Schuler's has grown into one of the premier restaurants in the Midwest. Hans's father Win (short for Winston) perfected the fine art of hospitality that Schuler's lives by today. The food is fantastic, the surroundings are classic and comfortable and the 125 people who work there will bend over backwards to make sure you have an outstanding experience.

So if you've heard of Schuler's and their incredible attention to quality, atmosphere and hospitality, you're halfway there. To get the rest of the way there, you'll probably need your car.

Supino Pizzeria
(313) 567-7879
2457 Russell St., Detroit, MI 48207
www.supinopizzeria.com

If you're at Detroit's Eastern Market and you've got a hankering for pizza, I know where you should go. Check page 87 for more details!

Story behind the name:

Hangry

We schedule our restaurant shoots either at lunch or dinner time. And by then, we are wiped out and h'angry (yes, the contraction for hungry and angry is h'angry). When food comes to the table, all bets are off and fingers will be eaten if they get in the way. H'anger can cause an all-out UTR feeding frenzy.

Chapter 96

Season 7, Episode 8

•Kalamazoo
•Cheboygan

In this chapter we visit a city that's so cool, they even wrote a song about it. Now, I just need to learn how to spell it. If you like credible colleges, bountiful breweries, creative cuisine and a diverse downtown all wrapped up in a cool, condensed, cosmopolitan culture, Kalamazoo is where you need to congregate. It may be a little hard to spell, but it's easy to love with all of its energy, art and awesome places that entertain. Western Michigan University and Kalamazoo College keep the city hustling and bustling while artists and artisans give the town a creative vibe like no other. Just look around at all the incredible murals downtown and you'll see why this city has such a big and friendly face.

Heritage Guitars
(269) 385-5721
225 Parsons St., Kalamazoo, MI 49007
www.heritageguitar.com

If you love guitars, history and Michigan, here's a place you probably already know about. But if you don't know about it, fear not, because you're about to find out about it right now.

I'm talking about **Heritage Guitars**, and if guitars could talk, this is a story they'd love to tell. In 1896 Orville Gibson started building guitars in Kalamazoo, and when the Gibson Guitar company decided to relocate to Nashville in 1984, a handful of master craftsmen stayed behind, pulled up their guitar straps and started producing some of the finest instruments ever to hold six strings. And to this day, they're using many of the same machines and methods.

During our visit, we were lucky enough to join Pete Farmer on an absolutely fascinating tour of the factory (that you can take, too). It's amazing how much of these guitars are still handmade and how much tradition has been passed down through the decades. Everyone from ZZ Top to The Rolling Stones have stood between these four walls to witness the care and craftsmanship that goes into every one of these instruments.

Not only are many of the original machines still in use, some of the original Heritage artisans are still there making musical magic. That's right, Jim Berline is still on the factory floor, greeting guests and putting his personal touch on the Heritage brand. He's dedicated his life to this craft and you can hear it in every guitar that leaves this historic site.

There's so much guitar DNA in this place and we met so many awesome and very talented people. Even if you never intend to pick up a guitar, the Heritage Guitar Factory is a fascinating place to check out. Who knows, you just might become a virtuoso like me… not!

The Crow's Nest Restaurant
(269) 978-0490
816 S. Westnedge Ave., Kalamazoo, MI 49001
www.crowsnestkalamazoo.com

Have you ever been to a restaurant where the food is great but the atmosphere and service aren't? Or where the atmosphere is really cool, but the food is so- so? Or the people are really nice, but the… you know where I'm going with this. Well, guess what? In K'zoo we found a place where all three are (as Goldilocks would say) "just right."

That's because at **The Crow's Nest** they believe that feeding and treating you like a good friend is the right thing to do. It's not just a place to get a bite to eat, it's a place to belong, feel connected, and enjoy some pretty creative cuisine. And thanks to Mike Louks and Kim Jean, I felt at right at home the second I walked through the door.

There's a real sincere earthiness about this place, and people will walk two blocks or even drive two hours to eat there. What's cool is that they've managed to turn this awesome eatery into everyone's neighborhood spot, no matter where you live. You can also tell that the people who work there love it, and that feeling totally carries over into the food and service. Everything on the menu is finer diner food done with a healthy and creative twist, and they didn't have to twist my arm to enjoy some of it. Let's face it, if you're gonna go out for a bite to eat it may as well be about something, and at The Crow's Nest, it's all about you. Bonus!

The Kalamazoo Wings
(269) 345-1125
3600 Vanrick Dr., Kalamazoo, MI 49001
www.kwings.com

Our next stop in K'zoo was to witness some topnotch hockey. That's right; we went to see the Wings play… the Kalamazoo Wings, that is. They're an action-packed minor league hockey team that packs more fun and excitement into every game than a basket full of biscuits. K'wings games are fast, furious and full of fun and surprises. If you go, be sure to keep your head up and your proverbial stick on the ice because you're going to have a blast.

Before they dropped the puck, I dropped in on the man who mans the mic for the mighty K'wings, Joe Roberts. Joe's energy and enthusiasm for this team is as big as the game itself. He loves what he does, and I can totally see why. The atmosphere at these games is absolutely electric and the fans are as loyal as they are into it. If you've never been to a minor league hockey game, it's all about getting the fans into the act with all kinds of cool stuff to entertain the whole family. There's often as much going on off the ice as there is on it. But don't be fooled; this is seriously good hockey. The K'wings are a feeder team to Tampa Bay, so you'll see some talented young guys trying to make their mark and move up the "Lightning" ladder. The K'wings have been in K'zoo since 1974, so they're a big part of this community.

The night we went it was Star Wars Night… bonus! So, in my best Don Cherry suit, I grabbed onto the Force and had a ton of fun with the fans. Once the game got started it was a wild and crazy, fast and furious fun fest. The players pounded the ice for the puck and the fans cheered and made more noise than, well, an arena full of hockey fans. If you're looking for a fun family experience, head to a K'wings game. It'll be a night so unforgettable, you won't forget to remember to go back. Oh, and speaking of experience, it's about time you did the same with K-A-L-A-M-A-Z-O-O. See? I really can spell it. :-)

In Northern Lower Michigan, at the mouth of the Cheboygan river is a town of the same name that's been calling our name to come back. So we did. That was easy! There's a bit of a mystery about what the name **Cheboygan** means. But to us here at UTR, it means a great northern Michigan town where you can relax, eat, play or even stay for a lifetime. Back in the day it was a huge lumber town. Now it's big on hometown atmosphere, awesome stores to explore, interesting eateries and a waterfront that's become a way of life. There are some who say the name comes from an Ojibwe word meaning "through passage." Well, if you are passing through, I suggest you stop.

The Michigan Cranberry Company
(231) 625-2700
9972 Alpena State Rd., Cheboygan, MI 49721
www.michigancranberry.us

What's under the radar for a lot of people (and also just plain under the water) is Michigan's cranberry harvest. Because in order to get those little berries off the bush, you have to flood the fields first!

You read right; if you've never seen a Michigan cranberry harvest (or just wondered why those guys in the Ocean Spray Cranberry Juice commercials are wading waist high in water) it's simply the best and most efficient way to bag these buoyant berries and bring them to market. A ripe and healthy cranberry is actually hollow in the middle, so when they flood the fields, the cranberries can be scooped right off the surface of the water. Wally Huggett and his wife Sharon own and operate **The Michigan Cranberry Company**, so before I commenced to capturing my own cranberries, I thought it best Wally and I had a quick *cran*versation.

Wally and Sharon moved up to the Cheboygan area when they discovered that cranberries love it there. They fixed up some fields for flooding and now they are one of the premier cranberry producers in the world. Cranberries are a super healthy super food and one of only a few berries that are native to this continent. After a few encouraging words from Wally and a quick lesson in ways to stay warm and dry in the water, I wiggled into some waiting waders and went for it. Even though these berries float, it's still a ton of work sucking them off the surface with huge hoses and into giant bins on a truck. It's also quite a sight to see. For annual fall harvest tours, check the Cheboygan Area Chamber of Commerce website or call them at (231) 627-7183.

The Brick Oven
(231) 445-1925
216 Sutherland St., Cheboygan, MI 49721
www.cheboyganbrickoven.com

Now, if you're a bread lover like me, you know that the stuff we break is sometimes the best part of the meal. Well, here's a family in Cheboygan who took their love for bread, built a brick oven and a business off their barn, and now breadies are beating down their door. Alishia Sanford, along with her mom and dad, Joanne and Tim, call their place (surprisingly enough) **The Brick Oven**, and all their loyal fans are just as fired up.

It all started way back in the 1970s when Tim was stationed overseas in Greece. He would pass by women in small villages baking fresh bread in big brick ovens. The smell and taste of that bread never left him. So years later he built his own brick oven, Joanne started experimenting with healthy, all-natural recipes and Alishia started marketing. Voila, a warm and delicious family business was born. They actually built the little bakery in their yard right off of their pole barn, so their commute to work is… hey look, we're here already.

Even though bread is a universal food and they are exceptional at it, they've also branched out to what have become some pretty popular pizzas. They even bake double ginger biscotti, a personal favorite of mine. These are the kind of artisan baked goods that make you wish you worked there so you could spend your days surrounded by their savory smells. No wonder Tim remained inspired for so many years. If you're a total bread-head like me, you'll be grateful that folks like Tim, Joanne and Alisha are baking their very best. If you do go see them, I'll know not to ask you to bring me a loaf. Because with baked goods like this, it'll probably never make it.

The United States Ski Pole Company
(231) 331-3076
1160 E. State St., Suite C, Cheboygan, MI 49721
www.usskipoles.com

When I'm skiing, the most important equipment is the poles: they help me not fall down. So if you're in search of a superior pole, head straight to Cheboygan, because right there is The United States Ski Pole Company. And when it comes to the perfect pole, the world's not only watching; top skiers everywhere are planting these babies and winning.

Andy Liebner is a young, talented and driven entrepreneur who came all the way back from Alaska to make his mark, plant his poles and put Cheboygan on the world stage of skiing. Even though Andy is a fifth generation Cheboyganonian, he's traveled the world as both a champion Nordic skier and even an Olympic coach. In all his travels he noticed that no one in the US was making a carbon fiber ski pole, so he set out to design and produce the perfect pole. Now skiers around the world are using poles made right here.

Andy showed us the patented process he uses right there in his shop to produce these superior poles, and even if I understood it, I don't think I could tell you how he does it. Suffice it to say that Andy knows exactly what he's doing and the worldwide ski community has taken note. You won't find poles made like this anywhere else on this continent.

As always, the people of our great state never cease to amaze me. Andy is following his dream around the world and making his product right here in Cheboygan. If you're looking for a superior ski pole, The United States Ski Pole Company has plenty. And as I always say, if you're looking for great place to live, work and play, don't move a muscle, because you're in Michigan.

Story behind the name:
Grateful Bread

Tom made a pun in the brick oven segment and it stuck. Grateful Bread is not the funniest joke you'll hear on UTR, but we love knee-slappers and groaners alike.

KOWALSKI

SAFIE'S
All Natural
HOME STYLE SW
PICKLED BEE
Net 32 fl. oz.
(946 ml.)
Safie Specialty Foods Compan

SANDERS
AMERICA'S ORIGINAL GOURMET
DESSERT TOPPING
MILK CHOCOLATE
HOT FUD
GLUTEN FREE

PISTACHIO COMPA
AMERICA'S OLDEST PROCESSOR
PISTACHIO NUTS

Chapter 97

Season 7, Episode 9

292

Iconic Michigan Snack Pack

Michigan has so many incredible iconic brands
that it would be virtually impossible and borderline
irresponsible to just pick four. But you know us, we're
totally irresponsible!

And we even gave it a snappy name. We're calling this chapter The Michigan Iconic Snack Pack, featuring four fantastic foods you can be proud of, because they're made right here. These classic Michigan munchables have stood the test of time, because time and time again, we pick them as our favorites. So, enough talking about our sweet and savory selections; let's start saluting them.

By the way, all these tasty iconic Michigan food products are located at fine retail establishments across our great state. Just find one, buy some and commence to snackin'.

Kowalski Sausage Company
(313) 873-8200
2270 Holbrook Ave., Hamtramck, MI 48212
www.kowality.com

Kowalski and quality… have you ever noticed those two words rhyme? Coincidence? I don't think so.

And if you want to know what quality smells like, just walk by the **Kowalski Sausage** Company factory in Hamtramck and the incredible aroma of sausages and smoked meats will totally give it away. Oh, that and the giant sausage being squared by a colossal fork is a bit of a giveaway, too.

For almost one hundred years now, the Kowalski family and company have been putting meat both on our tables and in our lunch boxes. Michael Kowalski and his sister Linda Kowalski Jacob are fourth-generation stewards of this family and Detroit tradition, and they have no plans to change anything anytime soon.

The day we were there they were making Kowalski's signature Hunter's Sausage. It comes from their grandfather's original recipe, and the two or seven I tasted were incredible.

We had so much fun touring the Kowalski factory and meeting all the proud people who get these quality meats to market. And spending time with Michael and Linda was great; they gave me a true taste of how proud they are to carry on a family tradition that's been such a big part of all of our lives. Of course, getting a true taste of some of their awesome sausage didn't hurt either. Here sausage… that's a good sausage… come to Tommy… d'oh!

Safie Specialty Foods
(586) 598-8282
25565 Terra Industrial Dr., Chesterfield, MI 48051
www.safiespecialtyfoods.com

Next up is a company that puts old world tradition in a jar. So when you open it, it tastes new world fresh. How do they do it? That's what we wanted to find out.

For almost eighty years the Safie family has been proudly pickling their products, and my palate tells me they've pretty much perfected the process. Their jars of freshly pickled vegetables somehow taste even better than the day they were picked. Now, if you're wondering what their family secret is, Mary Safie and Victoria Safie-Cusumano told me: it's pride and hard work.

The day we visited Safie Specialty Foods, they were bottling their signature pickled beets, which I found out I'd been eating for years and didn't even realize it. Every jar is lovingly hand packed by some of the friendliest and most dedicated people you'll ever find. Grandpa Dimitri started it all back during the depression as a way to feed his growing family. Now Safie is feeding thousands of us across the country.

It really was a pleasure watching these dedicated and skilled people process and prepare this parade of pickled pleasures. And we were welcomed with so many open arms that, quite frankly, we lost count. They were one of the greatest crews this side of the sun.

The Safie family is just one more example how pride, persistence and old world knowhow made for yet another iconic Michigan brand. So, if you ever get into a pickle, make sure you do it with Safie's, because not only will they taste good… you'll look good doing it, too. Bonus!

Germack Pistachio Company
(313) 566-0062
2509 Russell St., Detroit, MI 48207
www.germack.com

Sometimes you feel like a nut… and sometimes you don't. But, once you taste Germack roasted pistachios, you'll feel like a nut all the time (why do you think I eat 'em?)

That's right: number three in our Iconic Michigan Snack Pack is the Germack Pistachio Company, because they've been an important part of the Motor City for almost one hundred years now. They're located right in the heart of historic Eastern Market, and if you've ever popped one of these tasty gems in your mouth, chances are it was generated by Germack. And once these savory little nuts are roasted, they travel the planet reminding everyone that in Detroit, we do things right.

Frank Germack's family was the very first family to roast pistachios in the entire United States. He also explained that back in the 1930s they started dyeing the nuts red to cover up any imperfections. They were marketed as "Red Lip" Pistachios and became a huge success and party favorite. And if you've ever wondered how they crack open the nuts to make them easily edible, they don't. The nuts actually all open on their own simultaneously when they're still on the tree, making a thunderous sound in the orchards. That I'd like to hear.

Today Germack sells an incredible variety of nuts and creative mixes that are perfect for even the nuttiest of occasions. So, if you don't feel like a nut after reading this, I suggest you eat one Germack pistachio and call me in the morning. Then you can tell me how your trip to the store went to get more. Ha!

Sanders Candy Factory
(586) 464-5372
23770 Hall Rd., Charter Twp. of Clinton, MI 48036
www.sanderscandy.com/factory-tours

Well, just to be gastronomically correct, we saved dessert for last. And when it comes to sweet treats, Michigan's own **Sanders** is a homegrown sensation (or is it Saunders?)

Sanders, Saunders… no matter how you grew up saying it, we all knew exactly what it meant: incredible cakes, candies and dessert toppings. For over 140 years, Sanders has been a Detroit and family tradition that's made life here so much sweeter.

Today, thanks to Michigan's own Morley Candy Company, Sanders is making a huge comeback. New stores are opening up everywhere, and many of Sanders' original family favorites are back on the shelves and back in our hearts.

To help me wrap my head around this collection of confections (and hopefully get my hands on some chocolate) we went to the Morley Candy Factory and spent some sweet time with VP of Manufacturing Mike Koch.

Mike is a modern day Willy Wonka. The man knows his candy and loves what he does. Morley has been around since 1919 and Sanders since 1875, when Fred Sanders opened his first chocolate shop. Fred goes back so far that Thomas Edison made the motors for his candy machines and Henry Ford helped repair them. He's also credited with inventing the ice cream soda and even the famous Bumpy Cake.

After our captivating confection conversation, Mike took me on a fascinating tour of the factory that you can take, too. It's a great way to see how candy comes to be. So if you've got a sweet tooth, head over to the Sanders Factory Tour and take in the sites sounds and smells of Sanders candies. Just don't forget to send me a box.

Story behind the name:
Snack Attack!

After seven years on the road, we know a thing or two about road snacks. As soon as we return home from a shoot, Jim sets about cleaning the stray bags of snacks stuffed into the seat backs and errant pieces of candy under the seats. Jim is also the main enabler of snacks, because even when Tom and Eric say no to snacks at a gas stop, Jim still brings them fun things to eat.

Chapter 98

Season 7, Episode 10

Park Yourself

If the hustle and bustle of modern city living has you a bit hyper, hold on, because we're about to show you some great places to go park yourself, literally.

On UTR, when we want to relax and get green, we visit one of Michigan's incredible parks. And we've been to tons of them. So for this chapter, we visit some of our state's greatest places to play and get away. Some of these were featured in our first book, so we've included them here, too (bonus!). If they're from an episode already featured elsewhere in this book, we'll tell ya where to find 'em. First up, we discover some southern Michigan wildlife.

Detroit River International Wildlife Refuge
(734) 692-7608
www.fws.gov/refuge/detroit_river

If you're the kind of person who likes the wild life, Detroit's Downriver area is actually the perfect place to be. That's because it's home to the Detroit River International Wildlife Refuge, nearly six thousand acres of islands and coastal wetlands that stretch forty-eight miles along the Detroit River and Western Lake Erie shoreline.

This former industrial area and brown field has been completely transformed back to its pristine and natural condition. Standing there now, you get to experience these coastal forests and wetlands just as the Native Americans did hundreds of years ago. It really is an incredibly natural, beautiful and serene place to explore.

After spending some time there, not only will you realize what a great place this is to be, you'll also start to understand why places like this are so important to all of us.

Next up we're gonna take you for a walk on the moon right here in Michigan, and you won't even need a spacesuit. Bonus!

Rockport State Park (see page 121)
(989) 734-2543
101750 Rockport Rd., Alpena, MI 49707
www.visitalpena.com/adventures/rockport-state-recreation-area

Well, now that we've taken you to the moon, we're gonna visit a lake in the clouds that's surrounded by porcupine mountains. Wow, sounds like the lyrics from a Beatles song.

Porcupine Mountains Wilderness State Park (see page 163)
(906) 885-5275
33303 Headquarters Rd., Ontonagon, MI 49953
www.porcupineup.com/porcupine-mountains-wilderness-state-park

Feeling relaxed and green yet? Good, because now we're going to take you way out on Lake Michigan for a UTR adventure, island style!

South Manitou Island
Manitou Island Transit (see page 8)
(231) 256-9061
PO Box 1157, Leland, MI 49654
www.manitoutransit.com

Well, get ready to island hop, because we're heading to the Motor City for a beautiful island that's back on everyone's radar. Why you ask? You'll see.

Belle Isle State Park (see page 141)
(844) 235-5375
2 Inselruhe Ave., Detroit MI, 48207
www.belleisleconservancy.org

Now, last but not least we take a quick visit to a park in southwest Lower Michigan for some sun, fun and a whole lotta sand.

Warren Dunes State Park
(269) 426-4013
12032 Red Arrow Hwy., Sawyer, MI 49125

Our first stop in Harbor country was Warren Dunes State Park on Lake Michigan. If you're looking for a beautiful Florida beach, don't go to Florida (wrong peninsula), go to Warren Dunes. The beach is huge, the sand is incredible and it has something a Florida beach won't have: the beach backs up to some gigantic sand dunes. This is a great park and beach for families and, yes, even camera crews.

When you're exploring Harbor Country, the main road you drive is the historic Red Arrow Highway. It was named after some brave men from this area who fought in WWI. The Red Arrow runs north and south and takes you past beautiful scenery, funky little art shops and of course (you know us) some great restaurants. Yes!

Well, that about does it for this chapter of UTR Parks & Rec. Thanks for reading and be sure to visit a Michigan Park real soon. And while you're there, don't forget to make s'mores, because you never know who you'll run into.

Story behind the name:
Parks & Rex

Nine out of ten times, when we hear people say "Parks and Rec," it comes out "Parks and Recs." We hear REX. Makes us think of a park with a ton of T-rexes running around playing fetch with a border collie. If we could draw good, we'd make a cartoon of that. But we can't, so use your imagination.

Chapter 99

Season 7, Episode 11

Southeast Michigan

If you drive south, then east in Michigan, you come to a part of the state that has a very distinctive name. It's called "Southeast Michigan" and it holds the state's highest helping of humans. That's why there's always something happening there. That's right, when you collect this many cool and creative people in one place awesome things are bound to happen, and that's why we're back with five more fabulous finds that will have you heading there in a hurry.

Scott Colburn Boots & Western Wear
(248) 476-1262
20411 Farmington Rd., Livonia, MI 48152
www.scottcolburnwestern.com

Do you have an inner cowboy in you that's just dying to ride off into the sunset? Well, if you do, just head west to Livonia. That is, unless you already live west of there, then just go there. I guess I should have thought that one through a little more.

Yep, believe it or not, I said Livonia, because that's where you'll find Scott Colburn Boots & Western Wear, Michigan's wild west of western wearables. If it's got anything to do with ridin', ropin' or runnin' cattle, it's there. And it's been there for years. From fancy western duds to a full collection of working class cowboy, they'll get you ready to ride. Heck, even their selection of cowboy boots stretches a country mile.

I had a chance to ride shotgun with Sarah Colburn because her family founded the place. In the 1940s her father Scott Colburn began working with Henry Ford's personal dance master, Benjamin Lovette, on a Ford-sponsored program to teach square dancing in area schools. He became Michigan's first fulltime square dance caller and traveled the state. In the 1950 he started selling western wear and the rest, as they say, is history. Today Scott's wife Marge (a remarkable woman) and their daughters Sarah and Liz are carrying on his legacy.

Well, the intoxicating smell of leather finally took hold and it was time for me to either giddy up or shut up. So I set out to rope my inner wrangler. I must have tried on a dozen cowboy outfits that day. From John Wayne to Roy Rogers, they had them all.

If you're an Urban Cowboy like me. I reckon you better get your hide to Scott Colburns aforin I have to tan it fur ya. That's cowboy talk for "Come to Scott Colburn." They've got everything but the horse.

Jamaican Fenton's Jerk Chicken Restaurant
(248) 739-2558
28811 Northwestern Hwy., Southfield, MI 48034
www.fentonbrownsr.wixsite.com/fentonsjerkchicken

If you've ever been to Jamaica you know that they have a very distinctive dish there called Jerk Chicken, and I love it. But since I'm never much in the mood to leave Michigan, I thought I'd tell you where you can get the real deal right here.

Welcome to Jamaican Fenton's Jerk Chicken Restaurant, a casual corner where you can feast on all the creative cuisine from this Caribbean country. Now, if you've never had Jamaican food before, it's fun, flavorful and full of island spices. You can either eat right at the restaurant or take it home and add a little rum and reggae, and you'll feel like you're right back on the beach.

Fenton Brown is the authentic islander who owns this Jamaican inspired joint, and even though he serves up a fantastic "Jerk" Chicken, he's a real nice guy! Fenton is a gentle soul with a quick wit, infectious laugh and a genuine love for people. He also happens to be one heck of a great cook. He even took us back in the kitchen and showed us how he marinates the chicken overnight with his family's own secret blend of spices. Then Fenton proceeded to lay out a feast fit for a Jamaican king. Or a UTR crew!

The whole time we were there, folks were lined up to enjoy these island-inspired eats. If your edible endeavors are stuck in a rut, jump in the car and jam on down to Jamaican Fenton's Jerk Chicken Restaurant. It's a tropical treat that's a whole lotta fun to eat. Irie irie!

Stahls Classic Auto Museum
(586) 749-1078
56516 N. Bay Dr., Chesterfield, MI 48051
www.stahlsauto.com

If you have a chronic craving for classic cars and you want to do something about it, there's no reason to stall. That is until you visit this place!

Stahls Classic Auto Museum is a place you just have to see to believe. It's a one-stop eye candy auto shop where you can get your car fix permanently fixed. You'll see over 125 cars on display, ranging from an 1886 Daimler prototype to some pretty crazy contraptions, including a mechanical walking elephant.

And if you love the awesome autos from the 1930s and 40s, they're all over it there. Just add in some classic restored signs, neon and pristine gas pumps and you've got quite a captivating collection to comprehend. The museum even has a huge collection of antique mechanical music machines that still work.

John Lauter is the curator at the museum, and he was the perfect motor-head to help me get a handle on this great place. He took my car-challenged cranium on a fascinating ride down the road of automotive history. John, along with Stahls awesome army of volunteers, can answer almost any question you might have about these incredible contraptions.

Well, after a great conversation with John, he cut us loose to roam this ridiculously cool collection, and in no time at all we all picked our favorites. Mine was of course the incredibly lavish 1931 Cord L-29 LaGrande Boattail Speedster, because there's a complete bar hidden inside the passenger door (remember, Jim always drives).

Jim had his eye on the incredible 1919 Meisenhelder because of the little seat on the outside of the car where I could sit. Wait a minute!

As for Eric, his dream ride was the 1912 Rolls Royce Silver Ghost. It had a big and comfy back seat, perfect for naps! You know Eric.

This incredible collection is a true and inspiring American treasure that's right here in our own backyard. And there's so much to see that you'll most likely be planning your return before you even leave. So, stop by Stahls and spend some quality time looking back at the things that move us forward every day.

Leon and Lulu
(248) 288-3600
96 W. 14 Mile Rd., Clawson, MI 48017
www.leonandlulu.com

There's lots of really cool stuff happening in Clawson these days, but the first thing we did when we got to town was check in with Leon and Lulu. And we think you should too.

Leon and Lulu is a cool and funky lifestyle store where you'll find everything you need to make you and your abode extra awesome. But it's so much more than just a store. It's a destination that's become a sensation for people who have an eye for fun and interesting furniture, cool clothing and one of a kind accessories. Another great thing about this eclectic collection is that it sits in a fully restored vintage roller-skating rink. Just walking into the place is a genuine experience. Don't forget to look up, because there's eye candy everywhere.

Mary Liz Curtin is the heart, soul and sense of humor at Leon and Lulu. She's also one of the kindest and most creative people to ever open doors to the public. She and her husband Stephen are a blast furnace of awesome ideas. They even purchased the historic Clawson Theater right next door and expanded their offerings to include a restaurant and super cool special events. If you're looking to expand your horizons, these two are always planning happenings that will have you here in a hurry.

Trust me, just walking into this place pretty much guarantees you be walking in again. It's that cool. So next time you caravan to Clawson, feel free to congregate with other creative consumers at Leon and Lulu. Whether you buy something or not, they'll love you for it.

The Royal Eagle Restaurant at St. Sabbas Orthodox Monastery
(313) 521-1894
18745 Old Homestead, Harper Woods, MI 48225
www.theroyaleagle.org

Now, if you show me awesome people serving up great food for a good cause, I'm rushin right to it. And speaking of Russian, that's exactly what they serve at The Royal Eagle: gourmet Russian cuisine in absolutely serene and beautiful surroundings. And it's all done to help raise money for the St. Sabbas Orthodox Monastery. Actually the restaurant is right inside this incredible institution and all proceeds go directly to maintaining its magnificence. So not only will your visit be filling, it'll be fulfilling as well.

This inspiring structure is totally under the radar and completely tucked away on an unassuming side street in Harper Woods. You're driving down the street by nice little manicured lawns and suburban homes when all of a sudden… boom! A huge monastery.

You'll find over six acres of serenity, manicured gardens, towering blue and gold onion domes and, thanks to the Royal Eagle Restaurant, the aroma of Eastern European fare in the air. There are amazing treasures for your spirit and your palate.

I had the distinct honor to sit down with Father John Pachomy and Chef Petr Balcarovsky to find out more about both this Russian restaurant and magnificent monastery. The many monks who inhabit this holy house have a number of important responsibilities. Father John is the monastery's master gardener and the gardens are a true testament to his talents. And speaking of talent, Chef Petr was classically trained in Europe to tantalize even the most trying of taste buds. Our meal was, in a word, amazing.

Note: The restaurant does not have a license to serve alcohol, but fear not, my libation lovers. You are allowed to bring your own wine. And while you're there feel free to take some time, stroll the grounds and reflect. It's good for the digestion.

Sensational surroundings, an air of elegance and a higher cause you just can't beat. Now that's true UTR type dining. If you get a chance, check out the Royal Eagle Restaurant at the St. Sabbas Orthodox Monastery because, quite honestly, the food there is heavenly.

So grab your bucket, your bucket list and try a trip to SE Michigan. Oh, and you'd better bring the five-gallon bucket. You're gonna need it!

Story behind the name:
Dress Up Tom

Tom takes any chance he gets to dress up in an outfit. This episode, we went too far.

Chapter 100

Season 7, Episode 12

UTR
The Making of Special

Well UTR friends and family, believe it or not (and like it or not) program 712 (season 7, episode 12) was our 100th episode. That's right; we've made one hundred of these crazy shows. So we thought: what better way to celebrate than to have Jim, Eric and I sit down separately and talk about each other behind our backs. So we had the always awesome Christy McDonald from Detroit Public Television interview us one at a time to ask the who, what, when, where, why and how of what we do.

In this episode we divulged a lot about ourselves and the people, places and things that made it all possible. For example, we found out that Eric thinks I'm smart (go figure) and that Jim thinks Eric makes the show tons better. I happen to think that Jim and Eric are probably the most talented and genuine people I will ever have the privilege to work with. In every show we do the best we can because we are simply the best of friends.

We also revealed how we sit down as a group (what we call our Three Amigos meetings) and decide what to feature on the program. To be honest, our fans are a huge resource because they send us suggestions and information daily. Heck, we even admitted that Corn Nuts are the preferred snack on UTR adventures and that in the seven years we've been doing the show, Jim has probably vacuumed up as many as we've eaten.

Here's just a sample of what we shared:

Tom on why the show works: "I think the secret is that we don't take ourselves too seriously. We're just three regular guys having fun, working hard and sharing our discoveries. Plus, I can't act and I'm not smart enough to lie, so what you're seeing is real."

Eric on his most memorable moment: "I'd have to say that when Jim rode his bike off of the wooden track in Copper Harbor and fell (camera pack and all) fifteen feet to the forest floor, my heart stopped for a minute. But, in true UTR fashion, we were able to take a near death experience and turn it into some hilarious TV Magic. My favorite was expert Jim coaching Tom on how to do it just before he took the plunge. By the way, if Jim ever offers to show you the photo of his bruise, best to decline."

Jim on the people you've met doing this show: "We have met so many great people and made so many friends along the way, that when we come back to a town we take extra time to reconnect. But I have to admit, one person turned out to be extra special. In season four, we were shooting up in Oscoda and we filmed a resort called Mai Tiki. The day was cloudy and yucky, so I had to go back the next week to film b-roll images. I ended up starting a fantastic friendship with the owner, Teresa, and believe it or not, we are now married. All the people we've encountered are awesome, but this meeting resulted in a wedding, so that's the icing on the wedding cake.

Tom on why there's so much food in the show: "We discovered early on in season one that food is the single biggest trigger for human beings. Food inspires and motivates us. It's also a big part of everyone's travel plans. People will drive a long way for a great meal, so we try to include at least a couple great food finds in every show. Heck, Jim and I drove two hours one way just to try deep fried gizzards."

Eric on why he loves what he does: "Aside from getting to visit all of the cool places that we have, this 'job' has afforded me going on eight years at home right when my little girls needed me to be there. Tom, Jim and I work hard at what we do, but each of us has freedom and trust in one another and know that life and family are more important than work. What an adventure it's been!"

Jim on what's it like being on the road: "I love it. I love the travel, the meeting new people, reconnecting with the old ones. Knowing that what we do is going to inspire more people to explore Michigan."

And finally, as for who snores?

Jim says, "Eric and Tom."

Tom says, "Jim and Eric."

Eric says, "I have no idea. I wear ear plugs."

If you watch this episode, you'll also find out that Jim has a powerful passion for music; Eric is the best dad on planet earth; and when I was eight, my mom actually predicted I'd have a TV show someday. You'll also find out how grateful we are to have this opportunity. Thanks for watching our program and for reading this book. I sincerely hope we see you on the other side of show two hundres. Hoo boy! Time for another Three Amigos meeting.

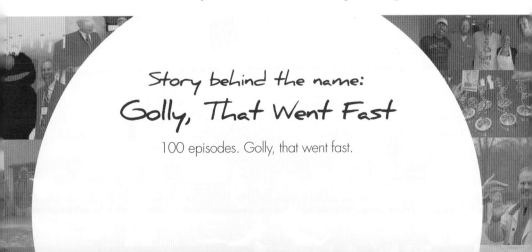

Story behind the name:
Golly, That Went Fast

100 episodes. Golly, that went fast.

Hemingwa

Chapter 101
(Bonus Chapter!)
Season 7, Episode 13

North by Northwest

"North by Northwest" is one of my favorite Alfred Hitchcock Movies. It also happens to be one of my favorite parts of Michigan's Mitten. Heck, Cary Grant was even from there… right?

Well, that may not be true, but what is true is that northwest Lower Michigan is one of the most pleasing places you can put your person on this entire planet. And if Cary Grant was from there he'd be plenty proud. Everywhere you turn there's beautiful natural surroundings, great towns to explore, awesome people doing incredible things and of course a cavalcade of culinary delights.

You could spend a lifetime loving this part of our great state, but we've only got one chapter, so let's git'er goin.

The Horton Bay General Store
(231) 582-7827
5115 Boyne City Rd., Boyne City, MI 49712
www.hortonbaygeneralstore.com

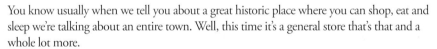

You know usually when we tell you about a great historic place where you can shop, eat and sleep we're talking about an entire town. Well, this time it's a general store that's that and a whole lot more.

If walls could talk, this place would be a prolific purveyor of the past. There's more history and folklore there than you can shake a time machine at. The Horton Bay General Store in Boyne City goes all the way back to 1876 and has been an important part of this entire region. Today it's a store downstairs, an incredible bed & breakfast upstairs and a tavern in the back where you can tell tall tales and even get some great food. What more can you ask of your local general store? From local baked goods and classic candies to even a vintage working soda fountain, it's all rustic and real.

Chip Lorenger is the owner of this Michigan treasure, and for over fifteen years, he's helped keep what he calls "the old girl" going. There's enough memorabilia and awesome artifacts there to start a thousand conversations, and the walls are adorned with photo after photo of Ernest Hemingway, who would frequent the store back in the day. Yep, this is a place that's stood the test of time because people like Chip have taken the time to continue its legacy.

The Horton Bay General Store is a living, breathing part of Michigan's past that continues to make new history every day. The great thing is you can go there and be a part of it. Who knows, in a hundred years someone could be in the store telling tall tales about you. You don't even have to be tall. Get it? Hoo boy.

Paper Station Bistro
(231) 242-4680
145 E Main St., Harbor Springs, MI 49740
www.paperstationbistro.com

Now if you take an old building and add a new menu and a cool couple to it, what do you get? Well in Harbor Springs, you get The Paper Station Bistro.

This cool and comfortable finer dinner is a relatively new place in town where the locals love to linger. Why? Well, I think it has something to do with the great food and atmosphere Mike and Damna Naturkas created. From burgers that'll break your heart to entrees that totally entice you, the food and drink there is what I'm talkin about. And when I'm done talking about it, I'm eatin!

Mike and Dawna came to Harbor Springs because they love the lifestyle and stayed because of the people. They wanted to give the community a casual and sophisticated place where they could share, connect and enjoy great cuisine and cocktails. The restaurant was named to honor the building's original endeavor, the Cleeland/Linehan newsstand, more than eighty years ago.

Another cool thing about the café is that while you dine you're surrounded by some pretty cool Motor City memories. From Iggy Pop and Jimmy Hoffa to an original Detroit Zoo Key and even awesome Olympia Arena, it's an artistic flash from Detroit's past.

On UTR we always look the places locals love, and if you think "love" is too strong a word, just try one of the burgers at The Paper Station Bistro. You just might ask it to marry you. And if you buy me one, I'll be your best man. Mmmmmmmm, burger!

Headlands International Dark Sky Park
(231) 348-1713
15675 Headlands Rd., Mackinaw City, MI 49701
www.midarkskypark.org

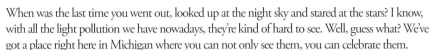

When was the last time you went out, looked up at the night sky and stared at the stars? I know, with all the light pollution we have nowadays, they're kind of hard to see. Well, guess what? We've got a place right here in Michigan where you can not only see them, you can celebrate them.

I'm talking about the Headlands International Dark Sky Park just west of Mackinaw City. At this six hundred acre wooded preserve along the Lake Michigan shoreline, these celestial beacons are bountiful. It's one of only a handful of parks like it in the entire world, and the heavens shine bright simply because of the lack of light in the area.

Mary Adams is quite simply star struck. She's a star lore historian, storyteller and author who's been immersed in the history of star knowledge for over thirty years. She's also the program director at the park and my personal gateway to the stars.

Mary, along with an amazing cast of volunteers, worked extremely hard to make this park a reality, and if time travel was possible, I know she'd do it all over again. Her passion for the night sky is so contagious that I went out the day after we got home and bought a telescope. And speaking of telescopes, the trip up to see the giant telescope they have at the park was one of the coolest things I've done on a long time.

This isn't just an open area where you stand around and stare at the stars. It's a state of the art facility that will host an array of programs and special starry events. The entire place is absolutely amazing. If it's a clear night and you want stars in your eyes, check out the night sky at the Headlands International Dark Sky Park.

Oh, and the first star you see, don't forget to make a wish. I did. I'm just afraid to take my hat off to see if it worked.

Gwen Frostic

(231) 882-5505
5140 River Rd., Benzonia, MI 49616
www.gwenfrostic.com

Do you ever wonder where hobbits, gnomes and leprechauns go when they want to express themselves artistically? Well, you're about to find out.

Gwen Frostic in Benzonia is an almost magical place where just a few steps slow you down and take you back in time. Tucked away on a wildlife sanctuary is her original shop built out of native stone, glass and wood. It's a building that brings the outdoors in and blends nature into its structure. It almost as if an elf commissioned Frank Lloyd Wright to build a summer home. It's there where you can watch Gwen's original art being immortalized on twelve vintage Heidelberg printing presses. Very cool to see!

Since the early 1950s, for a lot of people a trip to this part of Michigan meant a stop at Gwen's shop for her linoleum-block prints, handmade cards, papers and books. It's been a tradition for decades.

Even though Gwen Frostic passed away in 2001 she remains a true Michigan treasure. She was an artist, designer and philosopher whose legacy lives on, thanks to Kim and Greg Forshee and a dedicated staff of folks who believe in the power of her printed words and images.

Kim and Greg saved this business and Gwen's artwork from eventual extinction. They've put everything they have into preserving her wonderful work. And to prove that the family ink runs deep, Gwen's own nephew, Bill Frostic, is to this day the print master at the shop.

If you love nature and you'd like to experience the work of a world-renowned artist, you don't have to go far because Gwen Frostic's incredible work is tucked safely away right here in Michigan. Thanks, Gwen.

Crystal Coaster Alpine Slide at Crystal Mountain
(855) 995-5146
12500 Crystal Mountain Dr., Thompsonville, MI 49683
www.crystalmountain.com/activities/alpine-slide

Is your life going downhill? Well, if it's not it should be, because at Crystal Mountain in Thompsonville, going downhill is an uplifting experience!

When it comes to summer the best way to go downhill is on the cool and crazy Crystal Coaster Alpine Slide at Crystal Mountain. It's 1,700 feet of banks, dips, twists and turns through beautiful terrain that makes for one exciting ride. It's a great family fun experience that will have you and yours back for more.

Before I partook in this thrill packed pleasure, I rode the chairlift up to the top of the slide with Crystal Mountains PR Director Brian Lawson. Brian gave me some great tips on how to best slide down this safe and slippery slope. It's awesome. You're on what looks like a small sled complete with wheels and brakes. And the sides of the slide are high and wide. You'll see everyone from adults and teens to moms with their little ones on their laps. Even a few old-timers like me.

If you want to put a little speed into your summer, go ride the Alpine Slide at Crystal Mountain. It's a breathtaking blast for the whole family.

Story behind the name:

North by Northwest

We love Hitchcock. We really wanted to recreate the plane chase scene from the movie, but planes flown by a stunt pilot cost a lot. So we just talked about it and laughed. Then hit the road for Northern Michigan. See ya in season eight.

About the Authors

Tom Daldin is an Emmy award winning producer, actor and writer who has created programs that have aired across Michigan and the U.S. on PBS. He has also won a number of "best actor" awards in both commercial television and industrial films. When Tom isn't running around exploring cool people, places and things in Michigan, he's either enjoying time with his family, on his mountain bike or playing the drums real loud. Tom has a passion for the simpler things in life like nature, family, a great hockey game and, of course, a reasonably priced chicken salad sandwich. His greatest accomplishments in life are his children, Jeff, Anthony and Andrea, who have all turned out to be exceptional people. His true love is Cathy, his favorite color red, his inseam *34"* and if you ever see him on the street, please make sure to say hello and share what you love about Michigan.

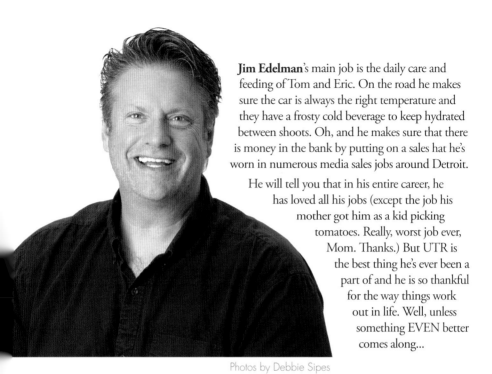

Jim Edelman's main job is the daily care and feeding of Tom and Eric. On the road he makes sure the car is always the right temperature and they have a frosty cold beverage to keep hydrated between shoots. Oh, and he makes sure that there is money in the bank by putting on a sales hat he's worn in numerous media sales jobs around Detroit.

He will tell you that in his entire career, he has loved all his jobs (except the job his mother got him as a kid picking tomatoes. Really, worst job ever, Mom. Thanks.) But UTR is the best thing he's ever been a part of and he is so thankful for the way things work out in life. Well, unless something EVEN better comes along...

Photos by Debbie Sipes

Eric Tremonti brought his love for positive storytelling to the UTR Michigan team after fifteen years in advertising production. Joining midway through UTR's first season, Eric wears multiple hats, including director, camera operator, producer, editor and post production manager. Eric will tell you that working on UTR is the second best job he's ever had, because it's given him the opportunity to spend more time on his first bestest job, that of world's greatest dad to his two young daughters. When he's not hard at work on either job, you can find Eric pursuing his passion for all things green in his garden and community farm plot. Eric is also a self-proclaimed super cooker guy and food aficionado... so it's no wonder he fits right in here at UTR World Headquarters.

UTR Shameless Sales Plug

How many times have you been reading an Ann Rice book, and—poof!—all of a sudden she includes a page devoted to buying Official Ann Rice Vampire Fangs? Or you're knee deep into the latest short story, 1,000 page thriller from Tom Clancy, and he stops in to sell you a pair of combat-worn aviator sunglasses?

That's right… zip, zero, nada.

We like to think that it's not because they have an ethical and pure approach to their craft of writing, but it's because they haven't thought of it yet.

Listen, we here at UTR Industries are never ones to abandon our craft either, but we also understand that at some point, you're going to need to buy one of the following:

> a hat
>
> or sweatshirt
>
> or apron
>
> or baby bib
>
> or T-Shirt
>
> or DVD of a TV show (allow us to make the case for it being one of our TV shows)…
>
> or a book that was the prequel to the book you're holding this very instant – The FIRST 50.

We have lots of cool and affordable stuff for sale in the UTR Store.

Check it out at UTRMichigan.com.

Cool stuff… it should be our middle name.

Index by City/Region

Index by Category

General Index